BIG MONEY WRITING PROFESSIONALLY

plots – how to make the sparkling dialo constantly seeking. course in each subj

This book belongs to:

....

TELLS HOW!

LIKE HAVI AN E AT Y SIDE

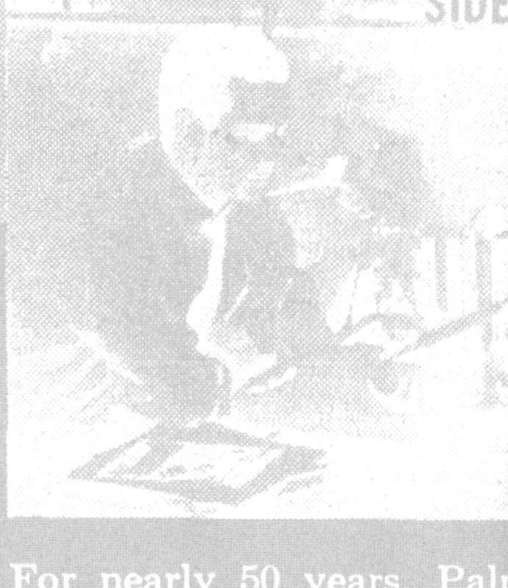

LATEST SALE OVER $1,000
"Most recent sale over $1,800. Your assistance has enabled me to appear steadily in national magazines."
L.A.–Trinity, Tex.

70 SALES IN 18 MONTHS
"Recently had a 5-page article in Readers Digest. Have made 70 sales in past 18 mos."
V.L.O.–Azusa, Cal.

REPORTS 1000TH SALE
"Just made the 1,000th sale of my writings. Am hitting plenty of national magazines."

For nearly 50 years. Palr has been helping ambitio women of all ages to write *sell*, and to *find buyers fo* tions. Although you stud your work is continuously supervised by a staff of

LEGENDS *of* LITERATURE

LEGENDS *of* LITERATURE

THE BEST ARTICLES, INTERVIEWS, AND ESSAYS FROM THE ARCHIVES OF *WRITER'S DIGEST* MAGAZINE

Including contributions from Stephen King, H.G. Wells, Kurt Vonnegut, Eudora Welty, Isaac Asimov, Harlan Ellison, Joyce Carol Oates, Edgar Rice Burroughs, and many more

EDITED BY PHILLIP SEXTON

WRITER'S DIGEST BOOKS

www.writersdigest.com
Cincinnati, Ohio

 Published by Writer's Digest Books, an imprint of F+W Publications, Inc., 4700 East Galbraith Road, Cincinnati, OH 45236. (800) 289-0963. First edition.

Distributed in Canada by Fraser Direct, 100 Armstrong Avenue, Georgetown, ON, Canada L7G 5S4, Tel: (905) 877-4411. Distributed in the U.K. and Europe by David & Charles, Brunel House, Newton Abbot, Devon, TQ12 4PU, England, Tel: (+44) 1626 323200, Fax: (+44) 1626 323319, E-mail: postmaster@davidandcharles.co.uk. Distributed in Australia by Capricorn Link, P.O. Box 704, Windsor, NSW 2756 Australia, Tel: (02) 4577-3555.

Visit our Web site at www.writersdigest.com and www.wdeditors.com for information on more resources for writers. For more fine books from Writer's Digest Books, please visit www.fwbookstore.com.

To receive a free weekly e-mail newsletter delivering tips and updates about writing and about Writer's Digest products, register directly at our Web site at http://newsletters.fwpublications.com.

11 10 09 08 07 5 4 3 2 1

Library of Congress Cataloging-in-Publication Data
Legends of literature : the best articles, interviews, and essays from the archives of Writer's Digest magazine / edited by Phillip Sexton. -- 1st ed.
p. cm.
Includes index.
ISBN 978-1-58297-473-6 (hardcover : alk. paper)
1. Authorship. 2. Authorship--Anecdotes. I. Sexton, Phillip. II. Writer's digest (Cincinnati, Ohio).
PN165.L44 2007
808'.02--dc22

2007010249

Edited by Michelle Ehrhard
Designed by Claudean Wheeler
Additional design by Kelly Piller
Production coordinated by Mark Griffin

Permissions

"How *Writer's Digest* Began" © 1970 by Richard Rosenthal. Reprinted with permission from the author.

"Started Writing at the Age of Ten" © 1921 by *Writer's Digest*.

"A.A. Milne" © 1922 by A.A. Milne.

"Shaw, the Dictator" © 1929 by Judge Henry Neil.

"Local Color" © 1932 by Erle Stanley Gardner; renewed 1959.

"Magic Out of a Hat" by L. Ron Hubbard reprinted with permission of Author Services, Inc., agent for the L. Ron Hubbard Library.

"Style" © 1938 by James Hilton. Originally published in *Writer's Digest* in 1938. Reprinted by permission of the Estate of James Hilton.

"The Detective in Fiction"; Copyright © 1932 by John Dickson Carr. By permission of Harold Ober Associates Incorporated.

"Within Quotes" © 1938 by Erle Stanley Gardner; renewed 1965.

"There's Money in Comics" © 1947 by Stan Lee.

Vonnegut on Writing © 1985 by Michael Schumacher.

"Controversy: Sharpest Sword of the Paperback Novelist" by Harlan Ellison originally appeared in *Writer's Digest* magazine. Copyright © 1963 by Harlan Ellison. Renewed 1991 by The Kilimanjaro Corporation. Reprinted by arrangement with, and permission of, the Author and the Author's agent, Richard Curtis Associates, Inc., New York. All rights reserved. Harlan Ellison is a registered trademark of The Kilimanjaro Corporation.

"The Horror Writer Market and the Ten Bears" by Stephen King. Reprinted with permission. © Stephen King. All rights reserved. Originally appeared in *Writer's Digest* (1973).

"This Thing Called Censorship" © 1922 by Smith C. McGregor.

"The Zen Writer"; Reprinted by permission of Don Congdon Associates, Inc. Copyright © 1958; renewed 1973 by Ray Bradbury.

"Hero, Heroine, Heavy" © 1943 by Leigh Brackett. Reprinted by permission of Spectrum Literary Agency.

Dedication

To writers
Known and unknown
Past, present, and yet-to-come
You inspire me

Acknowledgments

Thanks first, and always, to Mom and Dad. Also to the kind folks at Writer's Digest Books for once again allowing me to turn a personal passion into a real, live book. Of those, my greatest thanks go to Michelle Ehrhard, my editor, and Claudean Wheeler, designer-extraordinaire. Also, I'm grateful to those who have shared with me their love of writing and allowed me to return the favor: Irwin and Kathryn; Steve, Scott, Alice, Casey, Lauren, and Brad; Drs. Barnes and Lockridge; Jack Heffron, Richard Hunt, and the fabulous Michael Murphy clan. And for encouragement and support: Cindy, Mike, and Jennifer; Michelle, Tricia, Jeff, Melanie, Suzanne, Shawn, and Holly.

WRITER'S DIGEST

Contents

THE LEADING AND LARGEST WRITER'S MAGAZINE

Published monthly by the Automobile Publishing Corp., East 12th St., Cincinnati, Ohio. Subscribers sending change of address should allow two weeks for the change to be made, and supply both the old and new address. Est. 1919. Vol. 20. No. 6

PART II: ON THE CRAFT OF WRITING

PART III: PIECES OF HISTORY

PART IV: INTERVIEWS

AUGUST 2007

Introduction

PHILLIP SEXTON

What you hold in your hands is a time capsule of sorts. It's also love letter, a how-to guide, a history lesson, and a conversation among friends.

Perhaps you were expecting something more ... specific? But it is these things at the very *least*, and possibly more. The launch of *Writer's Digest*'s first issue, dated December 1920, provided a new forum for writers to express their interests and concerns, practical lessons for improving one's work, and new publishing opportunities called out monthly to reflect the most current markets.

Contributors to the magazine have run the gamut from little-known but highly skilled freelancers to best-selling authors. Both are well-represented in every year of *Writer's Digest*'s nine decades on sale. Many are included in this collection, but even they are a small sample of the writers who have provided memorable content over the years. There are so many, in fact, that a single book couldn't hold all their work.

Selection of the pieces included herein was driven by a number of factors, some practical, others more subjective in nature. When we're speaking of "legends," for example, it makes perfect sense to include articles and essays by such authors as H.G. Wells, Jack Kerouac, Stephen King, and Upton Sinclair. More surprising choices, however, might be Stan Lee, an interview with Hugh Hefner, and Rod Serling. And yet, these three individuals—comic book creator, publisher, and scriptwriter—made as big an impact upon their respective mediums as anyone possibly could. They are, inarguably, legends.

Some of the pieces that didn't make the final cut include essays and articles by Darryl Zanuck (Twentieth Century Fox film producer in 1944), William M. Gaines (publisher of *Mad Magazine*), George Romero (director of *Night of the Living Dead*), and Sylvester Stallone (keep in mind, he *was* nominated for a Best Original Screenplay Oscar in 1977). There were hundreds of others, but these few show the range of what *The Digest* (as it has been known to readers) has covered. You'll also notice that the majority of pieces are pre-1980. This isn't to suggest a dearth of material post-1980. In fact, contemporary issues of *The Digest* include as much, if not more, material from best-selling authors as ever. They are not, however, "rare" in any real sense, which is part of what drove the selection process.

And finally, some pieces were chosen based on their relationship to the author's development as a writer. For example, Ken Kesey's essay (page 63) was written just as *One Flew Over the Cuckoo's Nest* was being published. Kesey had no idea of the fame to come. Stephen King was in a similar situation. His piece (page 192) was written three months prior to the publication of *Carrie,* his first novel. *Writer's Digest* captured the thoughts of these authors and others just as they were beginning their journeys into legend.

But let's get back to our original statement: What you hold in your hands is a time capsule, a love letter, a how-to guide, a history lesson, and a conversation. And here's why:

The articles that follow act as a sort of snapshot, a time capsule reflecting the social mores, concerns, desires, and struggles of the time during which they were written. From sex and racial equality to censorship and war, each piece reveals the sensibilities of both the writer and the world around him.

The Digest always has, and always will be, a passionate advocate for writers and great writing. And, as such, this book is a celebration of both the contributors and the readers who have shared that passion for fine literature over the years. If you've read this far, you are probably one of them. Welcome to the love fest.

Much of the content that follows is specific to the practical needs of writers, helping them learn how to better create characters, craft dialogue, get published, etc. If you're not a writer, you may find these pieces particularly fascinating. Imagine having a conversation with Kurt Vonnegut in which he reveals his secrets for writing memorable fiction. Or discussing with Somerset Maugham the manner in which an author's personality can change our appreciation of his or her work.

It may be that history wasn't your favorite subject in school. That's okay. But literature shapes, and is inevitably shaped by, history. And it is through this lens that you may find history absolutely fascinating. The following pages contain articles that detail the need for screenwriters in the era of silent film, new job opportunities for women writers in the 1920s, issues of censorship as seen under two very different circumstances, the obligations of the writer during wartime, and much more.

And finally, *Legends of Literature* is a conversation among people who have, to one degree or another, devoted their lives to writing and reading, whether novels, short stories, films, plays, poetry, comic books, political discourse, or issues of social justice. It's a conversation we're all involved in, ongoing and unending. The pages that follow invite you to listen in, think, enjoy, and maybe—we might hope—add your voice to the discussion.

VOLUME LI JANUARY 1970 NO. 2

How Writer's Digest Began

RICHARD ROSENTHAL

1920 was a landmark year for both writers and writing. Edith Wharton discovered *The Age of Innocence. The Cabinet of Dr. Caligari* premiered in theaters. Agatha Christie introduced Hercule Poirot. Eugene O'Neill opened his first full-length play. New works appeared from H.G. Wells, F. Scott Fitzgerald, L. Frank Baum, and Robert Frost. The list goes on and on. It was also the year that Mario Puzo, Ray Bradbury, Isaac Asimov, and a little periodical called *Successful Writing* were born. *Successful Writing* quickly evolved into *Writer's Digest*, and in the nine decades since, *The Digest* has worked tirelessly to provide writers of all skill levels with the information they need to write well, get published, and live a rich, rewarding writing life. Forty years ago, then-publisher **RICHARD ROSENTHAL** shared with readers a brief history of how the magazine came to be …

It was post-World War I and the United States was in a mood to celebrate her newly found muscle on the world's battlefields. Everyone boasted, and we all wanted to tell the world "how we did it!" But the telling required words … and printing … and paper.

In the fall of 1920, Ed Rosenthal went to New York in search of paper for his Cincinnati-based printing and publishing companies. He found three sources so quickly that he decided (in the extra time he had) to chase a star that had been playing hide-and-seek with him for years.

He wanted to publish a magazine that would take the writer out of the garret and into the marketplace where the demand for his wares had never been greater. He wanted to show aspiring writers how to write for this new, hungry market and then how to sell to that market.

The climate for his invention hardly could have been better. He contacted all the writers he and his family knew, friends of writers, suspected writers, old writers, new writers—anybody who could reach that guy up there in the garret to tell him to come down and join the happy parade of the day. He succeeded.

He called his new publication *Successful Writing* and boldly asked twenty-five cents a copy from the buyer. He sold 1,400 copies of that December 1920 issue—enough copies to rush the second copy into print—and a third before he decided to change the title to *Writer's Digest*. While the reasons for the title change (the magazine has never "digested" articles or stories) have remained a mystery, the rest of the history is well documented in the magazine itself.

From that first issue—subtitled "A Monthly Journal of Information on Writing Photoplays, Short Stories, Verse, News Stories, Publicity, Advertising, etc."—to the one you are holding now, *Writer's Digest* has shown the writer his own best way to improve his craft and become a commercial success.

For instance, D.G. Baird, in his article "Cashing In on the Other Fellow's Ads" (September 1921), tells how he saw an unusual newspaper ad, clipped it, and found the person who created it. He then interviewed this person and sold the interview to *Printer's Ink*.

Or, for those readers who needed a special kind of push, Sinclair Lewis injected a large dose of adrenalin into their muses in the June 1931 issue with these words:

> To be not only a bestseller in America but to be really beloved, a novelist must assert that all American men are tall, handsome, rich, honest, and

> powerful at golf; that all country towns are filled with neighbors who do nothing from day to day save go about being kind to one another; that although American girls may be wild, they change always into perfect wives and mothers; and that, geographically, America is composed solely of New York, which is inhabited entirely by millionaires; of the West, which keeps unchanged all the boisterous heroism of 1870; and of the South, where everyone lives on a plantation perpetually glossy with moonlight and scented magnolias.

"The novel of labor and the laborer is more timely today than it ever was in this country. Labor will never again take a back seat in American politics." What this lead by Louis Zara said in his article "The American Labor Novel" in the January 1937 *Writer's Digest* was not only the loud, clear sound of the day but also a call to fellow writers to join in the great social cause of the 1930s—telling the story of the emergence of the blue-collar worker.

Succeeding years featured equally timely and provocative articles by everyone and anyone who could say well something about the joys or mechanics or frustrations or triumphs of writing.

As trends shifted, so did the editorial emphasis of the magazine. When the bright light of the pulp era dimmed, *Writer's Digest* warned its readers to sharpen their verbs, drop their adjectives, and start aiming at the burgeoning slick market.

Later (in the 1950s), specialty magazines began to flex their pages ... and *Writer's Digest* preached the specialization line. At about the same time, television (like all normal babies) cried night and day for *anything* even partially palatable. In those early days of television, *Writer's Digest* talked in the mysterious terms of this new market; how to write teleplays, continuity, jokes, questions for quiz shows and on and on.

The 1960s brought on a resurgence of the longer piece of writing—the book. *Writer's Digest* did whole series of articles on juvenile writing, mysteries, and the paperback phenomenon.

Alas, the 1960s also brought on the demise of some of the writer's institutions: *The Saturday Evening Post*, *Collier's*, *Coronet*, *Capper's Farmer*, *Household,* and too many others.

For the writer, the market scene shifted, and so did *Writer's Digest*. Trade journals and religious, juvenile, mystery, and confession magazines became the marketing hope for the new writer's place in the fun. Then new markets were "discovered," offering yet a new hope for the writer: advertising, publicity, political ghosting, newsletters, company publications, and dozens more in highly specialized areas.

Do any of these *new* markets sound familiar? They should. Advertising and publicity writing, for instance, is where we came in. Maybe "photoplays" will become the next *new* market for *Writer's Digest* readers.

Who knows? Whatever it is, *Writer's Digest* will be letting you know all about it, how to write for it, and where to find it.

The Forum

The thoughts expressed in these columns are those of our readers and do not necessarily coincide with the opinion of *Writer's Digest*.

FEBRUARY 1931

Please Cancel My Subscription Dept.

Dear Editor:

Some people has got more gumption than is good for those they do business with.

Not satisfied with sending youre paper to my boy, John Evan Stanton, till is cooked up a famely row, you keep on sending it till it makes troubel with the neighbors.

My neighbor come home last night and kicked on two accounts; 1st his supper wasen't ready, and second, he caught my boy mooning arround his wife and talkeing over what they read in youre paper.

My neighbor's wife throwed a full pott of beans at him and told him he got no litterary aspirashuns.

My neighbor dodged and my boy caught the Beans, Pot and All.

He ain't looked happy sense, but just the same, my neighbor's wife keeps on borrowing youre paper frum him regular.

I ask my boy ain't he ashamed of hisself the way the hull town is talking about him and my neighbor's wife, not to mention that Pot of Beans and All.

And my boy says some folks never would of been famus without some help frum scandal.

So will you just stop sending youre paper to my boy and save a lot of trouble to come.

TOM STANTON,
Stanton's Blacksmith Shoppe
309 North Division St.
DeRidder, La.

FEBRUARY 1932

Dear Editor:

It is a far cry from the stern, manly rejection slips of the 1890s to the simpering affairs of 1931. Editors in the old days spoke from the shoulder. Take the following for example. My first manuscript was an article slanted for *Leslie's* and entitled, "Up the Hill at San Juan—Why Not Over the Lawn to the White House?" About Roosevelt, you know. Three days after it was mailed it came back with a rejection slip reading:

"This magazine is not in the market for contributions of inferior literary merit. Anyhow, the Spanish-American war, is over."

It was a long pinkish slip printed in heavy, black type, and is known to collectors as the *Leslie* "comma after war."

Two weeks after I received it the comma was deleted by a five-to-four vote of *Leslie's* Editorial Board, and the slip leaped to instant value. I have refused ninety-five dollars for mine.

Another rarity in my collection is a robin's egg blue *Saturday Evening Post* slip of about 1906. So highly do I prize it that were Albert Payson Terhune to offer me half his kennels for it I should have to refuse.

Still to be found lying about, but rare enough to be worth hunting for, is the *Cosmopolitan* 1912, also known to collectors as the "monopoly grey." It reads as follows:

"Here's your manuscript. This magazine is being written by Jack London, Rex Beach, and Robert W. Chambers."

When Gouverneur Morris and Arthur B. Reeve smashed the combine, the "monopoly grey" became obsolete. I later saw this same slip bid up to seven hundred dollars at a sale of early Hergesheimer-iana. This famous author, as many know, was something of a collector himself.

I have stated earlier in this article that the rejection slips of the old days had a fine manly ring to them. This has gradually degenerated into the politely Chesterfieldian slip of today, meant to be mild and satisfying. Editors now return your manuscript with a bow that sweeps the floor and invite you to submit something else. My greatest fear as a collector is that they will at last grow so tender-hearted they won't reject anything at all. That they'll buy every last manuscript and publish them in a grade B magazine to be sold at half rates. When that time comes, *mes amis*—ah well, I shall at least have my souvenirs!

LEONARD L. SYSTER
Pennsylvania

MAY 1932

Dear Editor:

We are in a position to use a great quantity of feature stories with art and photographs of interesting subjects—girls, objects of unusual class and general happenings—suitable for use in the press.

We must have good, clear photographs that will make cuts for reproduction. It does not matter what part of the world they come from, for, though our own correspondents have Mexico and the Southwest thoroughly covered, good art is welcome though it emanate from Quintana Roo or Alaska.

We pay good rates, either on acceptance or on the tenth of the month. Unavailable material will be returned only if accompanied with stamped addressed envelope.

Unusual occurrences, "freaks," and interesting features are everywhere. We want them and we want them *now*. We can't guarantee to make anyone rich, *but* we will take all good art sent in. And we want it fast.

PAUL GIBSON, Managing Editor,
Southern Features
Laredo, Tex.

JULY 1932

Dear Editor:

Reared in a Methodist parsonage, I am surfeited on "hokum." The minister who baptized me was mean as "Old Scratch." He beat his horses unmercifully and was so strict with his children, they fairly despised him. Maybe that's the reason my baptism did not "take" so well.

I know dozens of preachers who murdered their wives by forcing childbirth upon them too often, while they, the preachers, stood in the pulpit and told their men how to lead "pure and holy" lives.

I want to live to see the motto, "What is home without mother?" replaced by "What is home without truth and consideration?"

I want to read a bestseller in which the heroine does not attain happiness by marrying at eighteen, producing a dozen nitwits, losing her teeth and hair before forty, dying at fifty, and having the following on her tombstone: "A faithful, unselfish wife and a loving, self-sacrificing mother."

The Good Book says the time will come when "Things that have been whispered in cellars shall be shouted from house-tops." You have started the shouting with that sparkling, courageous article, "Artistic Freedom or Hokum?"

However, to gain his point, Mr. Uzzell was probably guilty of over-emphasis. Truth in literature is not necessarily tragedy, sorrow, and one kind of Freudian misery piled on another.

Life is fine and beautiful in millions of ways, just as it is dreadful and repelling elsewhere. Artistic freedom is worth its goal. But writers, do not feel that you *must* be a crude realist to be honest. Truth is beauty, and beauty is soft and sweet as well as mean and dirty. Good writers see both, not just one.

MARGARET CHANDLER
Bowling Green, Ky.
First Prize Letter,
June Contest—Ed.

JANUARY 1934

Dear Editor:

Your article on Woodford's sex magazines was vile. Cancel my subscription at once. Your magazine should be barred from the mails. I am ashamed that I ever read *The Digest*.

MARGARET HILDETH BROOKES
Lexington, Ky.

Dear Editor:

I will not renew my subscription to *The Digest* if you carry any more articles on *beer*. I hate the vile stuff and don't want to promote the sale of it. I guess you'll soon be publishing articles on hard liquor.

MARY BONHAM
Chilhowie, Va.

Dear Editor:

I cannot understand how you carry an article on radio writing and promote such an un-American base influence as radio is in the American home. There are cursing and socialistic things said over the radio every day. I don't want your *Digest* any more if you carry such articles.

MRS. EVALINE CHAPMAN HARROD
Indianapolis, Ind.

Dear Editor:

I think your magazine is self-destructive. By publishing all the articles you do about requirements for *The Saturday Evening Post*, *The Rotarian*, *The Elk's Magazine*, *Liberty*, and all the other babbit profit-greedy magazines, instead of concentrating your activities on the revolutionary magazines such as *The New Masses*, *Anvil*, *New Republic*, etc., you are making way for worse and worse times which will end by eating you up. You are a slave and a reactionary. You won't face facts. Cancel my subscription. You boot licker.

EVAN HOLMES
New York City
General Delivery

MAY 1934

(Via cable collect)

Dear Editor:

I note in your April issue that Tahiti has the largest percentage of subscriptions to *Writer's Digest* per white population of any country STOP This is a misstatement STOP I am only white man here and I subscribe to WRITER'S DIGEST and have done so for past six years STOP Glad every mistake you make doesn't cost you as much as this one.

BETRAM ELLVINY SNELL
Novaya Zemlya
By Radio via Siberia

(WRITER'S DIGEST will refuse in the future corrections when sent cable or wire collect.—Ed.)*

**Sadder; wiser.*

SEPTEMBER 1934

Sir:

One of our inmates here receives your magazine every month, and becomes violently morose after reading a copy. Will you kindly discontinue his subscription. Thanking you, I am.

SIMON PEARLE, Warden,
State Institute for the Demented
Arkansas

The above letter has been framed, and a copy of it may be purchased by readers suitable for framing for 50 cents each.—Ed.

OCTOBER 1935

Sir:

Your magazine makes me sick. I would give five dollars if I were a subscriber so I could order you to cancel my subscription immediately. I never wrote a line in my life, and I bought a copy of your magazine one day by accident when I asked for *Reader's Digest*, which is a good magazine, and got yours instead.

Just for fun I kept it and took it home.

My husband, who is a normal, decent, and sometimes the best of all human beings, picked up your magazine from the table where I left it and read it through from cover to cover. It changed his entire life and it looks like it is going to change mine.

Anyway, my husband wrote a confession story and sold it, and then he wrote another story, a true one, mind you, about some people we know; my very best friends, and he intends to sell this one, too.

If he does, I'll be so ashamed of myself, I won't know what to do. I suppose you people think you are mighty smart. Your magazine gives people unethical and un-American ideas. I had my first serious quarrel with my husband in the six months we have been married and it's all your fault. The reason I went to live with my brother wouldn't have happened at all, if it wasn't for your terrible magazine. I hope something awful happens to you.

MRS. JENNY RAE RUEHLSON
Xenia, Ohio

SEPTEMBER 1938

Rummaging through old files, the editor of Houghton Mifflin found a letter which we thought might interest you.

Sir:

Within a week of my seventeenth birthday I shipped before the mast as sailor on a three top-mast sealing schooner. We went to Japan and hunted along the coast north to the Russian side of Bering Sea. This was my longest voyage; I could not again endure one of such length; not because it was tedious or long, but because life was so short. However, I have made short voyages, too brief to mention, and today am at home in any forecastle or stokehole—good comradeship.

As to literary work: My first magazine article (I had done no newspaper work), was published in January, 1899; it is now the sixth story in the *Son of the Wolf*. Since then I have done work for the *Overland Monthly*, the *Atlantic*, the *Wave*, the *Arena*, the *Youth's Companion*, the *Review of Reviews*, etc. besides a host of lesser publications, and to say nothing of newspaper and syndicate work. Hackwork for dollars, that's all, setting aside practically all ambitious effort to some future period of less financial stringency. Thus, my literary life is just thirteen months old today.

Naturally, my reading early bred in me a desire to write, but my manner of life prevented me attempting it. Common knowledge of magazine methods, etc., came to me as a revelation. Not a soul to help me.

Of course, during my revolutionaire period I perpetrated my opinions upon the public through the medium of the local papers, gratis. Once, by the way, returned from my sealing voyage, I won a prize essay of twenty-five dollars from a San Francisco paper over the heads of Stanford and California Universities, both of which were represented by second and third place through their undergraduates. This gave me hope for achieving something ultimately.

I am always studying. The aim of the university is simply to prepare one for a whole future life of study. I have been denied this advantage, but am knocking along. Never a night (whether I have gone out or not), but the last several hours are spent in bed with my books. All things interest me—the world is so very good. Principal studies are scientific, sociological, and ethical—these, of course, including biology, economics, psychology, physiology, history, etc., etc., without end. And I strive, also, to not neglect literature.

Am healthy, love exercise, and take little. Shall pay the penalty some day.

JACK LONDON
962 East 16th St.
Oakland, Calif.
March 1900

MAY 1939

Sir:

Some sixteen years ago, while I was still a member of Mr. Whisker's Naval Forces, I was coming back to the ship from Liberty one night. We were lying at the dock in Hoboken. Due to some strange impulse, I threw a very ripe tomato at the broad and authoritative back of a policeman. It was a bulls-eye.

I think then was the first faint stirrings of this thing called the "urge" to write. Unconsciously, I wanted to observe the action of an aroused limb o' the law. I did—with backward glances as I fled.

The net result of this episode was ten days in the ship's brig on b. & w. There were little round holes in the brig's door—twenty-two of 'em. Out of those ten days solitary confinement was born the plot of a yarn I am writing today. Sixteen years—a long time for a plot to chill—but that's the way they go.

I like to write sea stories—perhaps because I know more about the sea than anything else. When I write on I always buy a small model of the type of ship in my story: On it I ink in the name of my story craft. I have quite a collection with such names as "Peep O'Day," "Spindrift," "Nancy Clancy," "Rip Tide," "Katy Did," etc.

The 1939 Year Book was great. Long live you and your salty crew.

JUSTIN X. GOBB
(Chuck Wilson)
216 Pequot Ave.
New London, Conn.

JULY 1939

Sir:

Last night I crawled off a freight train on the outskirts of town. I was broke, hungry, dirty, and disgusted. In my grip I had, and still have—try to get it away from me—the 160,000-word manuscript of my first novel. Ahead of me I had a forty-block walk to town and all the problems incidental to being on the road—where to wash up, where to sleep, how to eat, etc., etc. In fact, except for its weight, I had hardly given the manuscript a thought since I left California.

Anyway, I headed for the "skidroad"; which in case you don't know, is that part of any town frequented by the "lower clawses," hoboes, itinerant working stiffs and would-be Jack Londons; and there after considerable high-class panhandling I connected with the price of a flop. It cost twenty cents, and consisted of a cot in a cubicle. There was no ceiling and only a candle for light. All night long I lay there listening to my neighbors grind their teeth, talk in their sleep, and clump up and down the hall in what sounded to me like deep-sea diving boots, listening and wondering which of the seven hells it was I had wandered into. Well, came the dawn. And a little back-door knocking for breakfast. Then calculations as to the distance to New York, plus a little inward moaning anent the parlous conditions of hitchhiking. And also some wonderment about the purpose of my trip. All of which resulted in a double strength *Mood Indigo*.

I had a contract and advance royalties from *Covici Friede*. They failed before my contract was completed. I had to finish the novel while broke, and I hadn't done a very good job of it either. I'd tried to get another contract and had been turned down four times, and once pretty hard. And so now I was headed for New York, where I could talk somebody out of another contract, was I? Nuts! Better to dump the manuscript in the nearest garbage can and go out and find me a job. Writing was for guys with college educations, for guys with a gift, for guys who could think straight. Writing wasn't for me.

And so I wandered into the public library and picked up a copy of *The Digest*; then pretty soon I wandered out again. But this time on the ball of my heel. Who said I couldn't write, that my stuff was screwy, that nobody wanted to read it anyway? How about Thomas Uzzell's "Try These On Your Next Story"? How about the tips in Bob McLean's "First You Go Up, Then You Go Down"? How about all the stuff I'd culled out of past issues of *The Digest*? How about my ten months work on the novel, and all the things I'd learned from it?

Huh! Look out New York, here I come!

Sincerely,

C.L. CLEAVES
En route

SEPTEMBER 1939

Sir:

When you decide to delete profanity from *The Digest*, please cancel my subscription. I will not read a magazine edited by a bunch of nincompoops who get scared every time a Garden Club lady yells "Fire!"

Another point: Too many of the letters you publish from authors are full of glee. It's eighteen years now that I've been putting one word after another and a third of my time is spent in the dumps.

Even a hop head feels low now and then—but a subscriber of *Writer's Digest*—never! That is, if one believes its editor.

You don't belong to the authors' union, pal, unless you're an expert nose diver.

MARTIN ELLSWORTH HARVEY
Rock Island, Ill.

JUNE 1942

Sir:

I've just been wondering, although it is none of my business, did the War take many men from the staff of *The Digest*. ...

ROSE STANTON LEE
Charlotte, N.C.

The Publisher is at Ft. Bragg. Eighteen men from our print shop are in various camps and countries.—Ed.

Sir:

Forty-two rejections later, and I received my first check for 120 dollars from Hazel Berge's Modern Romances. This is My Day, and I'm saying all the things first-salers say.

My first dollar goes for a renewal of my subscription to *The Digest*. Your magazine has been the index for all I have learned.

MRS. W.S. KNOX
Route 1
Sherman, Tex.

Sir:

Intellectual prostitution is wrecking the world at high printing press velocity. But what do you care?—eh? It's a big joke, isn't it? Write to sell. Write what? Poison. Write poison to sell. What do you care?—eh? Are you guilty?

JOHN
Box 535,
Easthampton, N.Y.

AUGUST 1942

Sir:

Before long the Board will have a weekly news release, and when we are ready to start it, we shall gratefully take advantage of your offer to run publicity for us in your magazine.

The best way for any writer to contribute of his talents to the war effort is to send to us a copy of our questionnaire, fill it out and return it us, and await assignments on specific projects which are being given us constantly by various government departments.

With thanks for your offer of cooperation.

REX STOUT
The Writers' War Board,
122 East 42nd St.
New York City

The Writer's War Board was originally formed in December, 1941, to carry out an assignment for the Treasury Department. In consultation with other government agencies and through the efforts of OCD, it was decided to broaden the scope of the Board's work, and to identify it with the Section of Volunteer Talents at the OCD. The Board is a two-way clearing house where writers can volunteer their services for war work and where government agencies can request the services of writers for specific tasks. Under the OCD, the Board has been furnished with a small office and staff in New York, and receives much volunteer assistance. The members of the Board are not paid. The "tops" in the profession work on it.

In its liaison work between the government and writers the Board has carried out assignments for the Army Air Force, the Navy, the Office of Facts and Figures, the Co-ordinator of Information, the Red Cross, the United Service Organizations, and the Maritime Commission.—Ed.

Sir:

I have been wondering what that express truck driver has been telling his friends since he carried the big wooden box to my front door nearly a week ago and calmly announced: "Typewriter, mister."

I distinctly remember having my pipe in my mouth at the time, so I couldn't have kissed him. That much is comforting, though I must have said and done other things that will be hard to live down. All I can remember at the moment is how the members of my family immediately scattered in all directions for hammer, screwdriver, scissors, and other tools when I discovered the little sticker, "WRITER'S DIGEST."

But phooey to truck drivers and other sane people. What do we care what they think?

Many thanks to you and the DIGEST for honoring me with eleventh place in the contest. It's a swell machine, and sturdy enough to eventually wear down the resistance of the Editor of *Liberty*—I hope.

VERNON E. HILL
112 East Newton St.
Tulsa, Okla.

OCTOBER 1942

Sir:

I like *The Digest* fine. But I do hate to see so much profanity. Even the women seem to think it proper to smear a little dirt in their writing. That is all the complaint I have to make. Other ways you put out a fine magazine.

Yours for clean reading, I am,

HENRY E. FOX
Plains, Tex.

DECEMBER 1949

Sir:

I read somewhere that if a writer sells five hundred dollars worth of "stuff" in a year, he is considered a professional. I'm inclined to believe that this is true. In adding up my 1949 sales, I came to the grand sum of $499.60. Anybody want to buy a story for forty cents?

NICK KOZMENIUK
9624-109A Ave.
Edmonton, Alberta, Canada

Sir:

Are there any writers, professional, or would-be, in this vicinity? I want to talk shop but am adrift in a sea of canasta players.

THELMA VERNER
Brenan Ave.
Gainsville, Ga.

Sir:

There is an old Chinese superstition that says: "If a stray dog comes to your back door, you will have good luck."

A few weeks ago the stray dog, a cute little mutt, appeared at my back door. The same day, the mailman brought my first check for a short story, in place of the usual rejection slip. Since then, I have had three more acceptances.

Here's my formula for other struggling writers. Hang a hunk of meat at the back door. Maybe the pooch will appear—along with the checks.

Incidentally, my wife wouldn't let me keep the dog.

LEE RUTTLE
3765-A Shafter Ave.
Oakland 9, Calif.

Sir:

I want to lodge a grievous complaint, not against editors—against editors' office boys. Of late, I note a growing tendency for magazines to return rejected manuscripts without the courtesy of sealing the envelopes.

Three out of five manuscripts come home unsealed, open to the not incurious eyes of postmasters, letter-handlers, mail-riders, family. They might as well be sent back in goldfish bowls.

H.E. THOMAS
Hazard, Ky.

FEBRUARY 1950

Sir:

Lee Ruttle, in your December number, says that, "If a stray dog comes to your back door you will have good luck." A mutt came to his door and he sold a story that day.

So, I hung out a hunk of meat and caught several cats. They came back in the night and howled on the fences and scratched in the grass. Since they kept me awake, I got up and looked over a reject, polished it, rewrote it in the otherwise quiet night, and sent it off. I wonder—will a cat do?

NED MAUSTON
1138 Screenland Dr.
Burbank, Calif.

DECEMBER 1951

Sir:

I am a member of the Milwaukee Metropolitan Crime Prevention Commission, a housewife, mother, and free lance writer, and in all these capacities I object to the cover from Theodore Pratt's novel used on the cover of your October issue. I am not prudish. I do not object to nudity depicted in an artistic manner, but the painting depicting "Cocotte" is sensual, voluptuous, carnal, fleshly, gross, salacious (all words from *Thesaurus*) and not a fit illustration for your type of magazine. As your subscriber, I take issue with your October issue—the cover, not the contents.

WANDA WATERS
7707 Stickney Ave.
Wauwatosa 13, Wis.

Sir:

Nobody asked me, but I'm telling you anyway. I don't like the "naked woman" on our fine mag!

VINNA MIDDLETON
Route 1, Box 2
Ashland, Ore.

Sir:

My *WD* for October did not arrive until the 17th of the month. There seems to be a very good reason for the late delivery. I am sure the letter-carrier thought the mag "too hot to handle."

Goodness knows, the gal on the cover needs a blanket; the camisole is too short. Which reminds me of the confused shopper who didn't remember if it was a casserole or a camisole he was supposed to get. Said the salesman: "It all depends—is the chicken dead or alive?"

MRS. W.F. HEPPENHEIMER
247 Webster Ave.
Jersey City 7, N.J.

JUNE 1960

Dear Editor:

For quite some time we have been trying to contact Jerry Siegel, formerly of 50 Knightsbridge Rd., Great Neck, Long Island, New York. Mr. Siegel happens merely to be none other than "the writer with the $100,000,000 brain—the original creator, with Joe Schuster, of *Superman*.

We are in possession of Siegel's manuscript, "Miracles on Antares" (the origin of which is described in the June, 1958 issue of *Future Science Fiction Magazine*) and which Nicholas Diamond assures us is "eminently appropriate" for immediate motion-picture production.

Must we call Superman personally, in order to locate his own creator? Can readers of *Writer's Digest* help?

G. BERNARD KANTOR
Ries-Kantor Promotions
533 West 112th St.
New York 25, N.Y.

Dear Phoenix (Pg. 6, March *WD*):

The things that got me off "quality" fiction were: (1) a story about the thoughts of a cow on its way to the slaughterhouse. Obviously this subject is fraught with emotionalism, for what greater depths of despair can there be? And (2) a story about a girl, with a large, lumpy lemon thrown in for symbolism. The girl was a large, lumpy lemon, too, so everything dovetailed neatly. Of course there was no resolution—her lumps and the lemon's lumps were as large and lumpy at the beginning of the piece as at the end.

I'll write me a story about sour grapes, and then I can turn purple with pleasure if I sell it.

DODY JENKINS SMITH
437 Parkwood Ave.
Kalamazoo, Mich.

Sir:

I am 7 years, 8 months, and 9 days old. I would be even older only it rained for 15 days in October and I don't count the days it rains on. Anyway, I wrote a story called "*Portrait Of A Man Sitting On a Flag Pole While His Wife Makes Flannel Cakes for Sixteen Hungry People In An Actors' Boarding House.*" My Pop says that's good title and that the trouble with most authors they make the title too short and if they made the title like mine they wouldn't have to write the story.

This story begins with two ghosts. The one ghost says to the other: "Do you believe in people?" The other ghost says: "There are two horses. Let's ask them." So they go to the horses who are looking at a stack of hay and the one ghost says: "That's a lot of hay," and the one horse says: "Well, that ain't money." And then along comes a dog and says: Hiyah, equines. How's the old hay balers?" And the one horse says, "Look, a talking dog." The one ghost says, "Where did you learn to talk?" and the dog says, "From people." And the ghost says, "Are there people?" The dog says, "Sure." The ghost says: "What do they do?" The dog says: "Well, right now, they mostly kill each other. But the guy that belongs to me, he is writing a book, Do you want to meet the guy?" The ghost said, "No, we already know a lot of ghosts that already wrote a book."

My November *Digest* came on the first and Hattie Bradfield got lost somewhere in the linotype machine, and my Pop says she probably got lost on Tenth Ave., or had to visit Elizabeth's room, whatever he means by that.

FRANKIE SCHINDLER
2220 South Elmwood Ave.
Berwyn, Ill.

WRITER'S DIGEST

PART I

Articles AND Essays

WHERE TO SELL STORIES, BOOKS, ARTIC

VOLUME II MARCH 1921 NO. 4

Started Writing at the Age of Ten

***WRITER'S DIGEST* EDITOR**

Interestingly enough, this off-hand, under-the-radar piece announced the arrival of one of twenteith-century America's greatest writers, four years before the publication of what many consider to be his masterpiece, *The Great Gatsby*. It paints a picture of F. SCOTT FITZGERALD that most wouldn't recognize: youthful, vibrant, and funny, without any trace of the alcoholism that eventually destroyed him.

F. Scott Fitzgerald, the brilliant young novelist whose short story, "Head and Shoulders," under the screen title of "The Chorus Girl's Romance," recently released by Metro and starring Viola Dana, is a young man whom obviously, the gods love. For Mr. Fitzgerald enjoys the unique and enviable distinction of being the youngest successful writing man in America, if not the world, with a novel and numerous short stories to his credit and more in demand.

Mr. Fitzgerald was born in St. Paul, Minnesota, September 24, 1896. This makes him not quite twenty-five years old—an extraordinary but incontestable fact. He was educated at the St. Paul Academy in St. Paul, Minnesota, during his early youth, after which he attended Newman School in Hackensack, New Jersey, and then entered Princeton University at the age of seventeen.

He elected literature as a profession at the age of ten, and at once started writing as though each day might be his last, with the result that at twenty-three Scribners published his first novel, *This Side of Paradise*, and the magazines commenced writing him letters for his work. During the war he served as a first lieutenant in the Forty-fifth and Sixty-seventh Infantry, and as aide-de-camp to General J.A. Ryan. He is a descendent of Francis Scott Key, who wrote "The Star-Spangled Banner," and his whole name is Francis Scott Key Fitzgerald. Mr. Fitzgerald was married on April 3, 1920, to Miss Zelda Sayre of Montgomery, Alabama, and for the rest, his own words can best describe his ingenuous personality:

"I wear brown soft hats in winter," he confesses. "Panamas in summer, loathe dress suits and never wear one, and prefer people with greenish-gray eyes." And again: "I'd rather watch a good shimmy dance than Ruth St. Denis and Pavlova combined!"

Could anything be more delightful? And this is the young man who wrote the story of the shimmy dancer who fell in love with the college boy as told in "Head and Shoulders," which was published in *The Saturday Evening Post*, and which Metro has released under the title of "The Chorus Girl's Romance."

VOLUME III JUNE 1922 NO. 7

A.A. MILNE

This autobiographical piece was written for *Writer's Digest* by the creator of Winnie the Pooh, four years prior to the little bear's creation. A.A. MILNE was already well known, however, for having written three successful novels and eleven plays. But in 1921, he produced a story that gave no indication of the gentle children's tale to come. The title? *The Red House Mystery*. The subject? Murder.

I was born in London on January 18, 1882, so I ought to be forty years old now—but nobody believes it. At the age of eleven I went to Westminster School with a scholarship and for a year worked very hard, but at twelve I began to feel that I knew enough and thereafter took life more easily. Perhaps the most important thing that happened there was that I began to write verses, parodies, and the like for the school paper. One evening when another boy and I were looking at a copy of a Cambridge undergraduate paper—*The Granta*—which had come to the school, he said solemnly: "You ought to edit that some day." So I said, equally solemnly: "I will." This sounds like the story of the model boy who became a millionaire; I apologize for it, but it really did happen. I went to Cambridge—in spite of the fact that everybody meant me to go to Oxford—and edited *The Granta*.

I left Cambridge in 1903 with a very moderate degree and a feeling in the family that I had belied the brilliant promise of my youth, and that it was about time I got to work and did something. Schoolmastering and the Indian civil service were two of the professions suggested. The first was not very exciting; the second meant more examinations to pass; so I said that I was going to London to write. I had enough money left over from my Cambridge allowance to keep me for a year, and by the end of the year I saw myself the most popular writer in London—editor of *The Times*, *Punch*, and *The Spectator*, member of all the important literary clubs, and intimate friend of Meredith and Hardy. My family was not so optimistic. They saw me at the end of the year deciding to be a schoolmaster. However, they gave me their blessing; and I went to London, took expensive rooms, and settled down to write.

By the end of the year, I had spent my money and I had earned, by writing, 20 pounds. So I moved to two cheap and dirty rooms in a policeman's house in Chelsea and went on writing. The second year, I made about 120 pounds and lived on it. In the third year, I was by way of making 200 pounds, for several papers were not getting used to me, but in February, 1906, a surprising thing happened. The editor of *Punch* retired, the assistant editor became editor, and I was offered the assistant editorship. I accepted and was assistant editor until the year 1914. Then for four years, I was in the Royal Warwickshire regiment and served on the western front.

When the war was over, I decided not to go back to *Punch*, with its regular weekly article, but keep myself free to write what and where and when I liked; risky, perhaps, at first, but much more fun. I have been doing this since, and have had no financial reasons for regretting it.

As to "The Red House Mystery"—I have always adored detective stories; I have always thought they must be great fun to write. One day, about three years ago, I thought of rather a good way of murdering somebody. Instead of leaving it at that, I went on thinking about it, and finally decided that it would make a good story. I began to write the first chapter and left the story to take care of itself. I hope it has done so successfully.

As regards more intimate matters, I have one wife, one son, one house, and one recreation—golf.

VOLUME IV OCTOBER 1923 NO. 11

Sex, Deftly Handled

H. BEDFORD-JONES, AUTHOR OF "THE FICTION BUSINESS," "THE SECOND MATE," ETC.

"King of the Pulps," **H. BEDFORD-JONES** was one of the early twentieth century's most respected—and highest paid—writers of pulp fiction. Although not as well known today as some of his contemporaries (including Walter Gibson, creator of *The Shadow*), Bedford-Jones overshadowed them all at the height of his popularity. He was known for producing a prodigious amount of quality material, almost all of which he sold for publication. Conservative estimates peg his output at more than twelve hundred magazine stories and seventy novels. And yet, as passionate as he was about his writing, he was equally as passionate about his beliefs. In the following article, he advises writers to avoid writing for the "sex magazines." That straightforward plea began a debate that played itself out in the pages of *The Digest*. The challenger? Dashiell Hammett—whose piece, and Bedford-Jones's response to it, follows this one.

There is a great deal of loose talk on this subject of sex and what attitude the writer should take toward it. Most of it is put on a purely sentimental or ethical basis. Mr. Bedford-Jones's article, though, is straight from the shoulder, and carries weight because he puts his whole case on good business grounds. We urge our readers to think twice, or better, read this article twice, before entering this market.—The Editor

There is a lot of money to be made by writers who can supply stories with a touch of sex, deftly handled.

In this obviously true statement, there is a great deal more than appears on the surface. It applies not only to magazines, but to books, as certain publishers who openly worship St. Pandarus have discovered. The two final words contain a very plausible and crafty snare for writers. In the hope that many other writers will read these words, I want to discuss the subject of sex literature, exactly as I see it, no preaching, but from a purely business aspect.

How does this growing flood of magazine and book publication, with a sex trend, affect those of us who make a living by writing—or want to? How does it affect our business, our rates, our editorial relations? It is the most deadly menace that writers have ever faced.

Now, it has certain claims to the consideration of writers. There is money in it, plenty of money. The publishers of any sex magazine emphasize its morality—that is, the fact that it must preach the bitter fruit of wrongdoing in order to get through the mails. We need not discuss this sort of argument. The plain fact is, as we all know, that these magazines are meant to be just as "snappy" as possible and still get by.

I'm not going to regard their morality, or lack of morality, at all. Let's look at this whole thing from a business standpoint, brethren.

In Europe, sex literature is decidedly on the wane. In Italy, a revulsion of popular sentiment allied to Fascism is sweeping it out of being. In Spain, readers have revolted against it in another way—it is dying of inertia. In France, the author of *La Garçonne* was expelled from the Legion of Honor; yet his book has not a tithe of the rotten degeneracy exhibited in Waldo Frank's *Rahab*, for example.

Now, why is all this true? Simply because the deadly menace to the writing craft has been perceived.

The menace is distinctly a commercial matter to be regarded as such by those of us who can gain no higher viewpoint.

First, this sort of literature fills a gap, supplies a demand; a large class of people desire it and buy it.

The same holds true of the white slave trade.

The publishers who specialize in this sort of book and magazine, the writers who produce it, aim first at pandering to the salacious reader, and second at masking this salacity behind a pretense of realism or cleverness or pseudo-morality.

This is perfectly legal and is a matter of business. The younger tribe of writers who make money by supplying mental aphrodisiacs for the bawdy trade loudly proclaim the triumph of art over censorship. They cannot claim that it is good business for them, however. It is a good business only for the pandering publisher. For the writer, it is business suicide. Why?

When the first flood of sex magazines came out, the better publications attempted to supply a check by means of a tacit blacklisting of the writers. This failed. Then, as now, much of the sex stuff came out under pen names. The writers who make a living from these magazines are usually good enough businesspeople to hide the fact, not from a sense of shame, but from a good business sense.

The Personal Danger

Let us avoid entirely the personal danger to the writer—the inner danger to himself. Let us regard only the menace to his pocketbook, his business, his future. If he is to make a living and a name for himself, the writer must look to ten and twenty years hence, not merely to the story he is writing today. This is vitally true. Tomorrow is built only on today. Now, the menace which faces the writer who is an intellectual prostitute is—aside from all questions of ethics or morality, but purely in a business sense—exactly that which faces the physical prostitute. There is no other analogy. There is glitter today, and tomorrow there is nothing. The writer may make a living but the publisher makes the big money.

And how is the writer of this stuff considered in the business world—in the world of writers? Exactly as a prostitute is considered in the social world.

You will cry out at this, but let's see. You say: "Look at Brown or Smith! Making slathers of money, and in the front of literature today! They are regarded by other writers as artistic masters—"

Hold on. How do you know they are so regarded—and by what other writers? You see a lot of log-rolling in a few magazines. Smith praises Brown's latest pornographic feat, and Brown praises Robinson, and all three get their friends into the action, and their publishers exert all possible pull to get the log-rolling printed in this or that "literary" periodical. The demimondaine says: "What clever writing!" The man or woman seeking vicarious sexual enjoyment chuckles and commends the story. I defy you to hear either it or the writer praised by anyone who amounts to a tinker's dam in the business world, the social world, the world of art or literature, or any other of the kingdoms of the world. So you must choose whether your writing, as a business, is to reach the people who are worthwhile and have a solid foundation, or to reach lower classes of people and get you nothing twenty years hence.

Does that verge on preaching? Then let's get back a bit. The magazine prostitutes, like their sisters in the flesh, reach out always for new blood—new writers. They do it in crude ways or in clever ways. One of them not long ago got a writer into its pages by sending him a list of reputable writers who had been signed up, with a statement of change of policy, etc. He found too late that it was all bluff—they wanted his name in their pages, even with a perfectly decent story under it.

"Deftly Handled"

Oh that clever phrase "deftly handled." The writer who would produce nothing raw is led on by an appeal to his artistry and craftsmanship. He is tempted by the money and publicity and the glitter, as viewed from a pinnacle of the temple; "cast thyself down—you can't hurt yourself, and look what you can gain!"

But you *can* hurt yourself, and you can hurt your business career past repair. I'm not preaching about your self-respect, but about your solid business standing. One of my proudest moments was when I met a certain great writer, to whom I thought myself absolutely unknown; and the talk touching upon a certain sex magazine, I answered a question by the remark that I knew little about such magazines and did not write for them. "Yes," came the reply. "Yes, I know you don't."

Regardless of the little circle of smelly writers who do log-rolling, your standing is thus indubitably affected if you go into this sort of work. How about your rates? Your pocketbook receives a more direct hit. You may not think it. You may think it a grand thing to be sure of selling all your stuff, to have a ready market, to get a steady two cents per word from a class of magazines constantly increasing in number and circulation.

It looks big. But count up the market thus afforded as against the market afforded by all other magazines. Count up the most you can earn by writing for the "best" sex magazines, and the most you can earn by writing for the best adventure or business or other fiction magazines. You'll see that if there's any cash balance, it's on the side of decency.

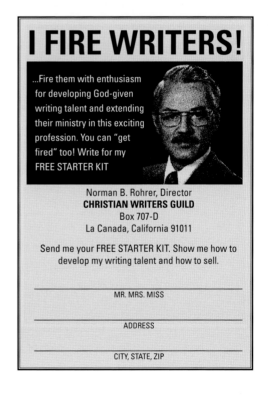

The effect on your business future is marked. You may start out, as many of us do, with the smallest little magazines, and work up to the top; but I defy you to start out with any sex magazine and work into any better class of writing. This is partly because your business future is governed by your associations; and with whom do you associate in the line of mental prostitution? With radicals, with social perverts, with moral lepers and anonymities—in short, with destroyers, not with builders.

But, you say, what of my art? Piffle. But, you say, the subject of sex is a realism that exists in the world; to neglect it, pretend not to see it, is absurdity!

Of course. Dead right. Now you're getting down to the basic principles. There's not the least objection against sex in literature. The objection is purely against its manipulation by unclean minds for unclean minds—as it is handled in our avowedly "sex" magazines and by our two or three pander-publishers. Then, you say, how to define the matter? Easily enough.

Artists recognize the principle that the nude in art is admissable, only if unconscious; self-conscious nudity is an appeal to the senses of the beholder and is banned. The same may apply to our writing. You can use almost any sex theme extant, if you use it with a clean heart and mind, and get it into the best magazines. A story, "The Lariat," in a recent issue of *Everybody's*, is a case in point. "Casanova's Homecoming" is a case in point of the contrary.

I submit that this prurient trend constitutes a menace to the business as a whole—to the entire writing game. We have seen it as a looming menace to the screen; and the screen, as a whole, has nipped it—as a matter of good business. More credit to the screen. Less credit to the publishers. Less credit to the log-rolling writers who declaim against the censorship. No writer has anything to fear from censorship unless his output contains something of which he is ashamed. Chew over that.

VOLUME V JUNE 1924 NO. 7

Shall We Write Sex Stories?

DASHIELL HAMMETT AND H. BEDFORD-JONES, IN DEFENCE OF THE SEX STORY

DASHIELL HAMMETT, author of *The Maltese Falcon, The Thin Man, The Glass Key,* and other classic mysteries of the "hard-boiled" variety, launched his writing career in the early 1920s. He was successful, to say the least, creating such classic characters as Sam Spade and Nick and Nora Charles. It's an odd bit of coincidence that *Black Mask* magazine published Hammett's first short story the same month that *Writer's Digest* ran H. Bedford-Jones's piece on writing for sex magazines (page 27). As detailed in that article, Jones had strong opinions regarding the use of sex in fiction. Hammett, however, disagreed, perhaps in part due to his penchant for crafting mystery stories in a more realistic, gritty vein. The text of his counterargument follows, along with Bedford-Jones's conclusive response.

A discussion of an article by H. Bedford-Jones which appeared in the October Writer's Digest, *titled "Sex, Deftly Handled." Mr. Bedford-Jones held that the writer could not afford to write them, as it affected both his reputation and his mental fiber.*

BY DASHIELL HAMMETT

Just a voice in disagreement with nearly everything that Mr. Bedford-Jones says in "Sex, Deftly Handled."

Literature, as I see it, is good to the extent that it is art, and bad to the extent that it isn't; and I know of no other standard by which it may be judged. As Jim Tully, writing recently of another who held opinions somewhat similar to Mr. Bedford-Jones, said: "It would be well for him to remember that art knows no morals—art being a genuine something—while morals differ in all lands."

If you have a story that seems worth telling, and you think you can tell it worthily, then the thing for you to do is to tell it, regardless of whether it has to do with sex, sailors, or mounted policemen.

Sex has never made a poor story good, or a good one poor; but if Mr. Bedford-Jones will make a list of the stories that are still alive after several centuries, he'll find that many of the heartiest survivors have much to do with the relations between the sexes and treat those relations with little of the proper Victorian delicacy.

Is Mr. Bedford-Jones in earnest, I wonder, when he places "The Exile of the Lariat" above "Casanova's Homecoming"?

Remembering, for instance, the meeting between Maurice and his mistress, and Arcade in "The Revolt of the Angels," would he, I wonder, put Anatole France among his "mental prostitutes"?

Does he believe that Shakespeare's *Henry VIII* is, because of its comparative sexlessness, a better play than Shakespeare's *Measure for Measure*?

And the associates he gives the writer for sex magazines: "radicals ... social perverts ... moral lepers ..." In Jack London's day, I understand, there were many good people who thought him a radical!

Now—that there may be no misunderstanding—here's exactly where Mr. Bedford-Jones's shoe pinches *me*, and where it doesn't. I've written altogether three stories that are what is sometimes called "sex stuff," and two—or possibly three—that might be so called if you stretched the term a bit. Against them, I've sold nine or ten stories in which no a single feminine name appeared; and half a dozen more in which only female characters were very minor ones. Then quite a few stories with the ordinary "love interest" and so forth.

The "sex stuff" is about 5 percent of what I have sold; and if figured upon what I have written, the average would be much lower—

Surely not a large "pinch."

REPLY TO MR. HAMMETT BY H. BEDFORD-JONES

Mr. Hammett is entitled to disagree; I like his honest opinion, and his argument is excellent. Unfortunately, it has nothing to do with the subject of my recent article, which was not "Sex," but "Sex, Deftly Handled."

A story worth telling, told worthily as possible—good gosh, Hammett, that's all any writer wants to do! The qualifier means a lot, however; that little "worthily" is the meat of the nut. Your letter itself shows that you're honest about your work, and you simply read too much into my article, which was no diatribe at all against sex in writing. Look at it this way. Suppose I let off a hot blast against smutty so-called "smoking room" stories; would you consider that I damned all after-dinner stories, which may be risqué and yet very witty? Not a bit of it. My argument is not against the story worth telling, but against the story deliberately written with a smutty pen to get the dinero. Your own record shows that you are not that sort of writer.

No, you can't lead me into that morass of morals and literature. I like a good sex story as well as anybody, if it's written with a clean mind. But, when it's written with a dirty mind, I don't like it—and you know perfectly well how much dirt is floating around in books and magazines, and how much of the stuff is put out deliberately as a mental aphrodisiac. Get my point better now?

VOLUME XIII FEBRUARY 1932 NO. 3

The Future of the Novel

H.G. WELLS AS TOLD TO M.B. SCHNAPPER

H.G. WELLS provided *Writer's Digest* with the following thoughts more than thirty years after having published *The Time Machine, The Island of Dr. Moreau, The Invisible Man,* and *The War of the Worlds*—the science fiction classics for which he is best known. In the years that followed until his death in 1946, he spent most of his time writing about social reform and the failings of capitalism. His thoughts regarding the future of mankind were strong ones, leaning toward socialism and the creation of a World State. Some of these thoughts are reflected in "The Future of the Novel." One year later, in 1933, Wells wrote *The Shape of Things to Come,* in which a council of scientists takes over the world in order to save mankind from itself.

There is realism and realism. Today, the fabric of the English and American novel has become realistic in everything but the actual naming of places and people. Thus we have the grocery store of No. 7, Blank Street, or the parish church of Dashington, against a background of trains running fair and square into London or Wichita. If the heroine sticks her head out of the train at New York's Grand Central station and says "Good-bye, dirty old Manhattan," no one hectors the author for "making a living" by unjust criticism (thrust into the mouth of a character who is a mere mask for himself) of the cleanest, biggest, etc., etc. The common sense of the reading and critical public long ago accepted the necessity of putting "real places" into fiction under their proper names and of admitting comment and discussion of them. Why should there be any objection to the same thing being done with the cardinal figures in the contemporary social landscape—the men and women who are molding the destinies of the nations?

To answer that is to realize very extensive changes that are in progress in the common texture of life today. In the days of Jane Austen it was possible to write a novel, giving the mental life of decent folk in England, with not a glance at political, social, or economic changes. Life and its processes had such an air of established stability upon her countryside that it was possible for her to ignore the battle of Waterloo and disregard the infinitely remote social distresses of manufacturing. Life went on inside a frame of public events so remote that no connection was apprehended between the two. If the squire babbled politics, what he said mattered no more than the odd things said by his lady when she had a fever.

And even in the great novels of the Dickens-Thackeray-George Eliot period, in Flaubert, in the chief novels of prerevolutionary Russia, in the Victorian novels of America, the march of large events was so remote that it could still be treated as the stars or Abyssinia or the structure of the atom are still being treated today—as irrelevant altogether. Even wars could be kept "off stage" in novels in English, at any rate until 1914. When they come in, as the war in North Italy comes into some of Meredith's novels, they come in *externally*, as scenery, as an uncontrollable outer event with which the action of the novel has no connection.

The common flow of human life—and therefore the normal novel—was going on right up to the opening decade of the twentieth century, with slight and negligible reactions from government or conspicuous personalities. Today that is no longer true.

Today, just as the world is growing smaller, as some say, because communications grow more rapid, so also public and collective life is growing intenser and penetrating private life more and more. We literary folk are in closer touch with the direction of affairs, and so is it with us. The personalities concerned are not only clearly and fully known, but they react more upon us. And the drive of change is far more perceptible. Institutions and standards that seemed to be established altogether and completely unchallengeable in the novel of fifty years ago are now challenged and changing; and the discussion of such changes, which was once unthinkable for ordinary people, is now a determining factor in their lives.

People like Lord Birkenhead abroad and Henry Seidel Canby in this country complain that in my novels, instead of picturing life, I discuss it. I certainly have it discussed. It is impossible to picture contemporary life without discussing it. People who are not discussing now are not alive. No doubt, it is hard to report people thinking in character, and I admit that I do it at times atrociously, but it has to be done. I plead the pioneer's right to be clumsy. Better be clumsy than shirk the way we have to go.

I happen to have lived as a novelist through the dawning realization of this change in the relation of private and public events, and to have felt my way before I saw it clearly toward the new methods this change has made necessary. I began, when I found that I wanted to convey the social scenery and put in some of its more characteristic peaks and prominences, by the old-established methods of the more or less modified real person under a false name.

I have found that method out. It is an utterly rotten method. And I wish all embryo as well as mature novelists would remember that. That method has been practiced by the masters before me; compare, for example, the Marquis of Steyne in *Vanity Fair*. Let me give quite frankly a particular case of my own. My chief character in *The New Machiavelli* was an ambitious young man who came into Parliament with a big Liberal wave in the opening decade of this country.

Such a young man was bound to get into some relations with the then-active Fabian Society and to be in touch with and meet and get points of view from the outstanding members of the Fabian Society—Mr. and Mrs. Sidney Webb. They all did. The influence of that organization was immense. If that phase was to be left out, the story would get so out of drawing as to be unreal. Well, I hold now that I ought to have put in Mr. and Mrs. Webb by name, just as I put in the Speaker or Palace Yard. They were just as much a part of the scene.

But, under the influence of the old tradition, I put in some people in the place of the Webbs, rather like them, but yet not exactly them. These phantoms who were like, but not yet identified with the Webbs, got worked into the story. I was amused to invent things about them, and I did so because I had released myself from direct statement. They are not the Webbs, but only Webby people. I succumbed to the temptation of making it rather a lark. But everyone recognized the "originals," so what was the good of the sham concealment? Everyone said, naturally enough, that I had made a malicious caricature. Everyone except Mr. and Mrs. Webb, who took it very cheerfully and charmingly and refused to make a quarrel of it to please their ardent friends. And there was a Balfouresque Mr. Evesham too in that novel. And these quasi-Webbs and this quasi-Balfour set all hunters of "originals" agog to hunt identifications up and down the wretched book. It is the sort of fun a Walter Winchell likes to have. For years, I could not write a book without having half the characters identified each with a dozen different "originals." And any figures left over at last, bless their hearts, were me!

This is not the way to handle the political novel. If a writer is to put in prominent people, he must put them in under their own names or destroy the reality of the human scenery altogether. There is nothing left for the novel nowadays but crime and adultery, if public life, economic forces, and the highly individualized personalities directing them are to be taboo. That is how the novel has gone in France. I do not believe it is going that way in England. I hope it is not in America.

In brief, the difference between the modern novel and the novel of the last century is this: that then, the drive of political and mercantile events and the acts of their directing personalities scarcely showed above the horizon of the ordinary life, and now they do. My refined contemporaries who explain to interviewers that there is nothing real in *their* novels are not really keeping close to simple humanity; they are merely keeping on the old course while humanity turns into the new.

VOLUME XIII JUNE 1932 NO. 7

The Tarzan Theme

EDGAR RICE BURROUGHS

When challenged to compile a list of fictional characters known the world over, only a handful come to mind. Mickey Mouse, certainly. Superman, of course. And then, there is Tarzan. His creator, **EDGAR RICE BURROUGHS**, was born on September 1, 1875. It wasn't until the age of thirty-six that Burroughs began writing—but even then, he had the gift. His very first novel, *A Princess of Mars,* was published in 1912. Soon after, he published *Tarzan of the Apes,* the first of twenty-three adventures starring the legendary hero. Though sources differ on exactly how many Tarzan novels have been sold, the most conservative estimate weighs in at more than thirty million copies in fifty-eight languages (including braille). Add to this thirty-eight movies, countless cartoons, television series, comic books, radio shows and newspaper strips, plus the ape-man's very own city (Tarzana, California), and it becomes clear that Mickey and Superman run a distant second and third. But what did Burroughs think of his omnipresent hero? Read on ...

Someone is always taking the joy out of life. For twenty years I proceed blissfully writing stories to keep the wolf from my door and to cause other people to forget for an hour or two the wolves at their doors, and then up pops the editor of *Writer's Digest* and asks me for an article on the Tarzan theme.

Frankly, there ain't no such animal; or if there is, I didn't know it.

Breathlessly, I flew to Mr. Webster, determined to create a Tarzan theme with his assistance; but I was disappointed in somehow not finding Tarzan in the dictionary. But I did find "theme." Webster calls it: "A subject or topic on which a person writes or speaks; a proposition for discussion or argument; a text."

That definition simplified my task, for under this definition the Tarzan theme consists of one word—Tarzan.

This is a helpful solution because it is easy and right now I am as busy as the well-known, one-armed paperhanger with the hives. I have to write two novels a year in addition to other writing; I am publishing my own books now, two a year, which entails a tremendous amount of detail; then there are seven newspaper strips a week in addition to motion pictures and radio. Being in the real estate business as a sideline adds to my labors, though not greatly for the past two years, as any realtor will tell you, unless paying taxes comes under the head of labor.

On top of all this, I have recently acquired by foreclosure a championship eighteen-hole golf course at Tarzana, California, which I have partially opened to the public for tournament play. A few days ago a good natured columnist commented on my activities in the *New York Evening Telegram* as follows:

> Edgar Rice Burroughs is marketing his book *Jungle Girl*, from his home in Tarzana, California. Mr. Burroughs is the nation's sixth largest industry, now that steel and railroads are slowing up.

Had he known about the golf course, I think he might have moved me up.

There is, however, one great advantage in all these activities. I have always required a great deal of exercise, but the amount that I must now take is considerably lessened by the fact that all these things, especially the real estate business, make me sweat without any other effort. Getting back to the theme—"a proposition for discussion or argument," says Mr.

Webster. The Tarzan stories are a means for avoiding discussion or argument, so that definition is out, and there only remains the last, "a text." As this connotes sermonizing we shall have to hit it on the head, which leaves me nothing at all to write about on the Tarzan theme.

Tarzan does not preach; he has no lesson to impart, no propaganda to disseminate. Yet, perhaps unconsciously, while seeking merely to entertain I have injected something of my own admiration for certain fine human qualities into these stories of the ape-man.

It is difficult and even impossible for me to take these Tarzan stories seriously, and I hope that no one else will ever take them seriously. If they serve any important purpose, it is to take their readers out of the realm of serious things and give them that mental relaxation which I believe to be as necessary as the physical relaxation of sleep—which makes a swell opening for some dyspeptic critic.

I recall that when I wrote the first Tarzan story twenty years ago, I was mainly interested in playing with the idea of a contest between heredity and environment. For this purpose, I selected an infant child of a race strongly marked by hereditary characteristics of the finer and nobler sort, and, at an age at which he could not have been influenced by association with creatures of his own kind, I threw him into an environment as diametrically opposite that to which he had been born as I might well conceive.

As I got into the story, I realized that the logical result of this experiment must have been a creature that would have failed to inspire the sympathy of the ordinary reader, and that for fictional purposes I must give heredity some breaks that my judgment assured me the facts would not have warranted. And so Tarzan grew into a creature endowed only with the best characteristics of the human family from which he was descended and the best of those which mark the wild beasts that were his only associates from infancy until he had reached man's estate.

It has pleased me throughout the long series of Tarzanian exploits to draw comparisons between the manners of men and the manners of beasts and seldom to the advantage of men. Perhaps I hoped to shame men into being more like beasts in those respects in which the beasts excel men, and these are not few.

I wanted my readers to realize that man alone of all the creatures that inhabit the earth or the waters below or the air above takes life wantonly; he is the only creature that derives pleasure from inflicting pain on other creatures, even his own kind. Jealousy, greed, hate, spitefulness are more fully developed in man than in the lower orders. These are axiomatic truths that require no demonstration.

Even the lion is merciful when he makes his kill, though doubtless not intentionally so; and the psychology of terror aids the swift mercy of his destruction. Men who have been charged and mauled by lions, and lived to tell of the experience, felt neither fear nor pain during the experience.

In the quite reasonable event that this statement may arouse some skepticism, permit me to quote from that very splendid work on animals, *Mother Nature*, by William J. Long, a book that should be read by every adult and be required reading in every high school course in the land.

> There are other and more definite experiences from which to form a judgment, and of these the adventure of Livingston is the first to be considered, since he was probably the first to record the stupefying effects of a charging animal. The great missionary and explorer was once severely mauled by a lion, his flesh being torn in eleven places by the brute's claws, and his shoulder crushed by the more terrible fangs. Here is a condensation of the story, as recorded in *Missionary Travels and Research in South Africa*:
>
> Growling horribly close to my ear, the lion shook me as a terrier does a rat. The shock produced a stupor similar to that which seems to be felt by a mouse after the first shake of the cat. It caused

> a sort of dreaminess, in which there was no sense of pain nor feeling of terror.

Compare this, then, with the methods of the present-day gangster who cruelly tortures his victim before he kills him. The lion sought only to kill, not to inflict pain. Recall the methods of the Inquisition, and then search the records of man's experiences with lions, tigers, or any of the more formidable creatures of the wild for a parallel in studied cruelty.

Let me quote one more interesting instance given in Mr. Long's book. We open at random to the experience of an English officer who, in 1895, was fearfully clawed and bitten by a lion, and who writes of the experience:

> Regarding my sensations during the time the attack upon my by the lion was in progress, I had no feeling of pain whatever, although there was a distinct feeling of being bitten; that is, I was perfectly conscious, independently of seeing the performance, that the lion was gnawing at me, but there was no pain. To show that the feeling, or rather want of it, was in now wise due to excessive terror I may mention that, whilst my thighs were being gnawed, I took two cartridges out of the breast pocket of my shirt and threw them to the Kaffir, who was hovering a few yards away, telling him to load my rifle.

Perhaps I am not wise in giving further publicity to these statements, since they must definitely take much of the thrill out of Tarzan stories by placing lion mauling in a category with interesting and pleasurable experiences.

Having demonstrated that the most savage animals in their most terrifying moods reveal qualities far less terrible than those possessed by man, let us see how association with these beasts combined with the hereditary instincts of a noble bloodline to produce in Tarzan a character finer than either of the sources from which it derived.

Necessity required him to kill for food and in defense of his life, the example of his savage associates never suggested that pleasure might be found in killing, and the chivalry that was in his bloodstream prevented him imagining such pleasure in youth without such example. His viewpoint toward death was seemingly callous, but it was without cruelty.

His attitude toward women and other creatures weaker than he was partially the result of innate chivalry, partially the natural outcome of a feeling of superiority engendered both by knowledge of his mental or physical superiority to every creature that had come within his ken and by heredity, and partially by an indifference born of absolute clean-mindedness and perfection of health.

His appeal to an audience is so tremendous that it never ceases to be a source of astonishment to me. This appeal, I believe, is based upon an almost universal admiration of these two qualities and the natural inclination of every normal person to enjoy picturing himself as either heroic or beautiful or both. Linked to these is the constant urge to escape that is becoming stronger in all of us prisoners of civilization as civilization becomes more complex.

We wish to escape not alone the narrow confines of city streets for the freedom of the wilderness, but the restrictions of manmade laws, and the inhibitions that society has placed upon us. We like to picture ourselves as roaming free, the lords of ourselves and of our world; in other words, we would each like to be Tarzan. At least I would; I admit it.

Unconsciously or consciously, we seek to emulate the creatures we admire. Doubtless there are many people trying to be like the late Theodore Roosevelt, or like Robert Millikan, or Jack Dempsey, or Doug Fairbanks because they greatly admire one of these characters. Fiction characters are just as real to most of us as are these celebrities of today or the past; d'Artagnan is as much flesh and blood as Napoleon. Perhaps the influence of d'Artagnan has had a finer influence upon the forming of character than has that of the great Corsican.

To indicate the force for good which a fiction character may exercise, I can do no better than cite the testimony of Eddie Eagan, Amateur Heavyweight Champion of the World, whose very interesting series of articles appeared in *The Saturday Evening Post.* As a boy, Eagan read the Frank Merriwell books, and his admiration for this fictional character shaped his future life. Among other achievements, Merriwell became an athlete and a Yale man, and these became two of Eagan's ambitions. Although a poor boy, Eagan worked his way through an education, first in college in Denver, then through Yale, and finally Oxford; and he became one of the greatest athletes of our times.

Years ago, when I came to a realization of the hold that Tarzan had taken upon the imaginations of many people, I was glad that I had made of him the sort of character that I had; and since then I have been careful not to permit him to let his foot slip, no matter what the temptation. I must admit that, at times, this has been difficult when I have placed him in situations where I would not have been quite sure of my own footing, and it has also not been easy to keep him from being a Prue.

On the whole, however, I must have been more or less successful for all ages and both sexes continue to admire him; and he goes his bloody way scattering virtue and sudden death indiscriminately and in all directions.

He may not be a force for good; and if he entertains, that is all I care about; but I am sure that he is not a force for evil, which is something these days.

VOLUME XIII JUNE 1932 NO. 7

The Detective in Fiction

JOHN DICKSON CARR

Though contemporary readers might not be familiar with **JOHN DICKSON CARR**, mystery lovers would be well advised to search out his works. Born in 1906, Carr is generally regarded as one of the greatest mystery writers of all time. He published his first novel, *It Walks by Night*, two years before the piece that follows. In the time between, he established himself as a master of the form, particularly those mysteries that involved seemingly impossible puzzles. His masterpiece—considered one of the best "locked room" mysteries ever written—is titled *The Three Coffins* (1935). In 1963, the Mystery Writers of America presented Carr with their Grand Master award. He died in 1977, after having published more than seventy novels, several dozen radio plays, nine short story collections, and an award-winning biography of Sir Arthur Conan Doyle.

The strangest thing about a good detective story is that it is really a detective story. That is to say, it possesses a detective with a modicum of intelligence, who actually solves the mystery. The real objection to most thrillers nowadays is not that the plots are bad, but that the detective is hopeless. He boggles and blunders along until somebody uncovers a clue which leads inevitably in the wrong direction. That always heads the sleuth in the right direction. Then, after more messing about with cigar-bands and persecuted heroines, the truth comes out. And no amount of ecstatic praise on the part of the author ("Inspector Whooze was a shrewd, patient, hardworking operative who always got his man") will convince the reader that Inspector Whooze belongs anywhere but in a kindergarten.

The reader, while as innocent as a child, is also as critical. He is quite willing to believe in Santa Claus, but you must at least give him a glimpse of the old gentleman's boots coming down the chimney.

And right there is where Inspector Whooze and his colleagues fail. They are not supermen. They are fashioned to resemble one's own next-door neighbor—which is precisely what the reader does not want. Something of the awe and terror of crime itself should cling round the figure of the detective: a grim shadow behind a curtain, who might himself be a criminal. Let the author invest him with this sense of gloom and the dark places of the brain, and we may safely leave all the wholesomeness to the murderer.

It will thus be apparent why, in all annals of detective fiction, there has been only one man. The lean hawk-faced gentleman from Baker Street—Sherlock Holmes of the evil laughter and the hypodermic needle—beside him, the rest of them are pygmies. It was not alone that with one glance he could tell that you were left-handed, asthmatic, henpecked, and a retired sergeant of marines from Afghanistan. It was rather the sense of overshadowing knowledge that emanated from him—and you understood that eerie power when night after night you saw the gaunt shadow pass the lighted window. In his efforts to convince you of a cold thinking machine, Sir Arthur Conan Doyle convinced you of a living man. He caught from London fog a terrible ghost of retribution, and in this day of "significant novels" and "memorable portraits," it is well to remember just who has created the one character that can never be forgotten.

Nowadays, writers of fiction try to show us what human, breathing, everyday people their detectives are. Consequently, the world regards them as wooden, unconvincing, and impossible. The good Sir Arthur went out of his way to insist in the dark, almost ghoulish qualities of Sherlock Holmes—consequently, the whole world steps right up to call him friend.

Now this is precisely the place where the author encounters his greatest stumbling block. Most readers, while cherishing and loving this version of the super-detective, refuse to believe that he can exist. "Improbable!" "Wild!" "Unbelievable!"—these are the bugbears against which the mildest of thrillers must contend. One police officer from real life, a certain Mr. Michael Fiaschetti, has rushed into print with a book called *You Gotta Be Rough*, wherein fiction (and very often, I fear, fact) has been given a terrific hauling over the coals. He becomes fairly violent in insisting that there is nothing thrilling about actual police work, and he talks with such bitterness against Sherlock Holmes that one is almost convinced he is personally acquainted with Mr. Holmes.

There is no denying his contentions. There could be none, with the stark and often powerful material he smashes at the reader—a parade of greed, lust, treachery, and grimness that turns the heart sick. It is drawn from that steaming region by the East River, where men are inured to mud and horror and the rat-tat-tat of machine guns. Everybody is crooked, including the police. The dope, the harlot, the squealer, the gunman crowd grimy elbows in his pages. It is a sort of ghastly twilight wherein the detective's only requirements are a heavy fist in brass knuckles and a quickness to dodge the whistling knife.

It is only when you read at great length in other chronicles of crime that you realize where there may be an error in these rather sweeping statements. His accounts are the tales of Gangland. There is very rarely anything like mystery in them, even to Mr. Fiaschetti. When gangs draw their guns, every pistol shot can be identified. There is a reason (and even the children know it) why each victim tumbles bullet-riddled into the street. I have walked through these roaring caverns of the East Side at twilight, alleys of blowing clotheslines under dim-lit tenements, of shrilling children and the tinkle of hand organs, of a stifling foulness, haunted by the hoot of boat whistles, and I have wondered how the watchful police system could control the menace of that tumult. They need strong fists. They need men who know every cranny of this snarling den, and the terrible shadow of the Chair.

But up beyond the Woolworth Building, beyond Park Place and uptown, there is a region where killers also walk. This is so in London, in Paris, in every city where the refinements of civilization have taught men the subtler arts of murder. Here there is no distinct "criminal class," mugged and fingerprinted, in which to seek familiar game. There is no apparent reason why Mr. X, retired cotton broker, or Miss Y, sedate schoolteacher, should be found shot through the head in Central Park. No brass knuckles, no knowledge of professional criminals, will solve this. And this, too, is life. It is the life with which the fiction writer most frequently deals: the tragedies of those who are not criminals—the unknown people, the respectable people—the people of the limousine and the tea service, who slay for motives older than bootlegging or gang war.

Mr. Fiaschetti beating the truth doggedly out of his suspects: This is one picture of a detective, so misleading because it is only half a picture. For all I know, it may be typical of the New York Police Department in every section of the city. But the other half of the picture you will find in actual records also. Read the accounts of Ashton-Wolfe, of Francis Carlin, of Dr. Hans Gross of Vienna; of Filson Young, Irving, Bolitho, Jesse, Post, Bjierre, and half a hundred others. Study the career of Dr. Alphonse Bertillion of Paris, the founder of modern criminology, and the subsequent amazing developments of Dr. Bayle and Dr. Locard. I state no personal opinion—there is the evidence, volume after volume in three languages, to attest their uncanny skill.

> Let us compare Paris to a clear pond, whose surface is unbroken. A stone is thrown into the pond, splashing and rippling the water in a widening circle—that is to say, a crime. The stone disappears. The ripples die away, and the surface is again unbroken. You would say that there is no trace left. But each ripple of the water stirred in passing, ever so slightly, the sand and mud of the banks; each ripple left its own mark, as a crime does, and by those tiniest of marks we identify the exact passage of the stone.

Had that remark been made by a detective of fiction, we should have regarded it as ingenious, but hardly sound. And yet this little bearded Frenchman, peering over his spectacles in the mysterious depth of his laboratory, made of it a working theory out of which terrifying marvels took form. That, if you will, is romance. It is not bounded by probability, as the fiction writers are, because it constitutes the glorious, mad romance of fact.

I am inclined to think that these detective exploits are one of the few branches of romance left to us. If you read some of these strange and eerie crimes, you will feel that sense of awe and terror of which I have spoken as the chief requisite of fiction. Crime is sordid, yes—like birth and money and fundamental things. But in the magical ingenuity by which the brain of man resolves it, we penetrate a world of romance not far from the Arabian Nights.

The children know it. The children love ghost stories and pirate stories, and tales of the goblin who lives under the stairs. And detective stories are only fairy stories for those who have grown up. There comes a time, in our electric-lit world, when we want to step out of our familiar door—out into a mysterious street where a mailbox becomes a dragon and men wear the monstrous shapes of a masquerade. If the mystery story gives us this, it is startling to reflect that the mystery story is not so strange or so incredible as these real streets of our familiar world. In marveling at fiction, we shall be taught a secret which in this age of sophistication we have nearly forgotten—I mean that we shall be taught the old secret, and great secret: to marvel at the truth.

VOLUME XIX SEPTEMBER 1938 NO. 10

Changes I Have Seen

UPTON SINCLAIR

By 1938, the year "Changes I Have Seen" appeared, **UPTON SINCLAIR** had already made a profound mark upon the American landscape. Born September 20, 1878, he was a tireless proponent of social activism, as well as an active member of the Socialist party. Most of his work focused upon exposing and addressing the social wrongs of his time. Sinclair is best known for his novel *The Jungle.* In it, he exposed the inhumane conditions found in the U.S. meatpacking industry. The resulting public outcry against these conditions was fierce—so much so that it contributed to the passage of the Pure Food & Drug Act of 1906. Sinclair also co-founded the American Civil Liberties Union's (ACLU) first permanent chapter in 1923. Fifteen years later, Sinclair wrote *Little Steel,* a detailed account of the legal and illegal methods used to ruin the steel industry unions. That same year, he published "Changes I Have Seen" in *Writer's Digest.* At the age of sixty, Sinclair's dedication to social reform remained unbowed. Five years later he won the Pulitzer Prize for his novel *Dragon's Teeth.*

When I was a boy, America was a land where money talked. Wherever you turned you heard people say it; they said it in loud and raucous tones, which hurt my ears. Money jeered, money bragged; money told me that I was nobody and that nothing I did or said amounted to anything. It never would, because I wouldn't make money, because I was such a fool as not to believe in money as the end and aim of civilization.

I was born in Baltimore, a great port which was making money after the Civil War. It had its merchant princes and its money kings, and I was so situated that I heard about them and sometimes met them. I listened to their conversation and discovered that it had to do with money, and the hereditary power and glory that money conferred upon its votaries and priests. I became in early childhood a reader of books, and learned about other worlds—of romance and adventure and heroism.

Then I was taken to New York, which was ruled by Tammany Hall, a racket, although that word had not been invented. I was in position to know the inside of that corruption, and I saw that it was all the pursuit and worship of money, the sacrifice of everything precious in life for cash.

At first I blamed the Tammany gangsters, the politicians; but then little by little I came to understand that the big business fellows were paying the politicians and making ten times as much out of it as the politicians. It was the bankers, the big-money men of Wall Street, who were buying America away from the people and making the word democracy a bad joke and a sham. So for many years I came to hate the Wall Street crowd, and when I met them and listened to them, I burned to put them in books and pillory them before the world.

It was only as I lived longer and grew wiser that I came to understand that men are what social systems make them, and that it was not the individual bankers and street railway magnates, but the system of production for profit which was destroying the American ideal of government of, by, and for the people.

I was eighteen years old when I became a "watcher" in a polling booth for a reform organization in New York and came very close to getting my head broken in the effort to keep a lot of marked Tammany ballots from being counted. So you see I have been in that fight for forty-two years now. You can still get your head broken any day or night; but even so, the mind of America is changing, and a part of me has sat up on a high hill and watched the procession go by, and seen it changing, ever so slowly—but a lot in forty-two years.

I attribute this change to the noble company of men and women of letters who have made their appearance on the scene during my time. Many of them did not know their own power and builded better than they knew. Mark Twain, for example. I don't think he knew he was a reformer, and when I met him, he was in sorrow and bitter despair about his country. But he loved kindness and justice and hated lying and knavery and all the systems of oppression, old or new. In stories like *The Prince and the Pauper* and *A Connecticut Yankee* he moved the imaginations of millions of people. (It is the imagination that rules in the end.) Likewise William Dean Howells; when I met him he was tired and subdued, but a book like *A Traveller From Altruria* went on working, and I hope still does so, in the cause of loveliness and fair dealing. That is why books are so important; they do not tire, and they go on working.

Younger writers came on, who were not tired and heartsick. I read Frank Norris's *The Octopus* and it shocked me mightily; I didn't know what to make of it because it was hard for me to believe that such things had ever happened in America, and—here is a strange and curious fact: I didn't know how to find out. The reviewers didn't know either—or at any rate they failed to tell me. And then came David Graham Phillips, a grand fighting man, who hated mammon-worship just as I did, and wrote a fighting book called *The Age of Gilt*. Phillips was happier than I in one way, that he was able to cut his stories to fit the magazines and was able to get his indictments of political and financial corruption even into *The Saturday Evening Post*—something which remains for all these years beyond my powers!

Jack London came three or four years ahead of me and poured out a flood of gorgeous stuff, most of it touched with revolt against the system, and some of it among the best fighting stuff we Socialists have. Jack helped to make *The Jungle* known, and ten years later, toward the close of his life, he wrote one of the most eloquent pieces of American prose as an introduction to my anthology of the literature of social protest, *The Cry for Justice*.

There were other writers; I should have to write quite an essay to tell about them all. There were not so many as I had hoped, for the World War came along, and it appears that a great war always brings in its train a period of disillusionment and cynicism. We had a decade of writers whose revolt against the world took the form of getting drunk and trying various forms of sex perversion. I won't name them, because they have punished themselves, and most of those who are still writing are now recognized for the reactionaries they always were.

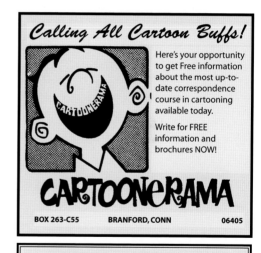

Now, *again*, America is taking heart, and dreaming of some kind of society in which there can be security and freedom for all the people—something which not even the rich can enjoy today. There are millions now who do not believe in money accumulation as the end and goal of human life. Good reason, you say, because they have no chance to succeed at it. But bitterness about one's personal fate is the first step to thinking and trying to understand a world in which one-third of the population is condemned to misery, no matter how hard they work and scheme and struggle.

In short, people are reading and thinking and talking about economics today. New writers are appearing and fighting for the right of independence and to say what they think about the system of exploitation, which has thrown some ten to twelve million permanently out of work, and is making it necessary for us to heap up a deficit of four billion of dollars a year to keep the ratio of unemployment from doubling itself. Thoughtful books and honest books, fighting books for the cause of social justice are pouring from the presses, both here and in England, and in all the countries where freedom to think and speak survives. I believe that America and the other democratic lands are soon to see a new birth of freedom, and I believe that the literary critics of that happier time will look back upon this age and call it the time of golden opportunity in the history of literature.

Among those who read these words are young writers who will thrill to the idea that their books may be read and their names be listed in that roll of honor. Get something vital to say and learn to say it with power and appeal. You may help to make the future of humanity happy and noble.

VOLUME XLIII JANUARY 1962 NO. 2

Are Writers Made or Born?

JACK KEROUAC

JACK KEROUAC is one of those few whose name not only brings to mind extraordinary writing, but also an entire literary movement. The influence of Kerouac's jazz-like writing style could be felt in the work of both his contemporaries and a generation of creators that followed, including Ken Kesey, Hunter S. Thompson, Allen Ginsberg, and Bob Dylan. His best-known work, *On the Road* (1957), perfectly captures his restless nature and dissatisfaction with the "traditional" values of 1950s America. In 1962, the same year the following piece appeared, Kerouac published *Big Sur*, a dark, harrowing chronicle of one man's attempt to overcome his personal demons of alcoholism, depression, and fame. It was a scene taken directly from Kerouac's life. Seven years later, at the age of forty-seven, Kerouac would die from internal bleeding caused by cirrhosis of the liver.

Writers are made, for anybody who isn't illiterate can write; but geniuses of the writing art like Melville, Whitman, or Thoreau are born. Let's examine the word "genius." It doesn't mean screwiness or eccentricity or excessive "talent." It is derived from the Latin word *gignere* (to beget) and a genius is simply a person who *originates* something never known before. Nobody but Melville could have written *Moby-Dick*, not even Whitman or Shakespeare. Nobody but Whitman could have conceived, originated, and written *Leaves of Grass*; Whitman was *born* to write a *Leaves of Grass* and

Melville was *born* to write a *Moby-Dick*. "It ain't whatcha do," Sy Oliver and James Young said, "it's the way atcha do it." Five thousand writing-class students who study "required reading" can put their hands to the legend of Faustus but only one Marlowe was born to do it the way he did.

I always get a laugh to hear Broadway wise-guys talk about "talent" and "genius." Some perfect virtuoso who can interpret Brahms on the violin is called a "genius," but the genius, the originating force, really belongs to Brahms; the violin virtuoso is simply a talented interpreter—in other words, a "talent." Or you'll hear people say that so-and-so is a "major writer" because of his "large talent." There can be no major writer without original genius. Artists of genius, like Jackson Pollock, have painted things that have never been seen before. Anybody who's seen his immense Samapattis of color has no right to criticize his "crazy method" of splashing and throwing and dancing around.

Take the case of James Joyce: People said he "wasted" his "talent" on the stream of consciousness style, when in fact he was simply *born* to originate it. How would you like to spend your old age reading books about contemporary life written in the pre-Joycean style of, say, Ruskin, or William Dean Howells, or Taine? Some geniuses come with heavy feet and march solemnly forward like Dreiser, yet no one ever wrote about that America of his as well as he. Geniuses can be scintillating and geniuses can be somber, but it's that inescapable sorrowful depth that shines through—*originality*.

Joyce was insulted all his life by practically all of Ireland and the world for being a genius. Some Celtic Twilight idiots even conceded he had *some* talent. What else could they say, since they were all going to start imitating him? But five thousand university-trained writers could put their hands to a day in June in Dublin in 1904, or one night's dreams, and never do with it what Joyce did with it: He was simply born to do it. On the other hand, if the five thousand "trained" writers, plus Joyce, all put their hands to a *Reader's Digest*-type article about "Vacation Hints" or "Homemaker's Tips," even then I think Joyce would stand out because of his inborn originality of language insight. Bear well in mind what Sinclair Lewis told Thomas Wolfe: "If Thomas Hardy had been given a contract to write stories for *The Saturday Evening Post*, do you think he would have written like Zane Grey or like Thomas Hardy? I can tell you the answer to that one. He would have written like Thomas Hardy. He couldn't have written like anyone else but Thomas Hardy. He would have kept on writing like Thomas Hardy, whether he wrote for *The Saturday Evening Post* or *Captain Billy's Whiz-Bang*."

When the question is therefore asked, "Are writers made or born?" one should first ask, "Do you mean writers with talent or writers with originality?" Because anybody can write, but not everybody invents new forms of writing. Gertrude Stein invented a new form of writing and her imitators are just "talents." Hemingway later invented his own form also. The criterion for judging talent or genius is ephemeral, speaking rationally in this world of graphs, but one gets the feeling definitely when a writer of genius amazes him by strokes of force never seen before and yet hauntingly familiar (Wilson's famous "shock of recognition"). I got that feeling from *Swann's Way*, as well as from *Sons and Lovers*. I do not get it from Colette, but I do get it from Dickinson. I get it from Céline, but I do not get it from Camus. I get it from Hemingway, but not from Raymond Chandler, except when he's dead serious. I get it from the Balzac of *Cousin Bette*, but not from Pierre Loti. And so on.

The main thing to remember is that talent imitates genius because there's nothing else to imitate. Since talent can't originate it has to imitate, or interpret. The poetry on page two of *The New York Times*, with all its "silent wings of urgency in a dark and seldom wood" and other lapidary trillings, is but a poor imitation of previous poets of genius, like Yeats, Dickinson, Apollinaire, Donne, Suckling. ...

-62- Genius gives birth, talent delivers. What Rembrandt or van Gogh saw in the night can never be seen again. No frog can jump in a pond like Basho's frog. *Born* writers of the future are amazed already at what they're seeing now, what we'll all see in time for the first time, and then see imitated many times by *made* writers.

So in the case of a born writer, a genius involves the original formation of a new style. Though the language of Kyd is Elizabethan as far as period goes, the language of Shakespeare can truly be called only *Shakespearean*. Oftentimes an originator of new language forms is called "pretentious" by jealous talents. But it ain't watcha write, it's the way atcha write it.

VOLUME XLIII SEPTEMBER 1962 NO. 10

The Day I Nearly Quit Writing

KEN KESEY

Everything, they say, happens for a reason. The following piece, written by **KEN KESEY**, seems to indicate that the old saying may be true. In it, Kesey details a story from two years earlier when, as a twenty-year-old from the Universityof Oregon, he attempts to gain employment as a copywriter for Capitol Records. His initial interview goes well. The work, however, is pedestrian and meaningless. But it appears to be his, if he wants it. Still, is it really even writing at all? And then, before he can even accept, something happens—something that puts Kesey back on course, turning him away from the easy paycheck and back toward what he was born to do. Two years later, the same year he wrote this article for *Writer's Digest*, Kesey published *One Flew Over the Cuckoo's Nest* and became a publishing legend.

It was like this: June of 1958 and there I am whooshing up the elevator of the Capitol Records building in Hollywood—a twenty-year-old publishing genius, hot out of University of Oregon writing classes, on my way up to an interview with, call them J.P. Cash and John D. Rockerroller. These two platter business highrankers need a man to handle the writing of the blurbs you skim over on the back of Capitol record jackets, and after talks with agents, personnel departments, etc., I'm high on the list as a candidate for the position. I'm sweaty but sharp-looking in my borrowed charcoal suit, and so business-like and important with my leather folio full of talent under my arm that when the elevator man stops he points to a frosted glass door and says, "Yes sir, right that way, sir."

I go down a long hall lined on both sides with the framed jackets of Capitol artists: famous singers with their mouths retouched, bandleaders in tasteful poses, and an occasional golden million-seller. Mighty impressive. These are the people I will be dealing with if I get the job. Maybe they're not Leadbelly or Mulligan or MJQ, maybe it's not Verve or Fantasy or Folkways ... but you've got to admit it's mighty impressive.

In the carpeted office behind the frosted glass, J.P. and John D. lean against filing cabinets as they ask me questions. Both are younger than I had anticipated, I remark. Only fair, they come back; I'm younger than they had anticipated.

The interview is friendly and casual, interrupted by secretaries in beige knit suits carrying monogrammed coffee cups, and phone calls handled with dynamic brevity: "... Hey Bert, yeah baby, you know how it bounces ... certainly; Dino and Frankie get their bite off the top ... certainly, you bet ... that's the kind, Bert; we'll see you hour an' a half at the Copper Skillet then okay?"

They divide up the stuff from my folio and frown over it while I study the grain of the desk, check my nails, count the holes in the acoustical ceiling, sneak glances at the readers (marvel at the way they are able to tap a cigarette ash dead center in a tray no bigger than a nickel, without ever looking up from the paper), and try to imagine what it is they are looking at now. The plays? The short stories? That description of a logger being sliced in half by a snapped donkey cable? Oh Jesus, that's probably the one, all right. That godawful thing. The description is *true*, damn it, but so out of place. It's too much, too gory. What was I thinking of, dragging some dirty, crumby illiterate choker-setter up here to bleed all over this Bigelow-on-the-floor? I must have been out of my head!

After a few minutes of reading they put the papers down and chew their lips in concentration. "You can *write*," John D. finally says, "but of course you can see *this* land lays a little different. It's pressure, everyday *zing wham bang* you get me? And not just *that*, but on a different plain *entirely*."

I nod and tell him I understand his position *perfectly*.

A minute of standstill. Then J.P. suddenly snaps his fingers at an idea. They will give me an assignment, a *bit* to work on. That's it! I can take a stab at one of the blurbs to see how the machinery rolls. *Fine*. He opens a door and calls to one of the girls to bring in that bit on Fred Waring for Christmas. She brings in a sheet of thin yellow paper with the names of thirty or forty Christmas carols carboned on it.

"This is a list of masters from a tape Waring and his Pennsylvanians have put together for our winter list. Now here's the deal: We don't know which songs will be picked for the album, but there will be only ten or twelve at the most. And the album is going to be called *Now Is the Caroling Season*. You got it? So what you do is you write, oh—leaving space for credits and probably a pen-and-ink—I should say approximately 250 to 300 words. Mood, setting—a little about Fred Waring, how great he is on a couple of particular songs. Have to be lucky. Of course, the title song will be there, 'Silent Night,' you know ... and tune the whole bit for the mother-grandmother-aunt ear, okay? Here. Use my desk and machine. John and I'll run grab some coffee and leave you to it. And don't you want to take off that heavy wool coat and get easy, man. Great day, this is Californee."

He slaps my back and I ask him if I could bum a cup of coffee for myself and he says, "Sure, you betcha."

I put my coat over a piece of abstract statuary and install myself behind the desk at the typewriter. My coffee arrives, complete with beige knit and a smile, and I crack my knuckles and tie into that machine, suddenly feeling calm and certain in my surroundings. In ten minutes I have a page that would make a D.A.R. official buy three copies of the record sight unseen or sound unheard. It has everything in it except the plum pudding. I give my new buddies a call and they return, impressed: "You're fast, man, and I *like* that." And once more I wait while they read a page of my work.

Only this time I relax and sip my coffee, confident of my effect. No bloody logger *this* time.

They finish the piece: "Great bit, man, *great*!" Backslapping, me shuffling around grinning, thinking to myself, why I didn't know it was *this* good? Though apparently it is, because they are going to go ahead and use it instead of the blurb they had been working on. And I get paid fifty bucks for it. Ten minutes writing on a record I've never heard about—a man I've never met, for fifty bucks. Will collectors someday browse Christmas record shelves in search of this, my first published work?

Whooshing back down the elevator I decide that tomorrow, on my follow-up interview when I'm to meet the Department Head to cinch the job (start at seven hundred, they said, with your own desk and beige knit coffee carrier), I'll wear my lightweight sport jacket and take it easy. To hell with this itchy wool; this is Californee!

And I'm still debating which necktie when I emerge from the electric eye door at the base of the building and see some kind of hassle is taking place down the block on Hollywood Boulevard. I find a crowd around a patrol car where two handsome, machine-made L.A. cops are trying to drag a young colored boy away from a lamppost. The boy has laced his fingers together around the post and he is welded there as though the long, copper-brown arms had melted and run to form an unbreakable circle. One of the cops has the boy's legs and the other has him around the waist, and they are pulling him horizontally from the post. All three participants seem remote and detached, unhurried in their combat. The cops pull steadily without visible anger, and the boy—perhaps fifteen, in faded jeans and a white T-shirt—looks from person to person in the crowd as though he is searching for someone he was supposed to meet at this corner.

A handsome woman in an airlines uniform explains that the boy has been hanging around this corner for almost a week, and that he seemed vague or doped or like that whenever someone asked what he was waiting for. So the authorities had been notified and when they arrived he fastened himself to that post. No one has been persecuting him, the woman feels compelled to repeat a number of times; no one has been discriminating against him or like that. No one is even *accusing* him of anything. The officers think, in fact, *everyone* who has been watching the poor soul these last few days thinks that the boy is in obvious need of help. And that, you see, is why they are taking him away.

The boy's eyes search out this cool, impersonal voice and for a moment he looks at the woman. The cops pull at his legs. The woman grows uneasy and goes into the travel agency office. The boy's eyes move on to the next person. His nose has started to bleed and the blood drops on the June-baked Hollywood sidewalk, and as I watch the drops of blood harden and turn brown there on the cement I'm reminded of a passage from Hemingway's *Soldier's Home*, where the hero looks down and watches the bacon fat harden on his plate while his mother is railing at him about his future. James B. Hall, my teacher at Oregon, pointed that passage out to me, and explained how many things that one sentence had going for it and just how much the written word was able to accomplish, properly applied. And this gets me thinking about what a good writer could do with a scene like the one before me, and thinking about the dozen different plots it could have and directions it could go and about how many things he could accomplish with it. And *this* gets me thinking about all the thousands of real glimpses that flash in front of you every day, all of them actual windows into stories and lives of people.

So I end up driving back to my apartment and spend the afternoon and most of the night writing a very bad socially symbolic story about Negroes as Negroes and cops as cops, getting to bed at dawn and consequently sleeping past time for my appointment at Capitol Records. I rush down to the drugstore and phone J.P. and make another appointment for the following day, but for some reason I miss this one also. I can't remember exactly why. I seem to recall a distinct lack of warmth in J.P.'s "Sure, you bet; we'll be waiting *anxiously* ..." and maybe I flubbed the second meeting because I felt they were miffed at me for missing our big meeting with the Department Head. But I can't say for sure; I'm hazy on that.

That first day, however, is still edged sharp as a knife in my memory: the awesome round building shaped like a mile-high stack of enormous long-play albums, the Hollywood sun on my charcoal suit, the elevator ride, all the people, all the talk—probably because the day was paradoxically significant: It stands in my memory as The Day I Nearly Quit Writing.

VOLUME LI JANUARY 1970 NO. 2

What Is the Writer's Social Responsibility?

NORMAN COUSINS

Out of all the "legends" in this book, it's no exaggeration to say that **NORMAN COUSINS**, born in 1919, is the one who actively did the most to make the world a better place. While serving as editor-in-chief of the *Saturday Review*, he is quoted as having said that "There is a need for writers who can restore to writing its powerful tradition of leadership in crisis." Clearly, he led by example. In addition to writing more than a dozen books and hundreds of editorials and essays, Cousins tirelessly championed nuclear disarmament, world peace, freedom, health, the environment, and more. No worthy cause went lacking for his attention. His efforts garnered him the Eleanor Roosevelt Peace Award (1963), the Family Man of the Year Award (1968), and—one year after writing the essay that follows—the United Nations Peace Medal (1971).

EDITOR'S NOTE:: *The February issue of* Writer's Digest *will present another viewpoint in Eudora Welty's answer to the question: "Must the Novelist Crusade?"*

When I refer to the social responsibility of the writer, I do not mean to suggest that he must be preoccupied with urban decay, teenage acidheads, thermonuclear warheads, and population bomb. What I do mean is that the writer should try to keep his windows and his options open. That is, he should not separate himself from major social influences. Whatever his literary field or approach, he will be a better writer if he is properly sensitive to the principal issues of the times.

An author—whether novelist, essayist, or poet—should write out of the richest possible mix: a mix that should by all means include a keen awareness of the main forces at play in the world. The writer's mind is, or should be, a kind of burning lens that bends inward and brings to a white-hot focus a great variety of previously unconnected facts, experiences, and impressions. The wider the cone of rays he brings to that focus, the more heat, light, and penetrating power he is likely to generate.

To me, then, the sin is not failure to write explicitly about this or that major social fact; the sin is, rather, to be so completely unaware of the phenomenon's importance that the question never comes up. It is also a sin, of course, to be perfectly aware of such facts, but to avoid them in one's writing because the fashionable subject this year is something else or because Big Brother does not want certain things mentioned out loud. Oliver Wendell Holmes, Jr., said it when he wrote, "As life is action and passion, it is required of a man that he should share the passion and action of his time, at the peril of being judged not to have lived." By this standard, a rather substantial number of writers are half-alive at best. A case in point: Two decades ago the editorials in the *Saturday Review* protested the nuclear obscenity with special emphasis on the emerging world arms race. In the late 1950s, we turned to the appalling long-range effects of the worldwide radioactive-fallout drizzle from above-ground nuclear tests. It seemed to us that the life-substance of two great nations was being devoted to the Bomb. Grown men were mortgaging their futures to build elaborate molehole "shelters." School children who were subjected to Civil Defense war drills were waking up screaming in the middle of the night. All this was the stuff of tragedy and collective madness.

Yet it soon came home to us that relatively few writers were concerning themselves *in print* about the apocalyptic challenge posed by the

Bomb and by nuclear power. I found, indeed, that some writers I knew felt we were becoming too "unliterary" because of our concern about the threat of fallout.

I might mention that one of *SR*'s major editors dissented strongly from my view, and we carried on a friendly joust in *SR*'s pages. His point, advanced with force and charm, was that none of us groundlings could ever know much about the Bomb and its possible spinoff problems. Instead of engaging in "hair-raising speculation" about fallout and such, those of us not at the center of government should, he said, "moderate their voices or remain silent."

In my editorial reply I tried to make the point that "this is the time for audible warning ... a time to split the sky with indignation over authorized madness and the towering assault on human destiny."

I cite the foregoing not to say I-told-you-so, or to say that the editor who differed with me was not a first-rate writer, thinker, and human being—for he certainly was all these. I cite the story, rather, because it illustrates several points about what I conceive to be the writer's responsibility.

First, the editorial colleague with whom I disagreed believed quite honestly that a writer—a literary man, that is—had no business bothering his head with "all that sort of thing." To him, the Bomb was just another blockbuster of a weapon whose disposition was the military's province. He felt there was really no point digging into the question of whether testing might kill or deform babies, for if there was any such danger, the military would have told us so. I'd like to think that this is by now an outmoded view, but sometimes I am not so sure.

Secondly, and as a corollary, he felt that whole realms of social and technical ferment were out of bounds to the cultivated man. His human sympathies were broad but belletristic, and the phrase "leave all that to the experts" about summed the matter up for him.

My friend's mistake, I submit, was that he ignored the writer's responsibility: He failed to concern himself with a major social fact-of-life because his conception of literature's role was, in this case, at least, too severely constricted.

There remains the other kind of default, which may well be an even greater sin. Many contemporary writers are in touch with the vibrant social realities but consciously sidestep any mention of them in their writing. Perhaps it's from simple fear of being called nasty names. Perhaps it's because the writer has an eye on the lucrative "shock-market" and feels "social" themes contain too much roughage for the average reader's diet. "I'm eating my heart out over the world situation," he will confide. "But of course, all that is death at the box office."

The danger is that such a writer will backpeddle so far in his haste to avoid "deep" social themes that he will lose all connection with the recognizable human scene. This isn't too bad, I suppose, if one is Wodehouse or Tolkien or Perelman, but most writers are not Wodehouses, nor should they try to be. Most serious fiction and nonfiction writers have been, I would think, men and women who cared strongly about the social-political life of their day.

At Least Awareness

Perhaps one reason for our chariness about "social responsibility" is that the phrase itself falls so strangely on American ears. The expression has a clanking sound to it and is redolent of old-line Soviet novels about love among the Stakhanovites, or turn-of-the-century American tales about pluck-and-luck types who put their pennies by and conquer the world of high finance. Maybe a better term for what I am getting at would be, simply, awareness of or openness to just about everything around us—the Bomb, malnutrition, and other social realities very much included.

Another approach would be to adopt Howard Mumford Jones's terminology. He once said that a "useful" writer is one "who dwells in the public world accessible to anyone who can read." If literature is not "useful" in this sense, Jones said, "it is likely to degenerate into an elaborate private game played with infinite relish by a selected few, but a game without general significance."

Instead of attaining this "general significance," too many authors nowadays, it strikes me, are writing out of their own egos instead of their consciences. Possibly they feel their egos are somehow coterminous with the whole human consciousness, and that this makes their writing universal. It succeeds only in reading like an exercise in Jungian solipsism—the novel thus becomes a mere spinning out of case histories. What we need are more writers who do not flinch from seeing themselves as spokesmen for human destiny; more writers able to get outside the "castle of the skin" and to concern themselves with the larger condition of man. As Emerson (dare one quote Emerson nowadays?) put it, "That is the vice—that no one feels himself called to act for man, but only as a fraction of man."

But why, one may fairly ask, place such heavy responsibility on the writer? With a President and a Congress, and all the other paraphernalia of representative government, does the writer really have a hand in shaping the political and social man? Anyone who has been close to the rotunda of any state capitol knows the unhappy answer to that question. The trouble with government is that there are too many hands on the lever—in fact, too many hands-on-hands. Some Presidents have tried to get around the pressures of office by using an ingenious system of dodges, stratagems, and pulls-vs.-counterpulls.

But such stratagems and fancy capework just won't work. In the end, the people begin to hold you to your word, and that seemingly wispy force, public opinion, prevails.

If the past few years have taught us nothing else, they teach us that the writer's real constituency is not men in positions of power but the American public, *the writer's constituency*. This is an obvious post-1968 point, but it can still use stressing. Power was shaped and exercised, it was recently believed, through arcane manipulations at the top. The public and its opinions were regarded by most "in" folk in somewhat the same way that ponderous, puckish Herman Hickman, the one-time Yale football coach, looked on Yale's graduates: "My job," he once said cheerfully, "is to keep the alumni sullen, but not mutinous." But as of the beginning of 1968, American public opinion came full size in the United States.

This is not without its effect on writers. *The writer has ready access to that newly emerged sovereign power, public opinion, and he is more than ever before a major figure in American and world society*. He may not yet realize this home truth, or if he does realize it, he may feel uneasy about coming to terms with it. But like it or not, the writer will, in the years just ahead, become more and more of a force in our national life.

Rights and Responsibilities

Needless to say, with such new power comes new obligations. Anyone who writes well but dishonestly will be like a child flipping levers at random on the command console at a missile base. More than ever before, a dishonest but superficially persuasive article or TV essay will have a perhaps unimaginably bad effect.

This would seem to suggest that our writers should do two things. First, try to take in as wide-angle a view of their times as they possibly can. Second, when they come to write of the things they know and feel, they will consult their consciences and not the box office.

What we need today are writers who can restore to writing its powerful traditions of leadership in crisis. Most of the great tests in human history have produced great writers who acknowledged a special responsibility to their times. They defined the issues, recognized the values at stake, dramatized the nature of the challenge. In terms of today's needs, the challenge to writers is to see themselves as representatives of the human community. For the central issue facing the world today is not the state of this nation or that nation, but the condition of man. That higher level today needs its champions as never before.

The danger so well described by the philosopher Whitehead—the danger that events might outrun man and leave him a panting and helpless anachronism—is by now much more than a figure of speech. We have leaped centuries ahead in inventing a new world to live in, but as yet have an inadequate conception of our own part in that world. We have surrounded and confounded ourselves with gaps: gaps between revolutionary science and evolutionary anthropology, between cosmic gadgets and human wisdom, between intellect and conscience. The clash between knowledge and ethics that Henry Thomas Buckle foresaw a century ago is not more than a mere skirmish.

What is it we expect of the writer who is confronted with this sudden, severe upset in the metabolism of history? No single answer can possibly have enough elasticity to be all-inclusive. But we can certainly expect him to reflect the new spirit of the age, which points to the convergence of man. We can expect him to become a herald of world citizenship. We can expect him to narrow the gap between the individual and society. We can expect him to shorten the distance between individual capacity and collective needs.

Our generation lacks a philosophy of vital participation in the world community. How much emphasis is there on the most important science of all, the science of interrelationships of knowledge, that critical area beyond compartmentalization where knowledge must be integrated in order to have proper meaning? Is there enough of a sense of individual responsibility for group decision? Is the individual equipped to appraise the news and to see beyond the news, to see events against a broad historical flow? For ultimate objectives have suddenly become present imperatives; they will be faced and attained in our time or they may not be attained at all.

These are vaulting responsibilities and the writer cannot be expected to assume the entire burden of human destiny. But at least those responsibilities offer something of a yardstick by which the writer can measure his own part and place in the total picture of our time.

Twenty-four hundred years ago, the world knew a Golden Age in which the development of the individual was considered the first law of life. In Greece, it took the form of the revolution of awareness, the emancipation of the intellect from the limitations of corroding ignorance and mental inactivity. Once again, in our time, there is within the grasp of man another Golden Age—if only he can recognize it and act upon it. And writers can chart the way.

VOLUME LI FEBRUARY 1970 NO. 3

Must the Novelist Crusade?

EUDORA WELTY

In this piece, EUDORA WELTY, born in 1909, also known as the "First Lady of Southern Literature," takes the question posed to Norman Cousins in the previous issue (see "What Is the Writer's Social Responsibility?," page 69) and provides a different, though no less passionate response. "Let us suppose," she says, "that we might help if we were to write a crusading novel. What will our problems be?" Can one, in fact, write a novel with a "mission"—the intent to better the world—and still be effective? Her argument is fascinating and persuasive. Welty's ability to craft honest, insightful fiction that moved readers without manipulating or overbearing them was her gift. For it, she won many awards, including the Pulitzer Prize for her novel *The Optimist's Daughter*, published three years after this essay.

Not too long ago I read in some respectable press that Faulkner would have to be reassessed because he was "after all, only a white Mississippian." For this reason, it was felt, readers could no longer rely on him for knowing what he was writing about in his life's work of novels and stories, laid in what he called "my country."

Remembering how Faulkner for most of his life wrote in all but isolation from critical understanding, ignored impartially by North and South, with only a handful of critics in forty years who were able to "assess" him, we might smile at this journalist as at a boy let out of school. Or there may have been an instinct to smash the superior, the good, that is endurable enough to go on offering itself. But I feel in these words and others like them the agonizing of our times. I think they come of an honest and understandable zeal to allot every writer his chance to better the world or go to his grave reproached for the mess it is in. And here, it seems to me, the heart of fiction's real reliability has been struck at—and not for the first time by the noble hand of the crusader.

It would not be surprising if the critic I quote had gained his knowledge of the South from the books of the author he repudiates. At any rate, a reply to him exists there. Full evidence as to whether any writer, alive or dead, can be believed is always at hand in one place: any page of his work. The color of his skin would modify it just about as much as would the binding of his book. Integrity can be neither lost nor concealed nor faked nor quenched nor artificially come by nor outlived, nor, I believe, in the long run denied. Integrity is no greater and no less today than it was yesterday and will be tomorrow. It stands outside time.

The novelist and the crusader who writes both have their own place—in the novel and the editorial respectively, equally valid whether or not the two happen to be in agreement. In my own view, writing fiction places the novelist and the crusader on opposite sides. But they are not the sides of right and wrong. Honesty is not at stake here and is not questioned; the only thing at stake is the proper use of words for the proper ends. And a mighty thing it is.

Because the printed page is where the writer's work is to be seen, it may be natural for people who do not normally read fiction to confuse novels with journalism or speeches. The very using of words has these well-intentioned people confused about the novelist's purpose.

The writing of a novel is taking life as it already exists, not to report it but to make an object, toward the end that the finished work might contain this life inside it and offer it to the reader. The essence will not be, of course, the same thing as the raw material; it is not even of the same family of things. The novel is something that never was before and will not be again. For the mind of one person, its writer, is in it too. What distinguishes it above all from the raw material, and what distinguishes it from journalism, is that inherent in the novel is the possibility of a shared act of the imagination between its writer and its reader.

"All right, Eudora Welty, what are you going to do about it? Sit down there with your mouth shut?" asked a stranger over long distance in one of the midnight calls that I suppose have waked most writers in the South from time to time. It is part of the same question: Are fiction writers on call to be crusaders? For us in the South who are fiction writers, is writing a novel *something we can do about it*?

It can be said at once, I should think, that we are all agreed upon the most important point: that morality as shown through human relationships is the whole heart of fiction, and the serious writer has never lived who dealt with anything else.

And yet, the zeal to reform, which quite properly inspires the editorial, has never done fiction much good. The exception occurs when it can rise to the intensity of satire, where it finds a better home in the poem or the drama. Large helpings of naiveté and self-esteem, which serve to refresh the crusader, only encumber the novelist. How unfair it is that when a novel is to be written, it is never enough to have our hearts in the right place! But goodwill all by itself can no more get a good novel written than it can paint in watercolor or sing Mozart.

Nevertheless, let us suppose that we feel we might help if we were to write a crusading novel. What will our problems be?

Before anything else, speed. The crusader's message is prompted by crisis; it has to be delivered on time. Suppose John Steinbeck had only now finished *The Grapes of Wrath*? The ordinary novelist has only one message: "I submit that this is one way we are." This can wait. When we think of Ibsen, we see that causes themselves may in time be forgotten, their championship no longer needed; it is Ibsen's passion that keeps the plays alive.

Next, we as crusader-novelists, shall find awkward to use the very weapon we count on most: the generality. On fiction's pages, generalities clank when wielded, and hit with equal force at the little and the big, at the merely suspect and the really dangerous. They make too much noise for us to hear what people might be trying to say. They are fatal to tenderness and are in themselves nonconductors of any real, however modest, discovery of the writer's own heart. This discovery is the best hope of the ordinary novelist, and to make it, he begins not with the generality but with the particular in front of his eyes, which he is able to examine.

Taking a particular situation existing in his world, and what he feels about it in his own breast and what he can make of it in his own head, he constructs on paper, little by little, an equivalent of it. Literally it may correspond to a high degree or to none at all; emotionally it corresponds as closely as he can make it. Observation and the inner truth of that observation as he perceives it, the two being tested one against the other: To him, this is what the writing of a novel is.

We, the crusader-novelists, having started with our generality, must end with a generality; they had better be the same. In the place of climax, we can deliver a judgment. How can the plot seem disappointing when it is a lovely argument spread out? It is because fiction is stone-deaf to argument.

The ordinary novelist does not argue; he hopes to show, to disclose. His persuasions are all toward allowing his reader to see and hear something for himself. He knows another bad thing about arguments: They carry the menace of neatness into fiction. Indeed, what we as the crusader-novelists are scared of most is confusion.

Great fiction, we very much fear, abounds in what makes for confusion; it generates it, being on a scale which copies life, which it confronts. It is very seldom neat, is given to sprawling and escaping from bounds, is capable of contradicting itself, and is not impervious to humor. There is absolutely everything in great fiction but a clear answer. Humanity itself seems to matter more to the novelist than what humanity thinks it can prove.

When a novelist writes of man's experience, what else is he to draw on but the life around him? And yet the life around him, on the surface, can be used to show anything, absolutely anything, as readers know. The novelist's real task and real responsibility lie in the way he uses it.

Situation itself always exists: It is whatever life is up to here and now, it is the living and present moment. It is transient, and it fluctuates. Using the situation, the writer populates his novel with characters invented to express it in their terms.

It is important that it be in their terms. We cannot in fiction set people to acting mechanically or carrying placards to make their sentiments plain. People are not Right and Wrong, Good and Bad, Black and White personified; flesh and blood and the sense of comedy object. Fiction writers cannot be tempted to make the mistake of looking at people in the generality—that is to say, of seeing people as not at all *like us*. If human beings are to be comprehended as real, then they have to be treated as real, with minds, hearts, memories, habits, hopes, with passions and capacities like ours. This is why novelists begin the study of people from within.

The first act of insight is to throw away the labels. In fiction, while we do not necessarily write about ourselves, we write out of ourselves, using ourselves; what we learn from, what we are sensitive to, what we feel strongly about—these become our characters and go to make our plots. Characters in fiction are conceived from within, and they have, accordingly, their own interior life; they are individuals every time. The character we care about in a novel we may not approve of or agree with—that's beside the point. But he has got to seem alive. Then and only then, when we read, we experience or surmise things about life itself that are deeper and more lasting and less destructive to understanding than approval or disapproval.

The novelist's work is highly organized, but I should say it is organized around anything but logic. Just as characters are not labels but are made from the inside out and grow into their own life, so does a plot have a living principle on which it hangs together and gradually earns its shape. A plot is a thousand times more unsettling than an argument, which may be answered. It is not a pattern imposed; it is inward emotion acted out. It is arbitrary, indeed, but not artificial. It is possibly so odd that it might be called a vision, but it is organic to its material: It is a working vision, then.

A writer works *through* what is around him if he wishes to get to what he is after—no kind of proof, but simply an essence. In practice he will do anything at all with his material; shape it, strain it to the breaking point, double it up, or use it backwards; he will balk at nothing—see *The Sound and the Fury*—to reach that heart and core. But even in a good cause he does not falsify it. The material itself receives deep ultimate respect: It has given rise to the vision of it, which in turn has determined what the novel shall be.

The ordinary novelist, who can never make a perfect thing, can with every novel try again. But if we write a novel to prove something, one novel will settle it, for why prove a thing more than once? And what then is to keep all novels by all right-thinking persons from being pretty much alike? Or exactly alike? There would be little reason for present writers to keep on, no reason for the new writers to start. There's no way to know, but we might guess the reason the young write no fiction behind the Iron Curtain is the obvious fact that to be acceptable there, all novels must conform, and so much be alike, hence, valueless. If the personal vision can be made to order, then we should lose, writer and reader alike, our own gift for perceiving, seeing through the fabric of everyday to what to each pair of eyes on earth is a unique thing. We'd accept life exactly like everybody else, and so, of course, be content with it. We should not even miss our vanished novelists. And if life ever became not worth writing fiction about, that, I believe, would be the first sign that it wasn't worth living.

With a blueprint to work with instead of a vision, there is a good deal that we, as crusader-novelists, must be at pains to leave out. Unavoidably, I think, we shall leave out one of the greatest things. This is the mystery of life. Our blueprint for sanity and of solution for trouble leaves out the dark. (This is odd, because surely it was the dark that first troubled us.) We leave out the wonder because with wonder it is impossible to argue, much less to settle. The ordinary novelist thinks it had better be recognized. Reckless as this may make him, he believes the insoluble is part of his material too.

The novelist works neither to correct nor to condone, not at all to comfort, but to make what's told alive. He assumes at the start an enlightenment in his reader equal to his own, for they are hopefully on the point of taking off together from that base into the rather different world of the imagination.

It's not only the fact that this world is bigger and that fewer constrictions apply that may daunt us as crusaders. But the imagination itself is the problem. It is capable of saying everything but no. In our literature what has traveled the longest way through time is the great affirmative soul of Chaucer. The novel itself always affirms, it seems to me, by the nature of itself. It says what people are like. It doesn't, and doesn't know how to, describe what they are *not* like, and it would waste its time if it told us what we ought to be like, since we already know that, don't we? But we may not know nearly so well what we are as when a novel of power reveals this to us. For the first time we may, as we read, see ourselves in our own situation, in some curious way reflected. By whatever way the novelist accomplishes it—there are many ways—truth is borne in on us in all its great weight and angelic lightness, and accepted as home truth.

Passing judgment on his fellows, which is trying enough for anybody, is frustrating for an author. It is hardly the way to make the discoveries about living that he must have hoped for when he began to write. If he does not pass judgment, does this mean he has no conscience? Of course he has a conscience; it is, like his temperament, his own, and he is 100 percent answerable to it, whether it is convenient or not. What matters is that a writer is committed to his own moral principles. If he is, when we read him we cannot help but be aware of what these are. Certainly the characters of his novel and the plot they move in are their ultimate reflections. But these convictions are implicit; they are deep down; they are the rock on which the whole structure of more than that novel rests.

Indeed, we are more aware of his moral convictions through a novel than any flat statement of belief from him could make us. We are aware in that part of our mind that tells us truths about ourselves. Yet it is only by way of the imagination—the novelist's to ours—that such private neighborhoods are reached.

There is still to mention what I think will give us, as the crusader-novelists, the hardest time: Our voice will not be our own. The crusader's voice is the voice of the crowd and must rise louder all the time, for there is, of course, the other side to be drowned out. Worse, the voices of most crowds sound alike.

Worse still, the voice that seeks to do other than communicate when it makes a noise has something brutal about it; it is no longer using words as words but as something to brandish, with which to threaten, brag, or condemn. The noise is the simple assertion of self, the great, mindless, general self. And for all its volume it is ephemeral. Only meaning lasts. Nothing was ever learned in a crowd, from a crowd, or by addressing or trying to please a crowd. Even to deplore, yelling is out of place. To deplore a thing as hideous as the murder of three civil rights workers demands the quiet in which to absorb it. Enormities can be lessened, cheapened, just as good and delicate things can be. We can and will cheapen all feeling by letting it go savage or parading in it.

Writing fiction is an interior affair. Novels and stories always will be put down little by little out of personal feeling and personal beliefs arrived at alone and at firsthand over a period of time as time is needed. To go outside and beat the drum is only to interrupt, interrupt, and so finally to forget and to lose. Fiction has, and must keep, a private address. For life is *lived* in a private place; where it means anything is inside the mind and heart. Fiction has always shown life where it is lived, and good fiction, or so I have faith, will continue to do this.

A Passage to India is an old novel now. It is an intensely moral novel. It deals with race prejudice. Mr. Forster, not by preaching at us, while being passionately concerned, makes us know his point unforgettably as often as we read it. And does he not bring in the dark! The points are good forty years after their day *because of the splendor of the novel.* What a lesser novelist's harangues would have buried by now, his imagination still reveals. Revelation of even the strongest forces is delicate work.

Indeed, great fiction shows us not how to conduct our behavior but how to feel. Eventually, it may show us how to face our feelings and face our actions and to have new inklings about what they mean. A good novel of any year can initiate us into our own new experience.

From the working point of view of the serious writer of fiction, nothing has changed today but the externals. They are important externals; we may have developed an increased awareness of them, which is certainly to the good; we have at least the same capacity as ever for understanding, the same eyes and ears, same hearts to feel, same minds to agonize or remember or to try to put things together, see things in proportion with. While the raw material of our fiction is changing dramatically—as indeed it is changing everywhere—we are the same instruments of perceiving that we ever were. I should not trust us if we were not. And we do not know what is to be made out of experience at any time until the personal quotient has been added. To convey what we see around us, whatever it is, so as to let it speak for itself according to our lights is the same challenge it ever was, not a different one, not a greater one, only perhaps made harder by the times. Now as ever, we must keep writing from what we know; and we must really know it.

No matter how fast society around us changes, what remains is that there is a relationship in progress between ourselves and other people; this was the case when the world seemed stable, too. There are relationships of the blood, of the passions and the affections, of thought and spirit and deed. There is the relationship between the races. How can one kind of relationship be set apart from the others? Like the great root system of an old and long-established growing plant, they are all tangled up together; to separate them you would have to cleave the plant itself from top to bottom.

What must the Southern writer of fiction do today? Shall he do anything different from what he has always done?

There have already been giant events, some of them wrenchingly painful and humiliating. And now there is added the atmosphere of hate. We in the South are a hated people these days; we were hated first for actual and particular reasons, and now we may be hated still more in some vast unparticularized way. I believe there must be such a thing as sentimental hate. Our people hate back.

I think the worst of it is we are getting stuck in it. We are like trapped flies with our feet not in honey but in venom. It's not love that is the gluey emotion; it's hate. As far as writing goes, which is as far as living goes, this is a devastating emotion. It could kill us. This hate seems in part shame for self, in part self-justification, in part panic that life is really changing.

Fury at ourselves and hurt pride, anger aroused too often, outrage at being hated need not obscure forever the sore spots we Southerners know better than our detractors. For some of us have shown bad hearts. As in the case of our better qualities, we are locally blessed with an understanding and intimate knowledge of our faults that our worst detractors cannot match, and have been in a less relentless day far more relentless, more eloquent, too, than they have yet learned to be.

I do not presume to speak for my fellow Southern writers, a group of individuals if there ever was one. Yet I would like to point something out: In the rest of the country people seem suddenly aware now of what Southern fiction writers have been writing about in various ways for a great long time. We do not need reminding of what our subject is. It is humankind, and we are all part of it. When we write about people, black or white, in the South or anywhere, if our stories are worth the reading, we are writing about everybody.

In the South, we who are now at work may not learn to write it before we learn, or learn again, to live it—our full life in the South within its context, in its relation to the rest of the world. "Only connect," Forster's ever wise and gentle and daring words, could be said to us in our homeland quite literally at this moment. And while the Southern writer goes on portraying his South, which I think nobody else can do and which I believe he must do, then if his work is done well enough, it will reflect a larger mankind as it has done before.

And so finally I think we need to write with love. Not in self-defense, not in hate, not in the mood of instruction, not in rebuttal, in any kind of militance, or in apology, but with love. Not in exorcisement, either, for this is to make the reader bear a thing for you.

Neither do I speak of writing forgivingly; out of love you can write with straight fury. It is the source of the understanding that I speak of; it's this that determines its nature and its reach.

We are told that Turgenev's nostalgic, profoundly reflective, sensuously alive stories that grew out of his memories of early years reached the Czar and were given some credit by him when he felt moved to free the serfs in Russia. Had Turgenev set out to write inflammatory tracts instead of the sum of all he knew, could express, of life learned at firsthand, how much less of his mind and heart with their commitments, all implicit, would have filled his stories! But he might be one of us now, so directly are we touched, with 113 years gone by since they were first published.

Indifference would indeed be corrupting to the fiction writer, indifference to any part of man's plight. Passion is the chief ingredient of good fiction. It flames right out of sympathy for the human condition and goes into all great writing. (And of course passion and the temper are different things; writing in the heat of passion can be done with extremely good temper.) But to distort a work of passion for the sake of a cause is to cheat, and the end, far from justifying the means, is fairly sure to be lost with it. Then the novel will have been not the work of imagination, at once passionate and objective, made by a man struggling in solitude with something of his own to say, but a piece of catering.

To cater to is not to love and not to serve well either. We do need to bring to our writing, over and over again, all the abundance we possess. To be able, to be ready, to enter into the minds and hearts of our own people, all of them, to comprehend them (us) and then to make characters and plots in stories that in honesty and with honesty reveal them (ourselves) to us, in whatever situation we live through in our own times: This is the continuing job, and it's no harder now than it ever was, I suppose. Every writer, like everybody else, thinks he's living through the crisis of the ages. To write honestly and with all our powers is the least we can do, and the most.

Time, though it can make happenings and trappings out of date, cannot do much to change the realities apprehended by the imagination. History will change in Mississippi, and the hope is that it will change in a beneficial direction and with a merciful speed, and above all bring insight, understanding. But when William Faulkner's novels come to be pictures of a society that is no more, they will still be good and still be authentic because of what went into them from the man himself. Mankind still tries the same things and suffers the same falls, climbs up to try again, and novels are as true at one time as at another. Love and hate, hope and despair, justice and injustice, compassion and prejudice, truth-telling and lying work in all men; their story can be told in whatever skin they are wearing and in whatever year the writer can put them down.

Faulkner is not receding from us. Indeed, his work, though it can't increase in itself, increases us. His work throws light on the past and on today as it becomes the past—the day in its journey. This being so, it informs the future too.

What is written in the South from now on is going to be taken into account by Faulkner's work; I mean the remark literally. Once Faulkner had written, we could never unknow what he told us and showed us. And his work will do the same thing tomorrow. We inherit from him, while we can get fresh and firsthand news of ourselves from his work at any time.

A source of illumination is not dated by what passes along under its ray, is not qualified or disqualified by the nature of the traffic. When the light of Faulkner's work will be discovering things to us no more, it will be discovering *us*. Even we shall lie enfolded in perspective one day: what we hoped along with what we did, what we didn't do, and not only what we were but what we missed being, what others yet to come might dare to be. For we *are* our own crusade. Before ever we write, we are. Instead of our judging Faulkner, he will be revealing us in books to later minds.

VOLUME LXVII MAY 1986 NO. 6

Your Future as a Writer

ISAAC ASIMOV

One of the world's most respected, popular, and influential science fiction authors, **ISAAC ASIMOV** produced more than five hundred books over his lifetime. And unlike many writers, he was equally adept at producing both fiction and nonfiction. A spiritual descendant of H.G. Wells (whom he quotes in the article that follows), Asimov was unrivaled in his ability to envision the future of mankind, making him uniquely qualified to predict what writers could look forward to in an era when more and more readers were being drawn away by the flash and dazzle of cable television video games. His belief that writers would become the necessary link between scientific advancement and society's understanding of it begs an obvious question: Was he right? And if not, is it only a matter of time?

1: Do you have a future?

You may have heard the statement: "One picture is worth a thousand words."

Don't you believe it. It may be true on occasion—as when someone is illiterate, or when you are trying to describe the physical appearance of a complex object. In other cases, the statement is nonsense.

Consider, for instance, Hamlet's great soliloquy that begins with "To be or not to be," the poetic consideration of the pros and cons of suicide.

It is 260 words long. Can you get across the essence of Hamlet's thought in a quarter of a picture—or, for that matter, in 260 pictures? Of course not. The pictures may be dramatic illustrations of the soliloquy if you already know the words. The pictures by themselves, to someone who has never read or heard *Hamlet*, will mean nothing.

As soon as it becomes necessary to deal with emotions, ideas, fancies—abstractions in general—only words will suit. The modulation of sound, in countless different ways, is the only device ever invented by human beings that can even begin to express the enormous complexity and versatility of human thought.

Nor is it likely to change in the future. You have heard that we live in an "age of communication," and you may assume, quite rightly, that amazing and fundamental changes are taking place in that connection. These changes, however, involve the *transmission* of information, and not its nature. The information itself remains in the form it was in prehistoric times: speech, and the frozen symbology of speech that we call writing.

We can transmit information in sign language, by semaphore, by blinking lights, by Morse code, by telephone, by electronic devices, by laser beams, or by techniques yet unborn—and in every case, we are transmitting words.

Pictures will not do; they will never do. Television is fun to watch, but it is utterly and entirely dependent on the spoken and written word. The proof is this: Darken the image into invisibility but leave the sound on, and you will still have a crude sense of what is going on. Turn off the sound, however, and exclude the appearance of written words, and though you leave the image as bright as ever, you will find you understand nothing of what is going on unless you are watching the most mindless slapstick. To put it even more simply: Radio had no images at all and managed, but the silent movies found subtitles essential.

There is the fundamental rule, then. In the beginning was the word (as the Gospel of St. John says in a different connection), and in the end will be the word. The word is immortal. And it follows from this that just as we had the writer as soon as writing was invented five thousand years ago, so we will have the writer; of necessity, for as long as civilization continues to exist. He may write with other tools and in different forms, but he will *write*.

2: *What, then, is your future?*

Having come to the conclusion that writers have a future, we might fairly ask next: What will the role of the writer be in the future? Will writers grow less important, play a smaller role in society, or will they hold their own?

Neither.

It is quite certain that writers' skills will become steadily more important as the future progresses—providing, that is, that we do not destroy ourselves, and that there is a future of significance, one in which social structures continue to gain in complexity and in technological advance.

The reasons are not difficult to state.

To begin with, technological advance has existed as long as human beings have. Our hominid ancestors began to make and use tools of increasing complexity before the present-day hominid we call *Homo sapiens* had yet evolved. Society changed enormously as technology advanced. Think what it meant to human beings when agriculture was invented—herding—pottery—weaving—metallurgy. Then, in historic times, think of the changes introduced by gunpowder—the magnetic compass—printing—the steam engine—the airplane—television.

Technological change feeds on previous technological change, and the rate of change increases steadily. In ancient times, inventions came so infrequently and their spread was so slow that individual human beings could afford to ignore them. In one person's generation, nothing seemed to change as far as social structure and the quality of life was concerned. But as the rate of change increased, that became less true, and after 1800, the Industrial Revolution made it clear that life—everyday life—was changing rapidly from decade to decade and then from year to year and, by the closing portion of the twentieth century, almost from day to day. The gentle zephyr of change that our ancestors knew has become a hurricane.

We know that change is a confusing and unsettling matter. It is difficult for human beings to adjust to change. There is an automatic resistance to change and that resistance diminishes the advantages we can obtain from change. From generation to generation, then, it has become more and more important to explain the essentials of change to the general public, making people aware of the benefits to be derived from change, and of the dangers that they must beware of as a result. That has never been more important than it is now; and it will be steadily more important in the future.

Since almost all significant change is the result, directly or indirectly, of advances in science and technology, what we're saying is that one particular type of writing—writing about science—will increase in importance even more quickly than writing in general will.

We live in a time when advances in science and technology can solve the problems that beset us: increasing the food supply, placing reproductive potentialities under control, removing pollution, multiplying efficiency, obtaining new sources of energy and materials, defeating disease, expanding the human range into space, and so on.

Advances in science and technology also create problems to bedevil us: producing more dangerous weapons, creating more insidious forms of pollution, destroying the wilderness, and disrupting the ecological balance of Earth's living things.

At every moment, the politicians and businesspeople and, to some extent, every portion of the population, must make decisions on both individual and public policy that will deal with matters of science and technology.

To choose the proper policies, to adopt this and reject that, one must know something about science and technology. This does not mean that everyone must be a scientist, as we can readily see from the analogy of professional sport and its audience. Millions of Americans watch with fascinated intentness games of baseball, football, basketball, and so on. Very few of them can play the game with any skill; very few know enough to be able to coach a team; but almost all of them know enough about the game to appreciate what is going on, to cheer and groan at appropriate times, and to feel all the excitement and thrills of the changing tides of fortune. That must be so, for without such understanding, watching a game is merely a matter of watching chaos.

And so it must be that as many people as possible must know enough about science and technology to be members of an intelligent *audience*, at least.

It will be the writer, using words (with the aid of illustration where that can make the explanation simpler or raise the interest higher, but *primarily* using words), who will endeavor to translate the specialized vocabulary of science and technology into ordinary English.

No one suggests that writing about science will turn the entire world into an intelligent audience, that writers will mold the average person into a model of judgment and creative thought. It will be enough if they spread the knowledge as widely as possible; if some millions, who would otherwise be ignorant (or, worse, swayed by meaningless slogans), would, as a result, gain some understanding; if those whose opinions are most likely to be turned into action, such as the political and economic rulers of the world, are educated.

H.G. Wells said that history was a race between education and catastrophe, and it may be that the writer will add just sufficient impetus to education to enable it to outrace catastrophe. And if education wins by even the narrowest of margins, how much more can we ask for?

3: *How do you prepare for your future as a writer?*

Nor is a world that is oriented more in the direction of science and technology needed merely for producing better judgments, decisions, and policies. The very existence of science and technology depends on a population that is both understanding and sympathetic.

There was a time when science and technology depended strictly on individual ideas, individual labor, and individual financial resources. We are terribly attracted to the outmoded stereotype of the inventor working in his home workshop, of the eccentric scientist working in his home laboratory, of the universe of ignorance being assaulted by devices built of scraps, string, and paste.

It is so no longer. The growing complexity of science and technology has outstripped the capacity of the individual. We now have research teams, international conferences, industrial laboratories, large universities. And all this is strained, too.

Increasingly, the only source from which modern science and technology can find sufficient support to carry on its work is from that hugest repository of negotiable wealth—the government. That means the collective pocketbooks of the taxpayers of the nation.

There never has been a popular tax, or an unreluctant taxpayer, but some things will be paid for more readily than others. Taxpayers of any nation are usually ready to pay enormous sums for military expenses, since all governments are very good at rousing hatred and suspicions against foreigners.

But an efficient military machine depends, to a large extent, on advances in science and technology, as do other more constructive and less shameful aspects of society. If writers can be as effective in spreading the word about science and technology as governments are at sowing hatred and suspicion, public support for science is less likely to fail, and science is less likely to wither.

Moreover, science and technology cannot be carried on without a steady supply of scientists and engineers; an increasing supply as the years go on. Where will they come from?

They will come from the general population, of course. There are some people who gain an interest in science and technology in youth and can't be stopped, but they, by themselves, are simply not numerous enough to meet the needs of the present, let alone the future. Many more youngsters would gain such an interest only if they were properly stimulated.

Again, it is the writer who might catch the imagination of young people and plant a seed that will flower and come to fruition. Thus, I have received a considerable number of letters from scientists and engineers in training who have taken the trouble to tell me that my books were what had turned them toward science and technology. I am quite convinced that other science writers get letters in equal numbers.

Let me make two points, however.

First, in order to write about science, it is not entirely necessary to be deeply learned in every aspect of science (no one can be, these days) or even in some one aspect—although that helps. To know science well can make you a "science writer," but any intelligent person who has a good layperson's acquaintance with the scientific and technological scene can write a useful article on some subject related to science and technology. He can be a *writer* dealing with science.

Here is an example:

Digital clocks seem to be becoming ever more common these days and the old-fashioned clock dial seems to be fading away. Does that matter? Isn't a digital clock more advanced? Doesn't it give you the time more accurately? Won't children be able to tell time at once as soon as they can read instead of having to decipher the dial?

Yet, there are disadvantages to a possible disappearance of the dial that perhaps we ought to keep in mind.

There are two ways in which anything might turn—a key in a lock, a screw in a piece of wood, a horse going around a racetrack, Earth spinning on its axis. They are described as "clockwise" and "counterclockwise." The first is the direction in which the hands on a clock move; the second is the opposite direction. We are so accustomed to dials that we understand clockwise and counterclockwise at once and do not make a mistake.

If the dial disappears (and, of course, it may not, for fashion is unpredictable, clockwise and counterclockwise will become meaningless and there is no completely adequate substitute. If you clench your hands and point the thumbs upward, the fingers of the left hand curl clockwise and those of the right hand counterclockwise. You might substitute "left-hand twist" and "right-hand twist," but no one stares at clenched hands as intently and as often as at block dials, and the new terms will never be as useful.

Again, in looking at the sky, or through a microscope, or at any view that lacks easily recognizable reference marks, it is common to locate something by the clock dial. "Look at that object at 11 o'clock," you may say—or 5 o'clock, or 2 o'clock, or whatever. Everyone knows the location of any number from 1 to 12 on the clock dial and can use such references easily.

If the dial disappears, there will again be no adequate substitute. You can use directions to be sure—northeast, south by west, and so on, but no one knows the compass as well as the clock.

Then, too, digital clocks can be misleading. Time given as 5:50 may seem roughly 5 o'clock, but anyone looking at a dial will see that it is nearly 6 o'clock. Besides, digital clocks only go up to 5:59 and then move directly to 6:00 and youngsters may be confused as to what happened to 5:60 through 5:99. Dials give us no such trouble.

One can go on and find other useful qualities in dials vs. digits, but I think the point is clear. An article can be written that has meaning as far as technology is concerned and will provoke thought and yet not require a specialist's knowledge. We can't all be science writers, but we can all be writers about science.

The second point to be made is that I do *not* say that writers won't be needed in increasing numbers in other fields.

As computers and robots take over more of the dull labor of humanity and leave human beings to involve themselves in more creative endeavors, education will have to change in such a way as to place increasing emphasis on creativity. No doubt, education by computer will become more and more important, and a new kind of writer—the writer of computer programs for education—will arise and become important.

Again, as leisure time continues to increase the world over, writing to fill that leisure time, in the form of books, plays, television, or movie scripts, and so on, will be needed in greater numbers.

In other words, more and more writers of more and more different kinds will be needed as time goes on; but, of them all, it is writers about science for whom the need will grow most quickly.

VOLUME LXXVI DECEMBER 1995 NO. 1

The Art of Hanging Out

GAY TALESE

GAY TALESE is often credited with having established the practice of New Journalism, or "literary" journalism. It is a credit he refuses to accept. And yet it cannot be denied that Talese brought something new to the field, almost immediately upon entering it. In the simplest terms, he took a rather straightforward job and turned it into an art form. In the article that follows, Talese describes his early days as a journalist and the methods that, developed over time, have enabled him to establish bonds of trust with an extraordinary range of subjects, resulting in diamond-perfect stories about everything from the public's changing sexual mores to the inner workings of the Mafia. One year later, Talese published his memoir, *Origins of a Nonfiction Writer* (1996), which further details his artistic evolution.

Part 1

I come from an island and a family that reinforced my identity as a marginal American, an outsider, an alien in my native nation. But while this may have impeded my assimilation into the mainstream, it did guide me through the wayward yet interesting path of life that is familiar to many searching people who become writers.

My origins are Italian, I am the son of a dour but debonair custom tailor from Calabria and an amiably enterprising Italian-American mother who successfully operated our family dress business. I was educated by Irish-Catholic nuns and priests in a poor parish school on the Protestant-controlled island of Ocean City, off the southern coastline of New Jersey, where I was born in 1932.

After school, I worked as an errand boy in my family's dress shop that catered to decorous women of ample figures and means.

Amid the low humming of the fans and the attentive care of my mother in the dressing rooms, they would try on clothes while discussing their private lives and the happenings and misadventures of their friends and neighbors.

The shop was a kind of talk show that flowed around the engaging manner and well-timed questions of my mother; and as a boy not much taller than the counters behind which I used to pause and eavesdrop, I learned much that would be useful to me years later when I began interviewing people for articles and books.

I learned to listen with patience and care, and never to interrupt even when people were having great difficulty in explaining themselves, for during such halting and imprecise moments (as the listening skills of my patient mother taught me) people often are very revealing—what they hesitate to talk about can tell much about them. Their pauses, their evasions, their sudden shifts in subject matter are likely indicators of what embarrasses them, or irritates them, or what they regard as too private or imprudent to be disclosed to another person at that particular time. However, I also overheard many people discussing candidly with my mother what they had earlier avoided—a reaction that I think had less to do with her inquiring nature or sensitively posed questions than with their grateful acceptance of her as a trustworthy individual in whom they could confide.

My mother's best customers were women less in need of new dresses than the need to communicate.

While I remember my father listening late at night to the news of World War II on his shortwave radio in our apartment above the store, a more intimate sense of the conflict came to me from a weeping woman who visited our shop one afternoon with word of her son's death on an Italian battlefield, an announcement that drew my mother's deepest sympathy and compassion—while my troubled father remained behind the closed door of his tailoring room in the rear of the building.

The exigencies of the war were of course evident and available everywhere; but I think large events influence small communities in ways that are uniquely illuminating with regard to the people involved, for the people *are* more involved in places where almost everybody knows everybody else (or think they do), where there are fewer walls behind which to hide, where sounds carry further, and where a less-hurried pace allows a longer look, a deeper perception and, as personified by my mother, the leisure and luxury of listening.

From her I not only learned this first lesson that would be essential to my later work as a nonfiction writer pursuing the literature of reality, but I also gained from my store-centered upbringing an understanding of another generation, one that represented a variety in style, attitude, and background beyond what I could have encountered in my normal experiences in school or at home. Among them were a presser who worked in the shop, a massive man with a shaved head and knife-scarred forearms, who had a small, feisty wife who regularly entered the steaming back room to berate him loudly because of his all-night gambling habits and other indiscretions.

I was reminded of her aggressiveness many years later, in 1962, while I was researching an article for *Esquire* on the ex-heavyweight champion Joe Louis, a man with whom I had cavorted through several New York night-clubs on the evening before our flight back to his home in Los Angeles. At the baggage claim area in Los Angeles, we were met by the fighter's wife (his third), and she promptly provoked a domestic quarrel that provided me with the opening scene of the magazine article.

After my colleague Tom Wolfe had read that article, he publicly credited it with introducing him to a new form of nonfiction, one that brought the reader into close proximity to real people and places through the use of accurately reported dialogue, scene setting, and intimate personal details, including the use of interior monologue—my mother would inquire of her friends: *What were you* thinking *when you did such-and-such?* and I asked the same question of those I later wrote about—in addition to other techniques that had long been associated with fiction writers and playwrights. While Wolfe heralded my Joe Louis piece as emblematic of what he called "The New Journalism," I think his complimenting me was undeserved, for I had not written then, or since then, anything I consider to be stylistically *new*, since my approach to research and storytelling had evolved out of my family's store, drawing its focus and inspiration primarily from the sights and sounds of the elderly people I saw interacting there every day like characters in a Victorian play.

But my memory of the white-gloved ladies remains benign, for they and the other people who patronized or worked in my parents' store (plus the curiosity transferred by my mother) sparked my early interest in small-town society, in the common concerns of ordinary people. Each of my books, in fact, draws inspiration in some way from the elements of my island and its inhabitants who are typical of the millions who interact familiarly each day in stores and coffee shops and along the promenades of small towns, suburban villages, and urban neighborhoods everywhere. And yet, unless such individuals become involved in crimes or horrible accidents, their existence is generally ignored by the media as well as by historians and biographers, who tend to concentrate on people who reveal themselves in some blatant or obvious way, or who stand out from the crowd as leaders, or achievers, or are otherwise famous or infamous.

One result is that "normal" everyday life in America is portrayed primarily in fiction—in the works of novelists, playwrights, and short-story writers possessing the creative talent to elevate ordinary life to art, and to make memorable the commonplace experiences and concerns of men and women worthy of Arthur Miller's plea in behalf of his suffering salesman: "Attention must be paid."

And yet I have always believed, and have hoped to prove with my efforts, that attention might also be paid to "ordinary" people in nonfiction, and that *without changing the names or falsifying the facts*, writers might produce what I call the "Literature of Reality." Different writers, of course, reflect differing definitions of reality. In my case, it reflects the perspective and sensibilities of a small-town American outsider whose exploratory view of the world is accompanied by the essence of the people and places I have left behind, the overlooked non-newsworthy population that is everywhere but rarely taken into account by journalists and other chroniclers of reality.

My first book, *New York—A Serendipiter's Journey*, published in 1961, presents the small town character of New York neighborhoods and reveals the interesting lives of certain obscure individuals dwelling within the shadows of the towering city. My next book, *The Bridge* (1963), focuses on the private lives and loves of steelworkers as they link a bridge to an island, altering the character of the land and its inhabitants. My first bestseller, entitled *The Kingdom and the Power* (1969), describes the family backgrounds and interpersonal relationships of my former colleagues on *The New York Times*, where I worked from 1955 through 1965. This was my only full-time job, and I spent all my years there in the main newsroom on Forty-third Street off Broadway. This newsroom was my "store." My next bestseller, *Honor Thy Father* (1971), was written in reaction to my defensive father's embarrassment over the prevalence of Italian names in organized crime. I grew up hearing him claim that the American press exaggerated the power of the Mafia and the role of Italian gangsters within it. While my research would prove him wrong, the book that I completed (having gained access to the Mafia through an Italian-American member whose friendship and trust I cultivated) was less about gun battles than about the island-like insularity that characterizes the private lives of gangsters and their families.

In response to the sexual repression and hypocrisy that was evident in my formative years, I wrote, almost in dedication to the patrons of my mother's boutique, *Thy Neighbor's Wife*. Published in 1980, it traces the definition of morality from my adolescence in the 1930s through the sexually liberating pre-AIDS era that continued into the 1980s—a half-century of social change that I described in the context of the ordinary lives led by typical men and women around the country.

The final chapter in that book refers to the research I did among nude sunbathers at a private beach located twenty miles downstream from my native island—a beach I visited without clothing and on which I would soon discover myself being observed by voyeurs standing with binoculars aboard the line of several anchored vessels they had sailed over from the Ocean City Yacht Club. In *The Kingdom and the Power*, I had referred to the journalism profession as voyeuristic. But here on this nudist beach, without press credentials or a stitch of clothing, my role was suddenly reversed. Now *I* was being observed, rather than doing the observing. And there is no doubt that my next and most personal book, *Unto the Sons* (1991), progressed from the final scene in *Thy Neighbor's Wife*. It is the result of my willingness to expose in a book of nonfiction myself and my past influences, without changing the names of the people or the places that shaped my character. It is also a modest example of what is possible for nonfiction writers in these times of increased candor, of more liberal laws without regard to libel and the invasion of privacy, and of expanding opportunities to explore a wide variety of subjects even, as in my case, from the narrow confines of an island.

Part 2

I left the island in the autumn of 1949 to attend the University of Alabama. As a journalism student I was usually ranked in the middle of the class, even during my junior and senior years when I was active on the college weekly and worked as the campus correspondent for the *Birmingham Post-Herald*. The faculty tended to favor the reportorial style of the conservative though very reliable *Kansas City Star*. They had definite views of what constituted "news" and how news stories should be presented. The five *W*s—who, what, when, where, why—were questions they thought should be answered succinctly and impersonally in the opening paragraphs of an article. Since I sometimes resisted formula, and might try instead to communicate the news through the personal experience of the single person most affected by it—being doubtless influenced by the fiction writers I preferred reading to the practitioners of "objective" nonfiction—I was never a faculty favorite.

It should not be inferred, however, that there was any unpleasantness between us, or that I was a rebellious student. They were reflecting an era that predated the rise of television as the dominant force in spot-news reporting. I was reflecting my own peculiar background in my ambivalence about who and what was important. In reading through old newspapers and other antiquated periodicals in the school library and elsewhere, as I sometimes did in my leisure time, it seemed that most of the news printed on the front pages was historically and socially less revealing of the time than what was published in the classified and the display advertising spread through the middle and back pages. The advertising offered detailed sketches and photographs showing the then-current fashion in clothing, the body styles of cars, where rental apartments were obtainable and at what cost, what jobs were available to the white-collar and the laboring classes; while the front pages were largely concerned with the words and deeds of many seemingly important people who were no longer important.

Throughout my college days that ended in 1953, and in the years following at *The Times*, I sought assignments that were unlikely candidates for page one. Even when I specialized in writing sports, whether it was at Alabama or at *The Times*, the final results interested me less than who played the game; and if given the choice of writing about people who personified the Right Stuff or the Wrong Stuff, I'd invariably choose the latter. If I wrote more compassionately about losers than winners during my sportswriting days, it was because the losers' stories to me were more interesting, a view I retained long after leaving the Alabama campus. As a *Times* sportswriter, I became enamored of a heavyweight fighter, Floyd Patterson, who was constantly being knocked down, but who kept getting up. I wrote more than thirty different pieces about him in the daily paper and its Sunday magazine, and finally did a long piece about him in *Esquire*, entitled "The Loser."

This was done when I was engaged in what Tom Wolfe called "The New Journalism," but, as I hope is obvious, that writing "style" is founded in old-fashioned legwork, hanging out with the story's subject day after day (just as I'd hung out in my parents' shop as a juvenile observer and listener). I have sometimes called it "The Art of Hanging Out," and it is an indispensable part of what motivates my work, together with that other element that I have maybe mentioned too much already, that gift from my mother: curiosity. My mother also knew that there is a difference between curiosity and nosiness, and this distinction has always guided me with regard to the people I interviewed and how I presented them in print. I never wrote about anyone for whom I did not have at least a considerable measure of respect, and this respect is evident in the effort I take with my writing and the length I will go in trying to understand and express their viewpoints and the social and historical forces that contributed to their character—or lack of character.

Writing for me has always been difficult, and I would not invest the necessary time and effort on people merely to ridicule them; and I say this having written about gangsters, pornographers, and others who have earned society's disapproval and contempt. But there was in these people also a redeeming quality that I found interesting, a prevailing misconception that I wanted to correct, or a dark streak upon which I hoped to cast some light because I believed it would also illuminate a larger area in which a part of us all live. Norman Mailer and Truman Capote have achieved this in writing about murderers, and other writers—Thomas Keneally and John Hersey—show it to us out of the gas chambers of Nazi Germany and the fatal fumes over Hiroshima.

Nosiness represents mainly the interests of the mean-spirited, the one-night-stand temperament of tabloid journalists and even mainstream writers and biographers seizing every opportunity to belittle big names, to publicize a public figure's slip of the tongue, to scandalize every sexual dalliance even when it bears no relevance to that person's political or public service.

I have avoided writing about political figures, for so much about them is of temporary interest; they are dated people, victims of the recycling process of politics, doomed if they openly say what they truly think. My curiosity lures me, as I've said, toward private figures, unknown individuals to whom I usually represent their first experience in being interviewed. I could write about them today or tomorrow or next year, and it will make no difference in the sense of their topicality. These people are dateless.

They can live as long as the language used to describe them lives *if* the language is blessed with lasting qualities.

My very first writing in *The Times*, in the winter of 1953 following my June graduation from Alabama, dealt with an obscure man who worked in the center of "the Crossroads of the World," Times Square. I was then a copyboy, a job I'd gotten after walking into the paper's personnel department one afternoon and impressing the director with my fast and accurate typing and my herringbone tailored suit (she later told me). Some months after I'd gotten the job, I was on my lunch hour, wandering awkwardly around the theater district when I began to concentrate on the five-foot high electric light sign that rotated in glittering motion the world's latest headlines around the tall, three-sided building overlooking Forty-second Street. I was not really reading the headlines; I was wondering instead: *How does that sign work? How do the words get formed by those lights? Who's behind all this?*

I entered the building and found a staircase. Walking up to the top, I discovered a large, high-ceilinged room, like an artist's loft, and there on a ladder was a man putting chunks of wooden blocks into what looked like a small church organ. Each of these blocks formed letters. With one hand he held a clipboard on which the latest headline bulletins were attached—the headlines changed constantly—and in the other hand he held blocks that he inserted into the organ that created lettering along the exterior wall's three-sided sign containing fifteen thousand twenty-watt bulbs.

I watched him for a while, and when he stopped I called to him, saying I was a copyboy from *The Times*, which was located a half-block away but which also owned this smaller building with the sign. The man greeted me, and, taking a coffee break, he came down the ladder and talked to me. He said his name was James Torpey, adding that he had been standing on that ladder setting headlines for *The Times* since 1928. His first headline was on the night of the Presidential election, and it read: *HOOVER*

DEFEATS SMITH! For twenty-five years, this man Torpey had been on that ladder, and even with my limited experience in New York journalism I knew that was some kind of story. After writing some notes about Torpey on the folded paper I always kept in my pocket, I returned to the main office and typed a short memo about him and put it in the mailbox of the city editor. I wasn't being paid to write, only to run errands and perform other menial tasks; but within a few days, I received word from the editor that he would welcome a few paragraphs from me on the high life of the lightbulb man—and this was published (without my byline) on the second day of November in 1953.

That article—and also my bylined piece in *The Times'* Sunday Travel section three months later about the popularity of the three-wheeled rolling chairs that people rode on the Atlantic City boardwalk—brought me to the attention of the editors. Other pieces followed, including a Sunday magazine article that *The Times* published in 1955 while I was on leave with the Army. The piece was about a woman old enough to be one of my mother's most venerable customers—a silent screen actress named Nita Naldi, who had once been Valentino's leading lady in Hollywood. But in 1954, decades after Nita Naldi's exit from the film business, it was announced that a new musical called *The Vamp*, inspired by the actress's life, and starring Carol Channing, would soon be coming to Broadway.

I had read this item in a tabloid's theater column one morning while riding the subway to work, months before leaving for the Army. The column mentioned that Nita Naldi was then living as a recluse in a small Broadway hotel, but the hotel was not named. New York then had close to three hundred small hotels in the Broadway area. I spent hours looking in the Yellow Pages in *The Times* newsroom when I was not otherwise occupied; then I jotted down the hotel numbers and later began placing calls from one of the rear phones that copyboys could use without being in visual range of the city editor's desk clerks, who like to assert their authority over copyboys.

I phoned about eighty hotels over a four-day period, asking each time to be connected to Miss Naldi's suite, speaking always in a confident tone that I hoped might convey the impression that I knew she was staying there. But none of the hotel people had ever heard of her. Then I called the Wentworth Hotel, and, to my amazement, I heard the gruff voice of a man say, "Yeah, she's here—who wants her?" I hung up. I hurried over to the Wentworth Hotel in person.

The telephone, to me, is second only to the tape recorder in undermining the art of interviewing. In my older years, especially while doing publicity tours for one of my books, I myself have been interviewed by young reporters carrying tape recorders; and as I sit answering their questions, I see them half listening, relaxing in the knowledge that the little plastic wheels are rolling. But what they are getting from me (and I assume from other people they talk to) is not the insight that comes from deep probing and perceptive analysis and much legwork; it is rather the first-draft drift of my mind, a once-over-lightly dialogue that too frequently reduces the exchanges to the level of talk radio on paper.

Instead of decrying this trend, most editors tacitly approve of it, because a taped interview that is faithfully transcribed can protect the periodical from those interviewees who might later claim that they had been damagingly misquoted—accusations that, in these times of impulsive litigation and soaring legal fees, cause much anxiety, and sometimes timidity, among even the most independent and courageous of editors.

Another reason editors are accepting of the tape recorder is that it enables them to obtain publishable articles from the influx of facile freelancers at pay rates below what would be expected and deserved by writers of more deliberation and commitment. With one or two interviews and a few hours of tape, a relatively inexperienced journalist today can produce a three-thousand-word article that relies heavily on direct quotation and (depending largely on the promotional value of the subject at the newsstand) will gain a writer's fee of anywhere from approximately five hundred to slightly more then two thousand dollars—which is fair payment, considering the time and skill involved, but it is less than what was being paid for articles of similar length and topicality when I began writing for some of these same national magazines, such as *The New York Times Magazine* and *Esquire*, back in the 1950s and 1960s.

The telephone is another inadequate instrument for interviewing because, among other things, it denies you of learning a great deal from observing a person's face and manner, to say nothing of the surrounding ambience. I also believe that people will reveal more of themselves to you if you are physically present; and the more sincere you are in your interest, the better will be your chances of obtaining that person's cooperation.

The house phone of the Wentworth Hotel, which I knew I had to use in announcing myself to Nita Naldi, did not present the same obstacle that a regular phone might have: I would, after all, be calling within her own building. *I was already there*, an undeniable presence!

"Hello, Miss Naldi," I began, having asked the operator to be directly connected without my having first announced myself to one of the hotel's desk clerks, a courtesy that—suspecting their mercenary nature—might have boomeranged to my disadvantage. "I'm a young man from *The Times*, and I'm downstairs in your hotel lobby, and I'd like to meet you for a few minutes, and talk about doing an article for the Sunday magazine."

"You're *downstairs*?" she asked, in a dramatic voice of mild alarm. "How did you know where I live?"

"I just called all the Broadway hotels I could."

"You must have spent a lot of money, young man," she said, in a calmer voice. "Anyway, I don't have much time."

"May I just come up to introduce myself, Miss Naldi?"

After a pause, she said: "Well, give me five minutes, then come up. Room 513. Oh, the place is a perfect mess!"

I went up to the fifth floor and will never forget the place. She occupied a small suite with four parrots, and the suite was decorated like a turn-of-the-century movie set. And she was dressed in a style that would have no doubt appealed to Rudolph Valentino himself, and perhaps *only* to him. She had dark arched eyebrows and long earrings and a black gown, and jet black hair I'm sure she dyed daily. Her gestures were very exaggerated, as in the silent screen era they had to be; and she was very amusing. I took notes, went back to my apartment after finishing work that day, and I wrote the story, which probably took three or four days, or even longer, to complete. I turned it in to the Sunday editor who handled show business subjects, and asked if he would be kind enough to read it.

A week later, he called to say he would like to use the article. His response marked one of the happiest days of my young life. The magazine would definitely publish it, he repeated, adding he did not know exactly when. It lay in type for a few months. But finally it did appear, on Oct. 16, 1955, while I was serving in the tank corps in Fort Knox, Kentucky. My parents sent me a telegram. I called them back from a telephone booth, collect, and my mother read the published article to me over the phone. It began:

> In order that Carol Channing be flawlessly vampish, beguiling, and pleasingly unwholesome as the star of the musical on the silent movie era which comes to Broadway November 10 and is called, not unexpectedly, *The Vamp*, she has had as a kind of adviser, aid-de-camp, critic, and coach, that exotic former siren named Nita Naldi. When it comes to vamping roles, no one is a more qualified instructor than Miss Naldi. In her heyday, in the 1920s, Nita Naldi was the symbol of everything passionate and evil on the silent screen. ...

And it ended:

> ... still very dark and buxom, Miss Naldi is recognized surprisingly often as she travels about. "Women don't seem to hate me anymore," she says with satisfaction. She is often stopped in the street and asked, "What was it really like kissing Valentino?" Young people will remark, "Oh, Miss Naldi, my father has told me so-o-o much about you!" to which the actress manages to respond graciously. Not too long ago a man approached her on the corner of Forty-sixth Street and Broadway and exclaimed in wonder, "You're Nita Naldi, the Vampire!" It was as if he had turned the clock back, restoring Miss Naldi to the world she had inhabited 30 years ago. Eager to live in the present, the actress replied in a tone that mixed resentment and resignation, "Yes, do you mind?"

My mother ordered several dozen copies of the magazine and mailed them out to all the customers who had known me as a boy in the store, and she included in her package my address at the base. In the fan mail I later received from them was also a letter from the city editor of *The Times* informing me that, after I was discharged and had returned to the paper, I would no longer be employed as a copyboy. I was being promoted to the writing staff, and assigned to the Sports Department.

In a postscript, he added: "You're on your way."

writer's digest

PART II On the Craft of Writing

VOLUME XIII JANUARY 1932 NO. 2

Local Color

ERLE STANLEY GARDNER

The foundation of **ERLE STANLEY GARDNER**'s writing career was built upon an extraordinary number of Western and mystery stories produced for the pulp magazine market of the 1920s. In order to make his tales as realistic as possible, Gardner would travel the world for months at a time. The article that follows details an epiphany he experienced while conducting this research. To the casual reader, his insight may seem minor, even trivial. But considered within the proper context of time and place, the impact is understandable—and no different, in fact, than our own initial realization of the power of the Internet. For the first time in history, the production and proliferation of books began to make "traditional" field research—even the research of lands thousands of miles away—unnecessary. One year later, Gardner wrote his first Perry Mason novel and the world grew even smaller.

When I first started in writing, I had a yen to write foreign adventure stuff. I knew something about the Chinese but nothing of China. Nothing daunted, I decided to write Chinese adventure stories.

Then I read what one of the writers' magazines had to say about the dire fate of the chap who "faked" his local color, and I got frightened. I'd always been one of the sort of chaps who hated to lose an argument. If I was going to have an argument with a reader who had been there, I wanted to win that argument.

So I decided I'd always know what I was talking about.

I knew something about the West, having rambled up and down the Pacific Coast for years on end, and I started in writing "Westerns." Then, when it looked as though detective stories were due for a boom, I started in getting gangster contracts, cultivating detectives, studying crime.

The more I studied, the more the passion for accuracy. I acquired quite a bit of underworld information. Too much, in fact. A certain detective, chasing down a puzzling case, crossed my back-trail and hunted me up—perhaps I should say "down." He wanted to know exactly how much I knew about a certain case, and he intimated that it would be far better for me to *talk* freely and confidentially.

As a matter of fact, I didn't know anything about the case except some underworld rumors. But I had been friendly with some of the people he wanted to investigate. I thought of the various possibilities of a "misunderstanding." Suppose my gangster friends should get the idea that I was imparting information? What then?

I decided to risk accuracy in favor of safety as far as the future was concerned. I had been writing a series of desert stories, and, in order to have my desert background absolutely true to life, I had acquired a camp wagon—a regular house on wheels—and I wrote most of my desert stories right out in the midst of the desert itself.

The camp wagon came in handy. I took a long trip out in the desert and didn't come back until the detective had switched his attention to another case.

Just recently, I went to China to write and study.

My friendship with the Chinese people goes back over quite a period of years, back to the time when I was starting in the law business, and some of my clients were Chinese. I'd made a stab at studying the language, jotting down a word here and there in a notebook, always with the idea that "sometime" I'd go to China.

Then, three years ago, I decided to make a real study of the language. I wanted to write "Chinatown" stories, and I wanted to be absolutely certain of the accuracy of my backgrounds. So I made arrangements for a teacher, and the wife and I set about learning how many different ways there were of saying "*ngow*" in the Cantonese dialect. There are plenty.

As we studied, the Chinese possibilities became more and more alluring. A year or so ago, the idea struck us that it'd be a good thing to go to China. Slowly the idea gathered strength. Some of our Chinese friends were in power in the government. We could manage a little Cantonese, enough to kid 'em along a bit, and they promised us that we'd see things the white man was seldom allowed to see.

So we went to China.

We went, not as tourists, but as friends of the Chinese. We lived with the Chinese, ate at the same table. In fact, we lived in houses where they didn't know anything about knives or forks. We went native.

And we had a series of vividly interesting, not to say exciting, adventures. We went up and down the coast on China Coasters. We traveled by sedan chair, rickshaw, and river boat, by train, steamer, and gunboat. We sat in on informal political discussions in which various factions shifted about into new positions that were destined to make history in China.

My notebook fairly bristled with information. We played tag with typhoons, delved into the underworld at Macao, were actually pursued by pirates in the delta of the Pearl River, went to inspect forts aboard a revolutionary gunboat, contacted the higher-ups of certain gangs of kidnappers in Shanghai.

Priceless bits of information rolled in with a regularity that kept me writing more in my notebook than I did to keep up my quota of fiction.

And we had some contact in the Sulu Archipelago, as well as with the headhunters of northern Luzon. We kept trying to break away from China, but always there was a perfectly wonderful experience just around the corner.

Finally, we took the bit in our teeth and bolted.

We walked right out on an experience that would have been almost an adventure book in itself and went directly to Zamboanga, over to Cotabato, then down into the Sulu Archipelago. We had further thrilling experiences among the Moros. The notebook expanded with additional information.

Finally, we broke away and went up to the mountain provinces. Here we contacted the Igorots, and the notebook swelled again. We secured photographs of the headhunters in their villages, received presents of spears, still bearing red rust, heard from the lips of the warriors themselves when those spears had been last used.

One of the headhunters even taught me the peculiar rhythm of beating the *gungsah* which marked the bringing in of an enemy's head. We learned how the spears are hurled, the head ax wielded.

I wanted to go to Manila. It seemed to have fiction possibilities.

We didn't have any particular contacts in Manila.

We knew a few of the army and navy crowd, but that was all—none of the natives.

We went to Manila, and set about getting some "local color" on Manila. And right then and there was when the trip blew up, when the "local color" became an elusive mirage, always glimmering in the distance.

I sensed there was quite a bit of interesting material there. But I couldn't find it. We stayed at the Manila Hotel, fought off heat and mosquitoes, yawned, hired cars and rode around the city, came back, yawned, and fought off more mosquitoes—or perhaps the same ones who had digested their former meals.

The facts that had come so thick and fast in the other places simply didn't come to us in Manila. We saw parks and buildings, interesting "types." We went out to dinner and gave dinner parties.

But there wasn't one blessed thing one could write about.

Then the wife made an excursion to the bookstore and picked up one of the recent books. It was illustrated with fine clear photographs, and it gave us all the information we were trying to get. More, it had lots of information about the Moros and the Igorots, information which we knew to be accurate because it tallied so accurately with what we had discovered for ourselves.

Always before, I'd scoffed at the writer who "faked" his local color. All right for him, if he wanted to do it, but I wouldn't descend to any such trickery. I'd know of what I wrote at firsthand, or I wouldn't write at all.

Yet here in this book was all the information I'd wanted to get on the political situation in Manila, written clearly and accurately. And it was information that I hadn't been able to get, even though I'd been on the ground.

And then I saw a great light.

Always before, we'd had contacts that took us out of the beaten, tourist track. Here in Manila we'd been simply sightseers. I thought back on the laughs we'd had at the "tourists" in China, the people who had eagerly boiled off the boats, gone directly to the European hotels, ventured forth in charge of "guides" or had "explored," finding their way, in either event, into the beaten ruts worn smooth by the feet of millions of other tourists.

They rode in rickshaws and sedan chairs, went to Chinese restaurants that made a specialty of serving European tourists, saw public buildings and parks, stared at the swarming multitudes, went back to the boat and sailed away, serene in the belief that they'd "done China."

That was exactly what we were doing in Manila—and, needless to say, we weren't getting anywhere.

So I walked down to the steamship office and bought a ticket back to China. I'm writing this in China now, getting finishing touches to some of the things we abandoned to rush to Manila.

It costs a lot of money for a writer to travel. Not only in the actual expense incident to the travel itself, but in the loss of income which is the inevitable result of trying to write stories in odd moments, under unfavorable conditions. Taken over a period of months, that loss of income, coupled with the expense of travel, makes a staggering figure.

And the writer who can only travel as a tourist had far better remain at home and devote his attention to the study of travel books.

I sensed that fact in Manila. A careful check-up has shown that it's an absolute fact.

Take China for instance. The Chinese are reserved. They're perhaps more misunderstood than any other race. They don't make friendships readily, they're secretive to a degree, and they distrust the motives of the seeker after information. Unless a writer had contacts there which would give him an entrée behind the scenes, he could live there for a year and never pick up anything worth writing.

That's indicated by the people themselves who live there, the Europeans. They don't associate much with the Chinese. They have their own district, just as the Chinese have their own districts in our American cities.

Many white people have lived in China for years without learning a word of the language, a bit of the customs of the people. They have learned how to order a number-one boy around in Pidgin English, and that marks the extent of their information.

Yet, if a writer knew the proper books to get, he'd find enough material about China to serve as background for all the stories he ever cared to write.

Take Macao and the pirates, by way of illustration.

As I've said before, the Chinese are secretive, suspicious, and reserved. They refer to themselves as the only real people. All others are "ghosts." They refer to us as "white ghosts" or "devil ghosts" or "pale ghost guys."

We had some contacts in Macao that simply couldn't have been picked up haphazard. I went to houses where I was the first "white ghost" who had ever been allowed to enter. The servants stared at me, open-mouthed.

I spent some little time with a character who was priceless from a fictional standpoint. Caution dictates that I say nothing which would even indicate his name or occupation. He showed me "behind the scenes" in Macao.

Yet Aleko E. Lilius has written a book which contains virtually all the information I was able to get about Macao. That book is for sale on the stands: *I Sailed With the Chinese Pirates* by Aleko E. Lilius.

And it's authentic. I know Lilius personally, crossed his back-trail in Macao and at Hong Kong before I'd even seen the man. He did just what he says he did—sailed with the Chinese pirates. He smuggled a camera along with him, took photographs. His book on Macao and the pirates is a veritable mine of information that took months of patient effort to assemble.

In fact, the average writer could never have developed the contacts Lilius had, even if he'd spent a lifetime in Macao. One appreciates the truth of this when one gets to know Lilius. He's a character, fully as interesting as any character of fiction. He's been in many different countries, had many and varied adventures. He's got a knack of acquiring adventures, a knack that comes in part through the fact that his head is utterly devoid of any bump of caution. Show Lilius a road that leads to adventures, and he plunges down it, heedless of burnt bridges.

And whenever you find a country that's sufficiently interesting to be worth a fig as a fictional background, you'll find that some adventurer of the type of Lilius has spent months of patient effort getting contacts that have put him "behind the scenes" and has published his adventures in book form.

One of the best-known writers of foreign adventure fiction has never visited the countries of which he writes. Yet his stories bear the stamp of authenticity in every detail. The reason isn't hard to find. When I visited this writer, he showed me his reference library, books dealing with the countries of which he wrote.

And he'd studied those books. Ask him anything about any phase of life in those countries, and he will rattle off the answer without even pausing.

In writing fiction, one must remember that it's the story that counts. The locale is only the background. In fact, one editor recently told me that he had had better success publishing foreign adventure yarns written by professional writers who had never visited the places they described than yarns written by those who had actually been to those places. The reason, he explained, was that the latter class lost sight of the story in putting in too much local color. It stiffened up the yarn, slowed the action, made it read like a travelogue.

Not that a man should pick up a travel book, read it through, and forthwith write a story whose setting is in the country described. Far from it. The facts gained by any one author in a travel book are always more or less colored. If a writer wants to use a certain locale he should carefully check over the available information, play one travel book against another.

But if he will study faithfully, he'll find that there's a lot more information open to him at less expenditure of time and money than if he visits a country as a tourist and tries to find out the facts for himself.

It figures out that there are three ways, good in the order listed, which a writer can secure his local color.

1. Fit himself to write of that country by dint of careful preparation, getting local contacts, familiarizing himself with the habits, customs, and language of the people he wants to visit, and then going to the country.
2. Purchase the books that deal with that country, and study those books.
3. Board a steamer, without any local contacts, go to the country and "look around."

The first method is, of course, the best. A person can draw a clearer picture of something he's actually seen or experienced than of something he's read about. But it's a method that takes time and money.

The second method is surprisingly efficient. Travel books have broken away from the conventional rut and are describing peoples and customs with a wealth of detail that was never dreamed of five years ago.

The third way is virtually valueless. I've about concluded that all tourist hotels are just about the same, that the average tourist sees nothing but the surface, never gets below that surface. He gets like his baggage, all plastered up with labels showing he's been different places, but with nothing else to show for it.

Civilization has spread pretty rapidly, and the science of fleecing tourists has become pretty well standardized. Stand in the lobby of the Hong Kong Hotel when a boat from the States comes into port, and you'll see what I mean.

Perspiring people, just a little bit awed, flocking in like sheep, being assigned to rooms, bathing, venturing down to the lobby again, thrusting cautious and curious faces out into the street, venturing out gingerly.

Stroll around to the typical tourist restaurants within two blocks of the hotel that night, and you'll see the more venturesome toying with awkward chopsticks at bowls of food that are seldom more than tasted. The more timid souls will be found in the hotel lobby, staring.

In short, if you want to write foreign adventure fiction, go ahead and write it. You can purchase that book by Lilius and learn more about the inside of Macao than you could by visiting it for a year if you didn't have an entrée. You can learn more about the Philippine islands from a reading of *The Isle of Fear* by Katherine Mao than you could by fighting mosquitoes at the Manila Hotel for a month.

And don't let anyone kid you that some of the most interesting foreign adventure stories aren't written by authors who have never been within a thousand miles of the places they describe.

If I ever go back to Manila, it won't be until after I've studied all I can learn about it, have made some contact there, and have an assurance that I can break out of the tourist rut and mingle with the natives.

If I can't do that, it's a cinch that some article writer has done it, and I can read his book and learn more about Manila than I could by fighting heat, mosquitoes, and sleepless nights, grinding out stories in the meantime on a portable typewriter, and gawking about me with eyes that can only see the surface.

My trip to China, to the Sulu Archipelago, and to the Igorot country was worth a thousand times the cost. My trip to Manila wasn't worth the hotel bill I paid. A trip to New Guinea would be only an expense.

I'm back in China.

VOLUME XVII JANUARY 1936 NO. 2

Magic Out of a Hat

L. RON HUBBARD

Twenty years prior to the publication of *Dianetics* and the beginnings of Scientology, **L. ("LAFAYETTE") RON HUBBARD** was a popular writer of pulp fiction. His best-known works from the era include *Fear* and *Final Blackout*. These humble beginnings, however, snowballed over more than fifty years, transforming Hubbard's literary works into a worldwide juggernaut, with his magnum opus, *Battlefield Earth*—a sprawling, one-thousand-page novel of the future—leading the fray. In 2005, Guinness World Records named Hubbard the most translated author of all time, with books published in sixty-five different languages. In the article below, the author shares some insights into his storytelling success.

When Arthur J. Burks told me to put a wastebasket upon my head, I knew that one of us—probably both—was crazy. But Burks has a winning way about him, and so I followed his orders and thereby hangs a story. And what a story!

You know of course how all this pleasant lunacy started. Burks bragged openly in *Writer's Digest* that he could give six writers a story apiece if they would just name an article in a hotel room. So six of us took him up on it and trooped in.

The six were Fred "Par" Painton, George "Sizzling Air" Bruce, Norvell "Spider" Page, Walter "Curly-top" Marquiss, Paul "Haunted House" Ernst, and myself. An idiotic crew, if I do say it, wholly in keeping with such a scheme to mulch editors with alleged stories. I spied a wastebasket in Burks's room and told him to plot me a story around it.

He ordered me to put a wastebasket on my head, told me that it reminded me of a *kubanka* (Ruski lid, if you aren't a Communist), and ordered me to write the story. I won't repeat here the story he told me to write. It was clean, that's about all you can say for it—(although that says a great deal coming from an ex-Marine).

This wastebasket didn't even look faintly like a *kubanka*. A *kubanka* is covered with fur, looks like an ice-cream cone minus its point, and is very nice if you're a Ruski. I wrote the story up that same night. Don't go wrong and find Art's article to see how he would do it. I'll show you the *right* way.

Burks told me to write about a Russian lad who wants his title back and so an American starts the wheels rolling, which wheels turn to gun wheels or some such drivel, and there's a lot of flying in the suggestion, too. Now I saw right there that Art had headed me for a cheap action story not worth writing at all. He wanted to do some real fighting in it and kill off a lot of guys.

But I corrected the synopsis so I didn't have to save more than the Russian Empire and I only bumped about a dozen men. In fact, my plot was real literature.

The conversation which really took place (Burks fixed it in his article so he said everything) was as follows:

BURKS: I say it looks like a hat. A *kubanka*.

HUBBARD: It doesn't at all. But assuming that it does, what of it?

BURKS: Write a story about it.

HUBBARD: Okay. A lot of guys are sitting around a room playing this game where you throw cards into a hat and gamble on how many you get in. But they're using a fur wastebasket for the hat.

BURKS: A fur wastebasket? Who ever heard of that?

HUBBARD: You did just now. And they want to know about this fur wastebasket, so the soldier of fortune host tells them it's a *kubanka* he picked up, and he can't bear to throw it away although it's terrible bad luck on account of maybe a dozen men getting bumped off because of it. So he tells them the story. It's a "frame" yarn, a neat one.

BURKS: But you'll make me out a liar in my article.

HUBBARD: So I'll make you a liar in mine.

So I started to plot the story. This hat is a very valuable thing, obviously, if it's to be the central character in a story. And it is a central character. All focus is upon it. Next I'll be writing a yarn in second person.

Anyway, I was always intrigued as a kid by an illustration in a book of knowledge. Pretty red pictures of a trooper, a fight, a dead trooper.

You've heard the old one: For want of a nail the shoe was lost, for want of a shoe the horse was lost, for want of a horse the rider was lost, for want of a rider the message was lost, for want of a message the battle was lost, and all for the want of a horseshoe nail.

So, it's not to be a horseshoe nail but a hat that loses a battle or perhaps a nation. I've always wanted to lift that nail plot and here was my chance to make real fiction out of it. A hat. A lost empire.

Pretty far apart, aren't they? Well, I'd sneak up on them and maybe scare them together somehow. I made the hat seem ominous enough and when I got going, perhaps light would dawn. Here we go:

"That's a funny-looking hat," I remarked.

The others eyed the object and Stuart turned it around in his hands, gazing thoughtfully at it.

"But not a very funny hat," said Stuart, slowly. "I don't know why I keep it around. Every time I pick it up I get a case of the jitters. But it cost too much to throw away."

That was odd, I thought. Stuart was a big chap with a very square face and a pocketful of money. He bought anything he happened to want and riches meant nothing to him. But here he was talking about cost.

"Where'd you get it?" I demanded.

Still holding the thing, still looking at it, Stuart sat down in a big chair. "I've had it for a long, long time but I don't know why. It spilled more blood than a dozen such hats could hold, and you see that this could hold a lot.

Something mournful in his tone made us take seats about him. Stuart usually joked about such things.

Well, there I was. Stuart was telling the story and I had to give him something to tell. So I told how he came across the hat.

This was the World War, the date was July 17, 1918; Stuart was a foreign observer trying to help Gajda, the Czech general, get Russia back into fighting shape. Stuart is in a clearing.

... and the rider broke into the clearing.

From the look of him he was a cossack. Silver cartridge cases glittered in the sun and the fur of his *kubanka* rippled in the wind. His horse was lathered, its eyes staring with exertion. The cossack sent a hasty glance over his shoulder and applied his whip.

Whatever was following him did not break into the clearing. A rifle shot roared. The cossack sat bolt upright as though he had been a compressed steel spring. His head went back, his hands jerked, and he slid off his horse, rolling when he hit the ground.

> I remember his *kubanka* bounced and jumped and shot in under a bush ...
>
> Feebly he motioned for me to come closer. I propped him up and a smile flickered across his ashy face. He had a small arrogant mustache with waxed points. The blackness of it stood out strangely against the spreading pallor of his face.
>
> "The ... *kubanka* ... Gajda." That was all he would ever say. He was dead.

Fine. The *kubanka* must get to General Gajda. Here I was, still working on the horseshoe nail and the message.

The message, the battle was lost. The message meant the *kubanka*. But how could a *kubanka* carry a message? Paper in the hat? That's too obvious. The hero's still in the dark. But here a man has just given his life to get this hat to the Czechs and the hero at least could carry on, hoping General Gajda would know the answer.

He was picking up the message he knew the hat must carry. He had killed three men in a rifle battle at long range in an attempt to save the cossack. There's suspense and danger for you. A white man all alone in the depths of Russia during a war. Obviously somebody else is going to get killed over this hat. The total is now four.

> I swore loudly into the whipping wind. I had no business getting into this fight in the first place. My duty was to get back to the main command and tell them Ekaterinburg was strongly guarded. Now I had picked up the cossack's torch. These others had killed the cossack. What would happen to me?

So my story was moving along after all. The fact that men would die for a hat seems so ridiculous that when they do die it's horrible by contrast, seemingly futile.

But I can't have my hero killed, naturally, as this is a first-person story, so I pass the torch to another, one of the hero's friends, an English officer.

This man, as the hero discovers later, is murdered for the *kubanka* and the *kubanka* is recovered by the enemy while the hero sleeps in a hut of a *muzjik* beside the trail.

The suspense up to here and ever farther is simple. You're worried over the hero, naturally. And you want to know, what's better, why a hat should cause all this trouble. That in itself is plenty reason for writing a story.

Now while the hero sleeps in the loft, three or four Russian Reds come in and argue over the money they've taken from the dead Englishman, giving the hero this news without the hero being on the scene.

The hat sits in the center of the table. There it is, another death to its name. Why?

So they discover the hero's horse in the barn and come back looking for the hero. Stuart upsets a lamp in the fight, the hut burns but he cannot rescue the hat. It's gone.

Score nine men for the hat. But this isn't an end in itself. Far from it. If I merely went ahead and said that the hat was worth a couple hundred *kopeks*, the reader would get mad as hell after reading all this suspense and sudden death. No, something's got to be done about that hat, something startling.

What's the most startling thing I can think of? The empire connected with the fate of the *kubanka*. So the Russian Empire begins to come into it more and more.

The allies want to set the Czar back on the throne, thinking that will save them later grief from the Reds. Germany is pressing the western front and Russia must be made to bear its share.

But I can't save Russia by this hat. Therefore I'll have to destroy Russia by it. And what destroyed it? The Czar, of course. Or rather his death.

The Czech army moves on Ekaterinburg, slowly because they're not interested so much in that town. They could move faster if they wanted. This for a feeling of studied futility in the end.

They can't find the Czar when they get there. No one knows where the Czar is or even if he's alive.

This must be solved. Stuart finds the hat and solves it.

He sees a Red wearing a *kubanka*. That's strange because cossacks wear *kubankas* and Reds don't. Of all the hats in Russia this one must stand out, so I make the wrong man wear it.

Stuart recovers the *kubanka* when this man challenges him. He recognizes the fellow as one of the Englishmen's murderers. In a scrap, seconded by a sergeant to even up the odds, Stuart kills three men.

Score twelve for one second-hand hat. Now about here the reader's patience is tried and weary. He's had enough of this. He's still curious but the thing can't go any farther. He won't have it.

That's the same principle used in conversation. You've got to know enough to shut up before you start boring your listeners. Always stop talking while they're still interested.

I could have gone on and killed every man in Russia because of that hat and to hell with history.

History was the thing. People know now about the Czar, when and where he was killed, and all the rest. So that's why I impressed dates into the first of the story. It helps the reader believe you when his own knowledge tells him you're right. And if you can't lie convincingly, don't ever write fiction.

Now the hero, for the first time (I stressed his anxiety in the front of the story) has a leisurely chance to examine this hat. He finally decides to take the thing apart, but when he starts to rip the threads he notices that it's poorly sewn.

This is the message in the hat, done in Morse code around the band (insert same):

"Tsar held at Ekaterinburg, house of Ipatiev. Will die July 18. Hurry."

Very simple, say you. Morse code, old stuff. But old or not, the punch of the story is not a mechanical twist.

The eighteenth of July has long past, but the hero found the hat on the seventeenth. Now had he been able to get it to Gajda, the general's staff could have exhausted every possibility and uncovered that message. They could have sent a threat to Ekaterinburg or they could have even taken the town in time. They didn't know, delayed, and lost the Russian Tsar and perhaps the nation.

Twelve men, the Czar and his family, and an entire country dies because of one hat.

Of course the yarn needs a second punch, so the hero finds the jewels of the Tsar in burned clothing in the woods and knows that the Tsar is dead for sure and the Allied cause for Russia is lost.

The double punch is added by the resuming of the game of throwing cards into this hat.

> After a bit we started to pitch the cards again. Stuart sent one sailing across the room. It touched the hat and teetered there. Then, with a flicker of white, it coasted off the side and came to rest some distance away, face up.
>
> We moved uneasily. I put my cards away.

The one Stuart had thrown, the one which had so narrowly missed, was the king of spades.

Well, that's the "Price of a Hat." It sold to Leo Margulies' *Thrilling Adventures* magazine of the Standard Magazines, Inc., which, by the way, was the magazine that bought my first pulp story. It will appear in the March issue, on sale, I suppose, in February. Leo is pretty much of an adventurer himself and without boasting on my part, Leo knows a good story when he sees it. In a letter to my agent accepting my story, Leo Margulies wrote: "We are glad to buy Ron Hubbard's splendid story 'The Price of a Hat.' I read *The Digest* articles and am glad you carried it through."

Art Burks is so doggoned busy these days with the American Fiction Guild and all that you hardly see anything of him. But someday I'm going to sneak into his hotel anyway, snatch up the smallest possible particle of dust, and make him make me write a story about that. I won't write it but he will. I bet when he sees this, he'll say:

"By golly, that's a good horror story." And sit right down and make a complete novel out of one speck of dust.

Anyway, thanks for the check, Art. I'll buy you a drink, at the next luncheon. What? Heck, I didn't do *all* the work!

VOLUME XIX MARCH 1938 NO. 4

Style

JAMES HILTON

Though **JAMES HILTON** wrote nearly two dozen books and won an Academy Award for screenwriting, he is best known for the classic novels *Goodbye Mr. Chips* and *Lost Horizon* (the first book ever published in paperback). In both, Hilton crafts characters that readers can't help but come to regard as friends and companions. Our empathy is assured, whether exploring mysterious Himalayan monasteries with Hugh Conway or suffering the horrors of war with Arthur Chipping ("Mr. Chips"). Familiar without being stock, pleasant without being cloying, both embody the qualities that Hilton so richly describes below.

On account, I suppose, of Mr. Chips, I have sometimes been asked how one creates a lovable character in fiction. My first answer is that the worst possible way would be to take pen and paper or typewriter and say to oneself: "I am going to create a lovable character."

As a matter of fact, the process of artistic creation is mysterious, even to the creator; there is, as G. K. Chesterton once said, all the difference in the world between knowing how things are done and knowing how to do them. The artist knows how to do them; he does not as a rule care whether he knows how they are done or not. He leaves that to critics, commentators, glossarians, footnoters, or his own biographer (if he is ever likely to have one)—but always with a wistful memory of Lord Balfour's remark in the British Parliament—"Gentlemen, I do not mind being contradicted, and I am unperturbed when I am attacked, but I confess I have slight misgivings when I hear myself being explained."

How many authors have had similar misgivings when enthusiastic admirers "explain" the significance of their characters, or when some well-meaning professor lectures learnedly on their writing methods! I once knew such a professor; he drew fascinating diagrams on a blackboard showing that so-and-so (I think it was Conrad) attacked his subject from the northeast corner; and the moral was that if we students only got ourselves in the right corner we might improve our literary output. The advice, however sound, was for me somewhat discredited by the fact that I did not want to write like Conrad anyway.

The only trick I know in writing is to have something to say, or some story to tell, and to say it or tell it as simply and effectively as possible. The proverb in *Alice's Adventures in Wonderland* cannot be bettered—"Take care of the sense and the sounds will take care of themselves." So far as "style" goes, I am a functionalist; if a sentence represents exactly the idea I wish to convey, I am satisfied with it. I dislike "style" that has a look or sound of having been stuck on afterwards, or "style" that employs unusual words with no intention but to startle the reader, send him to a dictionary, or give him the snobbish feeling that because he cannot properly understand what he is reading he is therefore improving his mind enormously. And I am ready to use any words that seem useful, whether the purists object to them or not—"intrigue" as a verb, for instance, which conveys to me a definite and needed shade of meaning between "interest" and "absorb."

As for creating character, I think it is one of those things that is not to be learned and cannot easily be counterfeited. Anybody, of course, can construct a dummy with an assortment of attributes attached to him like labels, and some writers have so successfully convinced the public that this is character-creating that the very word "character" has come to have a secondary meaning nowadays—i.e., we say a man is a "character" when we mean he is a little bit eccentric. Every stage actor knows how much easier it is to put over a juicy bit of character-acting than to portray an ordinary person who might be you or me; and most actors know also (to their own dismay) how readily the public is taken in by this sort of thing. A genuine creation should *have* character as well as *be* one; should have central heating, so to say, as well as exterior lighting. When Sir Walter Scott introduced any new personage into his novels he usually began with the hair and finished with the heels, making a complete inventory of dress and features all the way down; the result was that you felt you might possibly recognize the fellow if you were to ever meet him and he happened to be wearing the same clothes. But when Dostoyevsky or Dickens give you a character, you feel that you know him with your eyes shut. It is the difference between—"He had light blue eyes, lank hair, slightly stooping shoulders, and wore shabby tweeds"—and (I think Morley wrote this in one of his novels)—"Everything of him was *rather*, except his eyes, and they were *quite*." Please don't take this sentence as any sort of model; it is merely an example of how a good writer blows you a petal of meaning instead of feeling a whole forest for you—hoping you'll be just as satisfied, edified, and instructed.

So far, you may have noticed, I have been evading the question I began with—how a lovable character can be created. Frankly, I don't know. If you have a story to tell and tell it simply and without fuss, some of the characters may be lovable and others not so; you can hardly create them to specification. But sometimes, after you have finished with them, they ring a bell in your heart and afterwards in the hearts of your readers.

People love lovability; we all do; it is still human nature (even with a quarter of the world at war) to admire goodness. Our admiration, at its core, is sharp as a nerve; let them once touch that nerve, and stories have a good chance of being popular. But if there were any formula for touching it, believe the world of fiction would be swamped with "lovable characters." The truth is, the nerve is as secret as it is sensitive; try to create lovability to order and you will probably produce a mess of mawkishness that nobody will enjoy. The only recommendation I can give is that a writer should create the characters he has in mind and let them be lovable if they will.

VOLUME XIX AUGUST 1938 NO. 9

Within Quotes

ERLE STANLEY GARDNER

By 1938, **ERLE STANLEY GARDNER** was one of the country's most popular writers, having written more than one hundred short stories, three hundred novellas, and a dozen novels, six of which were made into films. And even in the midst of his extraordinary success, he was a friend to *Writer's Digest*, contributing articles and essays for a fraction of what larger magazines could pay him. What follows is one of his best: a comprehensive study of the mechanics of dialogue—at least as Erle Stanley Gardner saw them. He makes no pretense of being a teacher or advisor, knowing full well that what works for him may work for him alone. But the lesson is fascinating, nonetheless.

The people around The Digest *office are awfully proud of Erle Stanley Gardner. We had little, if anything, to do with his success, but we've kept abreast of his activities by watching the magazines and reading the pleasant little notes he sends the staff when he renews his subscription, or just "knocks out a letter to* The Digest*" telling us what's doing in Ventura and points east.*

Fifteen years ago, Erle was starting out on the long, hard road. He had no pull, no friends, and was a couple of thousand miles away from the nearest editor. Today he is one of the country's highest paid mystery writers, and his books have made a half dozen big box office movies. Generously, at a tenth of the rate he gets from Cosmopolitan, *Erle Stanley Gardener breaks down the secrets—trade secrets he has stored up about good plain and fancy dialogue writing. He hopes you can pick up a few tips from it, and so do we.*

I told the editor when he asked me for this article about dialogue, and I'm repeating it here and now: I won't put myself in the position of trying to tell other writers how to write.

I'm willing to discuss difficulties I've encountered in my work and the means I've taken to overcome them. If some other writer can profit by that, fine. I'm only saying, "These are little tricks of technique which have been of some value to me. I hope you like 'em." But I won't assume the attitude of saying, "This is how it should be done."

With that in mind let's look at this business of what goes inside the quotation marks.

For quite a while it had me licked.

Some fourteen years ago, when I was floundering around, keeping the kitchen stove hot with rejection slips, an editor wrote a caustic comment on one of my stories. This comment criticized the plot, the treatment, and the characters. It also commented on the dialogue. "The characters talk like dictionaries," the editor said.

In those days, I had a good mask I could put on when the occasion required. I pretended I took it in good part. I said he didn't make me mad—not the rage which would have had me sit down and write that I'd shown the story to two "disinterested" friends and they both agreed it was a better story than he'd ever published in his magazine, but the cold, white anger which made me vow to make that editor beg me for stories before I got done with him.

And then, because I'd put in quite a while practicing law in a courtroom and knew there were two sides to everything, I started examining that story to see what had given the editor the idea it was lousy and that the characters talked like dictionaries.

I don't know about you, but I could sit down and *think* I was writing a better story than the *Satevepost* ever *published*, yet have it loaded with faults that a kindergarten student would laugh at. Hypnotism, I guess. But I really and truly believed my yarns were masterpieces. (I remember one I wrote called "The Well of Silence" and ... well, I honestly expected that editor to grab a train and sign me up as soon as he read my yarn.)

Well, anyhow, the first real criticism I got was this withering blast. My characters talked like dictionaries, did they? Well, let's see ... Slowly I began to come out of my hypnotic trance. I read and re-read the story. Realization dawned on me. The characters *did* talk like dictionaries.

So I revised the yarn three times before I had it the way I wanted it. It was sixteen thousand words. I wasn't accustomed to typewriting and the ends of my fingers pulled apart from the nails. I taped 'em up with adhesive tape and stayed with it. I copied and revised that damned story three times in four evenings, a weekend and an afternoon which had been set aside for golf. And I sold it, and to the same editor who had poured such an acid criticism on my brainchild.

And when I showed that I could take straight-from-the-shoulder criticism, and buckle down and revise and send the revised story right back, I made an editorial friend. And I won a market.

That market was *Black Mask*. The editor was P.C. Cody, now in charge of circulation. When this story came out in *Black Mask*, Arthur E. Scott, who was then the editor of *Top Notch*, wrote me that he'd read it and thought I could write something which would be acceptable to him. I did. That, too, was pretty lousy. Years afterward he told me how utterly hopeless it had seemed when it came in, but it had the nucleus of a good idea in it, and so Scott took the time to write me a long letter pointing out where I had a good idea but had fallen down in my presentation.

This time I didn't get mad. I was commencing to see the light. I slaved over that story. It was called *The Case of the Misplaced Thumbs* and Arthur Scott's answer was a check for 320 dollars—and I was off.

As often happens to writers, it grew darker after the dawn. I had lots of rejection slips after that, but I knew that I could write. I'd seen my name in print. In short, I was bitten by the incurable bug, and after that discouraging experiences didn't have the same sting. I could take them standing up.

While Harry North was the editor of *Black Mask*, we got to the stage that writer and editor sometimes get—particularly if they don't know each other personally. I'd send him story after story. He'd send me rejection after rejection, nice letters of rejection, the story was good, but it didn't quite click. The characterization was bad—the dialogue wasn't quite right here, etc., etc. And he didn't like the revisions any better.

Lord only knows how those things develop, but occasionally a writer will find that he's written for some market regularly, and suddenly that market commences to get just a little upstage with him. This isn't right, and that isn't right, and the revisions aren't right.

Usually, those things end by the writer drifting away to another market. But, with *Black Mask*, the situation had rather an unusual ending—not that I would commend my reaction to be used on editors at large. But Harry North was essentially a hard-boiled guy who could dish it out, and, as events transpired, could take it. I remember I wrote a story for him titled "Three O'clock in the Morning." I worked like the devil to get that story so it represented my best work—whatever that meant. I sent it in to him with a short letter. Harry North replied with a check—no comments, just a check—and we were off again on another wave of prosperity, with me sending in stories and getting checks in return.

Sometime later, when "Three O'clock in the Morning" was published, imagine my consternation when I saw that Harry North had published my letter to him at the top of the story. His blurb read as follows: " 'Three

O'clock in the Morning,' " modestly asserts our Ventura contributor, in sending the yarn to the editor, "is a damned good story. If you have any comments on *it*, write 'em on the back of a check."

This is perhaps a roundabout way to approach the subject of dialogue. But what I'm trying to get at is that I learned what I know about writing the hard way. I stubbed my toe over every obstacle there was in the path of the beginning writer. Dialogue got me down and had me almost licked. Plots knocked me all over the ring and had me hanging on the ropes. The presentation of action threw me for a ten-yard loss every time I tried to carry the ball.

But I'm still here, happy, grinning, contented, battle-scarred, and making a living. I've found out enough about my old enemies so they don't knock me all over the ring now, although occasionally they land a good punch which has me pretty groggy for a while. But so far I've managed to escape the fatal count of ten—which should prove something.

So let's look at this dialogue business.

Years ago, when I realized that dialogue was one of my main troubles, I decided to take it to pieces and see what made it tick. I acted on the theory that if you wanted to lick an enemy, you first have to learn all there is about him. Study his strong points and his weak points. I started in with dialogue. I find that I still have my old notebooks. And, just in case you're interested, here's the way I approached the dialogue problem some fifteen years ago, with a few supplemental notes which have been added at a later date.

Here's the way the notebook reads:

DIALOGUE

OBJECT.

1. Portray character, reader isn't interested in what you tell him about the character of one of the actors in the story. He's more

convinced if he finds out for himself in the way he would do in real life. This is through conversation in relation to action.

2. To advance the action.
3. To avoid the historical slant.
4. Break away from author's personality.

HOW IT IS HANDLED.

1. Few lines idea in art.
2. Condensation.
3. Elimination useless repetitions and qualifications.

PERHAPS SET A PATTERN.

STRAINED ATTEMPT AT SMARTNESS DESTROYS ILLUSION REALITY.

POOR DIALOGUE DESTROYS PACE RHYTHM.

ENABLES BREAK UP SUBJECTIVE DISSERTATIONS TO HOLD INTEREST.

I think a writer should keep a notebook, not for the purpose of keeping plots alone, but to list points of technique which he picks up from time to time, and so he can review his own thoughts.

It's been quite a while since I worked out this first dialogue business, yet I can go back over a period of years and instantly recapture my thoughts of the moment.

I have a pretty large-sized notebook, filled with pages of self-criticism, suggestions from other authors, copies of interesting paragraphs from articles in writers' magazines, etc., etc.

So let's put this notebook classification of dialogue under a magnifying glass and see what we have. Under OBJECT, subdivision 1 is self-explanatory. So's 2. But 3 needs a little explanation. I had found that my stories weren't stories, but histories. I unconsciously approached the reader not from the angle of something which was happening, and in which he was an actor, but from the angle of something which had happened, and in which he was a tardy spectator. I'd already catalogued that as one of my faults. By advancing the story more through dialogue and less through statement I found I could eliminate a lot of that fault.

Subdivision 4 needs just a word. I used to get too much *me* in the story. It's well to be individual and show that individuality in your writing. But your characters must be individuals, entirely free of your apron strings. Don't cart them around, dump them in situations for a few pages, then pick them up, carry them into the next chapter, and dump them again. Let them move under their own power and take the story with them. And the way to cut the characters loose from your apron strings is through their dialogue, their oral reactions to the things the other characters are doing.

Now then, let's detour for a moment to the HOW IT IS HANDLED classification.

Subdivision 1. Ever notice how the artist who tries to sketch in everything he sees gets all bogged down in his own detail, how his pictures seem to lack a theme, how they shriek of such painful work that it's wearying to look at them, while some other artist makes two lines, throws in a patch of shadow, and it becomes a tree?

Well, in dialogue I found it worked better not to try to portray character and advance the story by working too much detail into the conversation. Sketch in a line and a bit of shading so that the reader sees the tree.

Subdivision 2. I found, to my surprise, that characters in stories almost never talk the way they do in real life. Listen to a friend. Figure the number of words in his ordinary conversation, then notice how you'd have to write what he said to get it published in a story.

Subdivision 3. The characters you like don't modify what they say with a lot of qualifications. They say "yes" and "no" and "drop that gun" and "what of it." They don't say, "Well, if it appears that Uncle John is dead, and since there is no other alternative, and because you represent the heirs, I'll agree; unless, of course, it should transpire that there's a will, in which event I'll reserve the right to withdraw from the agreement."

In other words, characters reach decisions (unless you're deliberately trying to portray a man who can't reach a decision). They express their decisions in a few definite words. The best illustration of this is in the movies. Go to a movie, enjoy it, then sit through the show a second time just to listen to the way the characters talk and what they say. You'll be astounded, if you haven't already consciously thought of it, to see with what few words the characters advance the plot, show their characteristics, and yet you feel that you're listening to really, truly, flesh-and-blood conversation.

You'll find that writing movie dialogue is a science, a science worked out until it has become an art.

"Perhaps Set A Pattern." This was the note I used to remind myself that the reader likes to identify himself with the characters, likes to figure that he'd have said about that same thing himself—if he'd thought of it. Therefore you want to figure the psychological reactions of the reader to what's taking place in the story, and when the hero says something, be sure he says it in a way which the reader might use as a pattern, something the way he'd like to talk in a similar situation. You'll make more reader friends that way—or that's the way I figured it when I was giving the session with the notebook.

Now, using so much of this framework as a basis of study, I can pick up any story written by any good author and find bits of dialogue that fit into this same pattern. In other words, successful authors have long ago encountered these same problems, solved them, and passed on to other problems. I don't say their reasoning and mine are identical, but so far as mine is correct I can ascertain that it's fairly well supported by illustrations.

Look at these examples, picked at random.

Take this from a yarn in *Country Gentleman* by Jerome Beatty:

> "Jumping Jupiter!" explained Dorothy. "You've been here two months, child, and you still believe Ed Deaver's hooey? Even the fan magazines don't print that yarn any more."
>
> "Well, wasn't she born on a South Sea isle and didn't she grow up among the carefree natives?"
>
> "She was born on a Kansas farm, that gal. I met a fellow the other day who went to college with her. He even was engaged to her—but she left him to go to Hollywood. That South Sea stuff, honey bunch, is publicity hokum."
>
> "Anyway, I think Bonita Belmore is just priceless—no matter where she was born."
>
> "She's no good. Anybody who would leave that boy for the movies–"
>
> "What boy?"
>
> "The boy from Kansas I was telling you about. The one she was engaged to. His name is Jimmy Dodd. You ought to see him, child; tall and kind of shy—and—well, he's all right, take my word for it."
>
> "I will. Are these manuscripts ready to be mailed?"

Get the way the story is advanced, the way you feel interested not only in the characters who are talking, but in the ones are being talked about? See the pair who are doing the talking without even knowing what they look like?

Or try this from *Cosmopolitan* by Margaret Culkin Banning:

> "Okay," said Mike, "but how about the bacon? Does the boy bring it home?"
>
> "He will. I don't have to worry about that. But even if he didn't, I wouldn't care. There are a lot of other things in this world more important than money!"
>
> "Name me two."
>
> "Figure it out for yourself," said Lily. She couldn't give him any more time. She had things to do.

Notice how cleverly that dialogue is worked in with a few swift lines and a bit of shading which makes you see a tree. Notice how it's condensed, how it gives you a picture of the characters, their environment, their problems ... and yet two people wouldn't have talked *just* like that. They'd have talked more, qualified their statements. There'd have been the "Well, well, well, what are you doing here? Haven't seen you for a long time, and you're looking fine." ... "You, too! Where's your wife? I haven't seen her for ages. Where are you keeping yourself these days, and why don't we have one of those get-togethers?" ... "Swell idea. The little lady was talking about you just the other day. Say, I tell you what, let's ..." etc., etc., etc.

On the other hand, you have to be careful with this crisp, clever dialogue. The big-name writers handle it as a barber handles a razor. It's edged. Properly used it's a wonderful tool. Get careless with it and it makes trouble. Some writers try so hard to be clever they create characters which aren't convincing. Their characters talk with such brittle-sharp conversation it gives the reader an inferiority complex. It takes just a dash of swift lines, written with a delicacy of touch.

Let's look at *This* Week and see how James Warner Bellah goes about his stuff:

"So," he said, "if you'll just see your way clear to a settlement of four million dollars, round figures, we'll set the day."

Her voice was desperately low: "Do you mean to say that you are asking me to marry you—without feeling one thing for me?"

He said, "We're well-bred people. Love is for barmaids."

She said, "Go away quickly, Michael."

He raised his eyebrows. "I say, you Americans are frightfully touchy about money, aren't you?"

"Go away, Michael," she said.

In that scene the author was sketching in a bit of background. He wanted to show the reader the character of the girl, the thing she was trying to forget, her reason for being where she was and feeling as she did. It was a device to relieve the story from any possibility of a historical drag and make the reader feel right at home with the characters. In those few lines you've learned a lot about what the author wants you to learn, and, mind you, you've done it for yourself. He doesn't say, "The girl was sensitive, romantic, impulsive, yet firm. She had been places, was wealthy, a romanticist, yet she had seen the sordid rear its ugly head when she had been expecting romance—as though some jack-in-the-box had thrust up a screaming caricature of ugliness when she had opened a box which might have contained an engagement ring." He lets you find all this out for yourself, and, as a result, you feel this girl is one of your friends, rather than a friend of the author.

Remember sometimes when an officious friend, a too-friendly friend, had dwelt at length upon the charms of some young woman whom he was going to have you meet? "You'll be crazy about her, Jack, my boy. She's young, willowy, a swell sport, good company, honest and sincere without being Victorian about it. She knows her way around and doesn't ask odds of any man ... and I've told her about you, what a swell egg you are, about that time you took the ball around the end and ran for. ..."

Let him keep that up a bit and you don't give a damn whether you ever meet the little lady. When you do, you look for the gold and the diamonds of her character and see only wistful eyes and a turned-up nose and a hint of a freckle. You think, "Oh, splash." And she, looking at you with those wistful eyes, is thinking, "So this is the big, handsome brute? I feel like telling him, 'Go cure your halitosis with Listerine. Put Mum under your armpits and wash with Lifebuoy soap. Then come back in two years. Perhaps you are perfect, but you don't look it, and who gives a whoop anyway?' "

But suppose this friend had kept his trap shut and just introduced you to a snub-nosed gal with freckles, who looked just like any other of the sex that invariably gives a right-hand turn signal when they're really going to turn left—and she'd seen only a big palooka with a cleft chin which she really didn't like and eyes that were like her spaniel's, and you'd started talking, and found out, a bit at a time, that the girl was *different* and she'd learned that you had a *commanding personality* ... and what ho, my lads, we're off to another romance. Ike, gimme that ring out of hock and take this overcoat instead.

Or, let's look at examples from some of the action type of magazines, where you'll find that dialogue has to have a certain punch.

Take this for example:

> "... beefed to Doran, and Doran tried to get Smith pulled off the case and thought he did. Then Morrow got killed. Get that?"
>
> "I hear you talk."
>
> "Then Smith picked up a guy ... etc."

The above is from a yarn by Roger Torrey in September, 1937, *Black Mask*. See how the mere statement, "I hear you talk," in answer to the question of the man who was spilling a lot of facts, shows the character of the listener, casts doubt upon that of the talker, and keeps the element of mystery and suspense in the story?

Or, take this from a story by Carroll John Daly in *Dime Detective* (and any student who wants to get virility in dialogue and action can always count on Carroll John Daly having a sleeve pretty well filled with Aces).

> "Am I to understand that you have taken Richard Havermore prisoner, and that you know personally where he is, and that you intend to torture him to death?"
>
> "That's it exactly," he said slowly.
>
> And that was all. He'd made his own trap, put the cheese in it, then stuck his face in for that cheese. My gun was out again, up and down—and his lean body crashed upon the table.

Notice how Daly advances the plot with a statement of facts, and this illustrates it with a comment on action which lifts the reader right out of the chair.

One of the best ways of handling dialogue is to intersperse just the right amount of narrative action between the passages of dialogue. That keeps the story moving and the conversation from becoming monotonous.

I can illustrate with another passage from that same story of Daly's:

> I twisted two guns into my hands. He looked blank and chirped in a bird-like voice that could be heard all over the place: "You police—no?"
>
> "No is correct." Then I stepped forward, lifted my gun up and down. It was the blow with my gun that knocked him to the floor, but it was his own idea to hit it with his face.
>
> A voice called: "That sounds like you, Williams."

Or, take a specimen from a story by William E. Barrett in *Detective Stories*:

> "I'm Chet Chandler, McQuillen," he said, "and I can do you some good. Let me have your story."

> He was brisk and businesslike; a slender, well-groomed young man with level eyes and a jaw that he didn't develop by "yessing" people. I liked him, but I couldn't see any reason why he should be my lawyer.
>
> "Nobody that's heard my story has liked it," I told him.
>
> The corners of his eyes wrinkled up pleasantly.
>
> "Give me a crack at it."
>
> I shrugged. After all, it was no secret. I'd been telling it to the cops all night. With a cigarette burning cheerfully, I went into it again. He followed it all the way and interrupted only when I skipped over the descriptions. He wanted everything, and when I finished, he smoked quietly for a few minutes before he opened up.
>
> "Would you be interested in learning that the fifty dollar bill you had was part of the Baintree ransom money?" he said.
>
> I stiffened at that. "That Missouri kidnapping?"
>
> "Yes. Know anything about it?"

Notice that the conversation isn't really the conversation a person accused of crime would have with an attorney. It's a condensed version which, nevertheless, makes you feel you've heard a long conversation. You sense the reserved, self-sufficient character of the storyteller when he says, "Nobody that's heard my story has liked it."

And, for sheer picture-painting, character-sketching conversation, take this from a story by Leslie T. White in *Dime Detective*:

> The wagon cop frowned, moistened the stub of his pencil. "How'n hell do you spell 'malicious'?"
>
> "Make it resistin' arrest, instead," the patrolman growled and walked away.

And if you want a nice illustration of how a little comment on the part of the author, interspersed with bits of conversation, can give added meaning and emphasis to what's being said, notice this from a yarn by S. Omar Barker, in *Adventure*:

> "You're a damn fool," observed Butch Gates. His tone was impersonal, but there was no hint of either condescension or contempt in it. Then, as if an afterthought, he added: "Both of you."

These are typical examples of the best dialogue technique. Don't think they're easy to find. If you want to see the game from the other side of the fence and realize what an editor has to contend with, just pick up a few magazines and say to yourself, "I'll just pick out a few examples of outstanding dialogue technique."

Story writing has improved a lot since I broke into print. My early stories wouldn't get by today. Competition is more keen. Quality has progressed. The acceptable story of today must be better written than the acceptable story of fifteen years ago. But don't let that discourage you. There are many more markets. Try your best to put dialogue with a punch in your stories and you'll find editors will "write their comments on the back of a check."

And, for beginning writers who are keeping up a brave front and holding a stiff upper lip, but who secretly are tired to death of getting courteously insulting slips stating that stories are returned, not because they lack merit, but simply because they are unavailable, I have one or two suggestions.

Study plot. What is it? What is its function? What is it supposed to accomplish? How is it built up? Study dialogue. Analyze it. Strip it down to essentials. Study action—what makes for action in a story? How does one get virility and sense of speed in a yarn?

Then, with those three things in mind—plot, dialogue, and action—write a yarn and send it out.

See what happens.

And more power to you!

VOLUME XXIV JULY 1943 NO. 8

Hero, Heroine, Heavy

LEIGH BRACKETT

Though **LEIGH BRACKETT** was only one of several well-known female writers working in the mystery, science fiction, and fantasy fields of the early and mid-twentieth century, she was certainly among the most highly regarded. Her first novel, *No Good From a Corpse*, was published the year after the article that follows. A mystery of the hard-boiled variety, it caught the attention of Hollywood director Howard Hawks. Hawks hired Brackett to work with William Faulkner on the screenplay for Raymond Chandler's *The Big Sleep*. That collaboration resulted in what many consider the best piece of film noir ever made. Brackett continued writing until her death in 1978. Her final work was the first draft of the screenplay for George Lucas's *The Empire Strikes Back*.

You look so familiar, spread out down there in the gutter. That's where I used to spend most of my time, too, when I was still taking it from Big Boss Plot.

Well, climb up on your feet again, pal, and take heart. I'll let you in on something.

This guy John L. (The Formula) Plot—is a phony. He isn't tough at all. In fact, he's a pushover once you get his number. And I'll tell you how I got his number.

I went over his head. I went to the people. And the people, boys and girls, is where every writer has to go sooner or later if he wants to eat and maybe someday be a genius, even if it's only Genius, j.g.[1]

Since I did that, Plot hasn't bothered me. I've got him licked. My stories sell, a couple of editors, God bless 'em, have said nice things about me, and sometimes I feel pretty happy about the whole thing. I even think I may be a real writer, with a genuine excuse for filling up printed pages.

I like to write. I wouldn't trade writing for any other job on earth. Being a Voice of the People is quite an undertaking, even if you're only a feeble squeak.

When I first started in this racket, I was duly impressed by Plot.

So I knuckled under to The Formula. I read all the books about him. I took a course about him. I met his mob, and attained a degree, a most flattering degree, of familiarity. I called Complications by their first names. I clapped Twists on the shoulder. (Don't get ahead of me, sonny.) I played around with Climaxes, Denouements, Beginnings, Middles, and Ends.

Writing was pure physical agony. All those Twists and Climaxes and things wouldn't cooperate. The minute I sat down at the typewriter they got sullen and fractious. I had to coax, kick, and beat every last one of them into position.

Anyway, I finally took my troubles to a certain more-than-worthy gentleman who advertises inside the back cover of *Writer's Digest*. In his office at that time was Henry Kuttner, that eminent breeder and fancier of the better type monsters. Hank insisted on reading each and every one of my yarns and telling me what was wrong with it.

The dialogue always went something like this:

BRACKETT: Well, what's the verdict on this one?

[1]Junior Grade

HANK: Same thing. It isn't a story. It doesn't live.

BRACKETT: (*groans*) But *why*? I sweat blood over that one. The plot's okay, isn't it? The hero has a problem, he fights it, he wins. What's wrong?

HANK: Oh, the plot's fair enough, technically. Trouble is, you have a Hero, with capitals. A great big beautiful thing with steely eyes and muscles out to here, who's so stiff with guts and nobility he can't sit down. You've got a villain who is simply reeking with Villainy, for no particular reason except that the Hero has to have some excuse for existing. You've got a Heroine—well, let's just forget her.

BRACKETT: (*wails*) But those characters—I took their outsides from people I've met. I've done everything the books say, given them tags and motivation and everything. They all react to the plot ...

HANK: The plot should react to them. You bone up a situation and then sling a sawdust dummy into the middle of it, and right away it starts doing the customary things. They don't live. And if they don't live, neither does the plot.

The funny part of it was that I was just as bored with my story people as he, and everybody else. That should have tipped me off, right there. I wrote about Heroes, Heroines, and Heavies because The Formula told me to.

No matter how I struggled, it always came out the same way. Dead. Dead and reeking. And Hank would say patiently, "Draw from life," and I would cry, "But I do!"

And believe it. Honestly, sincerely believe *that I was drawing my characters from life.*

That psychological block, that semantic lesion, cost me more in time, money, and punishment than I can bear to think about. Looking back, I wonder how as big a fool as I was could have avoided being drowned by now knowing enough to come in out of a California dew.

There are two reasons for my unconscious stupidity. The first is purely cultural. The popular magazines, the average American novel, and above all the motion pictures, have a certain definite set of stock figures. They all use them, shamelessly and with conviction. There are exceptions, of course, and of late Hollywood, notably Warner Bros., has managed to let go of some of its cherished clichés. But by and large, there isn't much change.

We, the public, absorb these fictional creatures from the time we're able to read the funnies and toddle to the Saturday matinees. We know a hero when we see one. We know that all heroines are beautiful and perfect beyond compare, except for the few poor sweet things who have been tricked into evil ways through no fault of their own. We know all about bankers, taxi drivers, doormen, hotel clerks, farmers, cowboys, Marines, white-haired mothers who sacrifice all, gangsters, cops, chorus girls, and so on. We know all about courage, gallant death scenes, noble renunciations, the cowardly end of the rat who sins against the Hays Code[2]. We know all about love. Oh yes we do, too!

Or else we're the other kind. We're smart and adult. We read Serious Novels. We know that decency, bravery, the better side of humanity is all a sham and a delusion. We know all about repressions and Freud and the evils of the social system, and every other system. We wallow in mire up to our ears, and to us the odor of a leaky sewer main is the only true, genuine perfume on earth.

Oh sure. Whichever set we belong to, we know people all right, all right!

The other reason, and the more important one, is social. And it hasn't anything to do with class or money or position. It's almost as universal

[2]A set of principles by which the motion picture industry agreed to govern itself in 1930.

as sex, and a damn sight harder to handle. It's the trained, conditioned illusion of life that we grow up with.

A child is born. His parents belong to a certain group, engaged in a certain occupation, or none, professing a certain religion, or none, having a certain set of moral standards, or none. The child grows up, believing this particular small section of human thought and behavior to be the norm. He, his people, his way—that's the savvy, the know-how. Everything outside is wrong, in greater or less degree. He doesn't like it. He doesn't understand it. He shuts his mind to it. He puts labels on people and sticks them carefully in pigeonholes, and when he wants to know what sort of a man or woman Soandso is, he just reads the label and that's that. Period. He doesn't have to talk to Soandso. He doesn't ever have to see him. He knows. All right. So the child, having in him the influences of conditioned social thinking and the sturdy, indestructible images of the printed pages and the silver screen, grows up and decides to be a writer.

He is immediately confronted by the question, "What shall I write about?" Well, people, of course. Every dope knows that. You get a guy with the right ideas, strong and brave and incorruptible, a beautiful gal for him to love, and a villain to make things hot. You throw in a cop, maybe, or a taxi driver, for comic relief, and a couple of minor characters to be noble and get killed, or ignoble and ditto. That's all simple. What you really need is a Plot. A good, strong, airtight Plot, with complications and twists and climaxes and a wow finish.

Of course, all the plots have been used over and over again, but what are you going to do? You've *got* to have a plot.

So he writes his plot, and pretty soon he knows all the phrases like "too slight" and "doesn't hold interest." He thinks the hell with it, the doors are closed to new talent, they just won't give me a break.

I'm not quite sure when or how I began to hoist myself over that mental wall. Probably it was contact with a few strange (to me) and vital individuals whose reactions I couldn't classify that gave me the boost I needed. Anyhow, I did climb over, and bingo! I discovered humanity.

Not all at once, or course. But I began to realize that people aren't Characters. They don't wear tags or fit pigeonholes. They aren't Heroes, Heroines, or Heavies. They're just human beings. They won't conform, and apparently they never heard of Plot or the rigid law laid down to govern human reactions in fiction. They aren't right. They aren't wrong. They just live.

I began to get really interested. I read books on psychology and crime, especially murder, not with an eye to judging but to understanding.

And people say there isn't anything to write about! They get stuck for plots. They scream about unfair discrimination against new talent. And all the time, right in front of their doors, in the buses and drive-ins and markets, in kitchens and palaces and homes and tenements, yes, even in Hollywood, people are living out all the plots that can ever be conceived or written.

Not thinking about them, but living them. Getting married, having babies, dying, planning murders, committing them, thinking about suicide and sex and beauty and the hereafter, loving, hating, laughing, working, sweating, and hoping. All kinds of people—stupid, brilliant, kind, cruel, and all of that mixed up in all of them along with fear and bravery, the desire to hurt, the desire to help, the desire to breed, the desire to be happy, the desire to escape.

When I found all that out, something happened to me. I said the hell with Plot. I'm going to write stories about people that interest me, the way I see them. I'm sick of formula. I'm sick of Hero, Heroine, Heavy. I'm sick of neat, tidy, emasculated emotions, with every little puppet jerking through the paces of what ought to be and not what is. I'm sick of Characters.

I'm going to write about men and women, all classes, types, and conditions, within the limits of my own capabilities. People with faults, with nasty tempers, with weaknesses and loves and hates and fears and gripes against each other. People I can believe in because I know and understand them. People who aren't like anybody else's characters because they are themselves, like 'em or don't.

And above all, people who are in the mess they're in because of legitimate action or emotion; who are opposed to each other in bitter antagonism because they're the kind of people they are; and who slug their way out on their own two feet with no help from me or the Great God Plot.

So I did, as well I could with what talent, brains, and experience I had to offer. I enjoyed myself. And all of a sudden I began to sell. I didn't set the world on fire, but I had fewer duds, and more fields of thought were opening up every day. Then I realized something else.

Plot wasn't an enemy any more.

I was astonished. The old boy hadn't let out a peep. I'd been so doggoned interested in my people, so busy watching them love and hate and laugh and sweat, that I hadn't had any time to think about him at all, and now he was no tougher than a cup of custard. I had him licked.

The whole thing is so painfully clear. I'd been working it backwards. First the plot, then the characters. Why I didn't realize years ago what a fool stunt that is, I'll never know.

Plot isn't a separate entity, a thing you can stand up like a lab skeleton for study. Plot is people. Human emotions and desires founded on the realities of life, working at cross purposes, getting hotter and fiercer as they strike against each other until finally there's an explosion—that's Plot.

Don't take my word for it. Look back over your favorite books and movies. What is it you remember? D'Artagnan battling the Cardinal's guards, Beau Geste dying with a dog at his feet, Sam Spade sending Bridget to the gallows—or the mechanical tracks by which Character A was brought into juxtaposition with Character B?

Plot or "Plotto"[3] won't help you out of a mess. The only recourse you have is your people. "Plotto" is a good springboard for ideas, yes. But you wouldn't want to take a plot out of it and then write people around it. Your man Joe Doakes is in such-and-such a hole. How to get him out? The answer is simple. Let Joe get himself out. You know Joe, inside and out. You don't have to consult a book or a formula about how he ought to get out. He'll do whatever it's in him to do, being the kind of a guy he is. Let him do it.

When you're dreaming up a story, start with people. If they're real, and strong, and want what they want, they'll beat the hell out of the plot all by themselves. They'll get into fresh situations, and get out in fresh ways, because they're not dummies being shoved around in a formula cage. They're men and women, with minds of their own.

Throw away the clichés, the stock figures, the romantic illusions. Motherhood does not automatically make all women saints. The poor are not models of pure nobility, all hotel clerks are not pansies, and believe it or not, the rich are frequently as decent human beings as you and I.

Park your prejudices on the shelf for a while. Stop viewing everything in the light of right or wrong, praise or blame, and just try to understand. Condemning John Dillinger is easy enough, but it isn't interesting and it isn't constructive. Understanding why John Dillinger became Public Enemy Number One is far more important. Meet the people. Listen to them tick. Learn to like them, not theoretically and at a distance, but close up, forebearing their faults because you have them too.

That doesn't mean that you have to go slopping around in a puddle of baffled sentimentality, like Saroyan[4], with the brotherly love running

[3] "Plotto" was a method of plot development by formulaic means created by William Wallace Cook in 1928. It was popular among pulp fiction writers for years. In 1941, the *Plotto* "how-to" manual was republished as *Plotto: The Master Book of All Plots.*

[4] William Saroyan (1908 – 1981) was a depression-era author and playwright whose stories celebrated optimism in the midst of tragedy. One of his best-known works is the play *The Time of Your Life* (1939).

out of your ears. It doesn't mean you have to throw away your ideals, or acquire habits you don't like or Live for Experience. You don't have to embrace everything you see. But unless you know people, feel with them, understand them, you can't call yourself even an attempt at a writer, or a human being, either.

It isn't a sure-fire formula I'm handing out, this People are Plots idea. I wish it were. I wish I didn't make mistakes and write trash and slip from time to time into rank commercial formula. I wish I could rise above my own limitations. But I can't. I can only try to grow up as high as possible, and hope that my upper limit won't be too low down.

In the meantime, I'm happy. I can write stories now, stories I like and believe in. My people take care of that. And there's the whole wide world just outside, an endless treasury of beauty and violence, laughter and pain. The real thing, the McCoy. All I have to do is open my mind and heart and let the stories walk in.

Climb down, kiddies. Especially those of you who don't, as I didn't, even realize your seclusion. Go to the people. They're the only place you'll ever have to go as a writer.

VOLUME XXIV DECEMBER 1943 NO. 1

Write About What You Know

W. SOMERSET MAUGHAM

By 1943, **W. SOMERSET MAUGHAM** was unquestionably recognized as one of the most popular authors of his time. His writing style was spare: simple and direct—at times, even detached. And yet he crafted characters, emotions, and situations that rang so true, you couldn't help but believe them to exist. Maugham himself would most likely shrug at the compliment and simply attribute the extraordinary verisimilitude of his work to one simple rule. "Write about what you know." Sex, sickness, violence, poverty—there was no personal experience too private to turn into a good bit of fiction. From *Of Human Bondage* to *The Razor's Edge* and *Ashenden* to *The Painted Veil*, recognizable elements of Maugham's life entered into everything he wrote. Here, he explains why.

I have just been reading some short stories that a young man, twenty years of age, sent to me. He tells me that he wants a candid criticism; but I know, as he in his heart knows, too, that what he really wants is praise. The stories are not badly written; he has taken the trouble to learn the elements of grammar, a precaution that young writers, both male and female, too seldom take; and his characters, though shopworn, are sufficiently individualized for the purposes of a short story; but he has chosen to write of subjects which, it is only too evident, he knows absolutely nothing about. That is precisely the error that so many young writers make, and it is because I can do nothing but point it out that I have been obliged to write the same letter over and over again.

It is, at first sight, strange that they should do so, since one thinks it much easier to write about what you know than about what you don't. The explanation, I suppose, is that they find the familiar commonplace and think that romance must be sought in the exceptional. That is why they are so fond of writing about painters, actors, singers, and fiddlers.

In one of the stories I have just been reading, a middle-aged farmer's wife, who, we are told, is a gifted pianist, suddenly writes a remarkable sonata and gets a distinguished conductor to orchestrate it. It doesn't require much knowledge of music to know that even a heaven-sent genius couldn't write a good sonata unless he had studied harmony and composition, and if it is a good sonata what would a conductor be doing in transforming it into a symphony? Another story deals with painters in Paris. I would bet a considerable sum that the author has never been to Paris or even stepped inside a painter's studio. I know the paintings he describes as great masterpieces. They were painted half a century ago and now hang in the deserted rooms of provincial museums. Old ladies still think them good.

The fact is that when you write about things you don't know, you fall into ludicrous errors. Of course, a writer cannot have a firsthand knowledge of everything, but his only safety is to find out everything he can about the subject he proposes to treat. Sometimes he thinks himself obliged to fake things; but to do that with plausibility needs skill and experience, and it isn't really worth doing, for it is seldom completely convincing; and if the writer cannot convince his readers successfully, then he is done.

Now, the only way I have ever discovered he can do that is to tell the truth, as he sees it, about what he knows; and the point of this statement lies in the words *as he sees it*. There are no new subjects (and incidentally there is none so stale as the great singer, the great painter, or the great violinist); but if a writer has personality, he will see the old subjects in a personal way, and that will give them an interest. He may try his best to be objective, but his temperament, his attitude toward life, are his own and color his view of things.

Let me give an example. James Farrell in *Studs Lonigan*, aiming at complete objectivity, has drawn a picture of lower-middle-class life in Chicago that gives an impression of complete verisimilitude. It is photographic, and they say the camera cannot lie. I suggest that another writer with a different personality could take the same environment, and even the same characters, and produce a picture that would be almost completely different.

My point is simple: The value of a piece of fiction depends in the final analysis on the personality of the author. If it is interesting, he will interest. It is true that the young writer cannot expect to have a personality that is either complex or profound; personality grows with the experiences of life; but he has some counterbalancing advantages. He sees things, the environment, in which he has grown up, with the freshness and the energy of his youth; he knows the persons of his own family and the persons with whom his daily life since childhood has brought him in contact with an intimacy he can seldom hope to have with people he comes to know in later years. Here is material ready to his hand. If his personality is so commonplace that he can see this environment and these people only in a commonplace way, then he is not made to be a writer and his is only wasting time in trying.

It is far from my meaning that he should not exercise his imagination. His imagination will work upon the facts and shape them into a pattern of significance or beauty. His imagination will enable him to deduce new facts from the facts he has observed. A writer need not devour a whole sheep in order to know what mutton tastes like, but he must at least eat a chop. Unless he gets his facts right, his imagination will lead him into all kinds of nonsense, and the facts he is most likely to get right are the facts of his own experience.

But now I must write that letter criticism and the chances are that this boy will think I'm just an old fool who doesn't know what he's talking about.

VOLUME XXVIII NOVEMBER 1947 NO. 12

There's Money in Comics

STAN LEE

Even if you don't know **STAN LEE**, who was born in 1922, you can't help but know his work. In 1961, Stan "The Man," along with artist and co-creator Jack Kirby, reinvigorated a flagging comic book industry with the Marvel Comics release of *The Fantastic Four #1*. Shortly thereafter, he created *Iron Man, The X-Men, Thor, The Incredible Hulk* (also with Kirby), *Spider-man* and *Dr. Strange* (with artist Steve Ditko), *Daredevil* (with Bill Everett), and hundreds of other characters. No one in the history of comics (or possibly any other form of literature, for that matter) has had as big an impact upon popular culture, save—perhaps—Walt Disney.

What's even more incredible, however, is the age at which Lee began to make his mark. He wrote the following while working as editor and art director of Timely Comics, Inc., the company he would eventually transform into Marvel Comics. He was twenty-five.

Well, what are you waiting for? They've been publishing comic magazines for more than ten years. They've been buying scripts for these magazines from freelance writers for that same length of time and paying good rates for them. There are ninety-two comic magazines appearing on the stands every single month—and each magazine uses an average of five stories. It's a big field, it's a well-paying field, and it's an interesting field. If you haven't tried to crack the comics yet, now's the time to start.

No matter what type of writing you specialize in—adventure, detective style, romantic stories, or humorous material, there is some comic magazine which uses the type of story you'd like to write. And, once you've broken into the field, you'll find that your assignments come to you at a fairly steady pace.

The pay is good. A competent writer can write about ten pages a day for six to nine dollars per page, depending upon the strip he is writing and the quality of his material. So, this comic field certainly bears a pretty close scrutiny from any writer who's interested in receiving meaty checks, and in receiving them often. (And I've yet to see the writer who *isn't* interested!)

"But I'm not good at drawing! How can I work with an artist on a comic strip?" How often I've heard that said by writers!

Look! You don't have to be able to draw flies! You do need an imagination, and the ability to write snappy dialogue and to describe continuity. And what writer won't lay claim to *those* talents?

Comic strip writing is very comparable to radio writing, or to writing for the stage. The radio writer must describe sound effects in his script, and the playwright must give staging directions in his play. Well, the comic strip writer also gives directions for staging and sound effects in his script, but *his* directions are given in writing to the artist, rather than to a director. He must tell the artist what to draw, and then must write the dialogue and captions.

A sample page from a script of *The Blonde Phantom* follows. This is an actual page, just as it was typed by Al Sulman, the writer. You will notice that the page is roughly divided into two sections, the left-hand section containing the instructions for the artist, and the right-hand section containing the dialogue. There are no set rules as to margins and borders, the important consideration being to make sure that the script is written clearly and can be easily understood by the editor and the artist.

One interesting aspect of writing a comic strip is seeing how the artist finally interprets your script. Syd Shores used the above copy [see sidebar on pages 170–171] to draw one page for *Blonde Phantom Comics*, issue #15. As you can see, the artist relied on the instructions that Alan Sulman typed on the left side of the script.

But there's more to comic strip writing than just knowing on which side of a page to type artist's instructions. Let's try to analyze some of the factors which go into the making of a good script.

1. *Interesting Beginning*. Just as in a story, the comic strip must catch the reader's interest from the first. The very first few panels should show the reader that something of interest is happening or is about to happen.

2. *Smooth Continuity*. The action from panel to panel must be natural and unforced. If a character is walking on the street talking to another character in one panel, we wouldn't show him horseback riding in the next panel with a different character. There *are* times when it is necessary to have a sudden change of scene or time, however, and for such times the writer uses captions. For example, if we have Patsy Walker lying in bed, about to fall asleep, in one panel, and want to show her eating breakfast in the next panel, the second panel would have an accompanying caption reading something like this: "The next morning, after a sound night's sleep, Patsy rushes to the kitchen to do justice to a hearty breakfast." Thus, by the use of captions, we are able to justify time and space lapses in our panels.

3. *Good Dialogue*. This is of prime importance. The era of Captain America hitting the Red Skull and shouting, "So you want to play, eh?" is over! Today, with the comic magazine business being one of the most highly competitive fields, each editor tries to get the best and snappiest dialogue possible for his characters. In writing a comic strip, have your characters speak like real people, not like inhabitants of a strange and baffling new world!

4. *Suspense Throughout*. Whether you are writing a mystery script or a humorous script, the same rule applies: Keep it interesting throughout. Any comic strip in which the reader isn't particularly interested in what happens

in the panel following the one he's reading isn't a good comic strip. All of the tricks you have learned and applied in writing other forms of fiction can be used in comic writing insofar as holding the reader's attention is concerned. But remember, giving the reader well-drawn pictures to look at is not enough; the reader must *want* to look at the pictures because he is interested in following the adventures of the lead character.

5. Finally, a *Satisfactory Ending*. An ending which leaves the reader with a smile on his lips and a pleasant feeling that all the loose strings of the story have been neatly tied together can cover a multitude of sins. It has always been my own conviction that a strip with an interesting beginning, good dialogue, and a satisfactory ending can't be *too* bad, no matter how many other faults it may have.

One point which I can't stress too strongly is: *Don't write down to your readers*! It is common knowledge that a large portion of comic magazine readers are adults, and the rest of the readers who may be kids are generally pretty sharp characters. They are used to seeing movies and listening to radio shows and have a pretty good idea of the stories they want to read. If you figure that "anything goes" in a comic magazine, a study of any recent copy of *Daredevil Comics* or *Bat Man* will show you that a great deal of thought goes into every story; and there are plenty of gimmicks, subplots, human interest angles, and the other elements that go into the making of any type of good story, whether it be a comic strip or a novel.

Another important point to remember is: The only way you can learn about comics is by reading them. So far as I know, there are no schools which give specialized courses in comic strip writing and no books which can be of too much help to you. Constant reading of the various comic magazines is the only way to develop a "feel" for what constitutes a good comic strip.

Another consideration of prime importance is: Decide which comic magazine you want to write for *before you do any writing*. The various magazines in the field have editorial differences which are almost amazing. A story which Timely Comics would consider exciting might be deemed too fantastic by True Comics, Inc., and Classic Comics, Inc., would have very little use for the type of story preferred at Fiction House! Each comic publishing company has its own distinctive formula and the only way to really grasp this formula is to read the magazines.

Most everybody knows something about the organization and workings of an ordinary fiction publishing company. But to most people, writers included, a comic magazine publishing outfit is cloaked in mystery. Let me tell you a little about how a comic house operates so that you'll have a better general knowledge about this large but comparatively unknown field.

The guy you're most interested in at a comic publishing house is the editor. "How does he differ from editors of other types of magazines?" Here's how: The editor of comics is more of a coordinator. He not only considers the merits of a script, but also who is going to draw it and whether it is written in a manner that will suit the artist's style of drawing.

If the artist who draws *Hedy De Vine* has difficulty drawing crowd scenes and specializes in close-up shots of beautiful women, then the

PANEL DESCRIPTION SAMPLE

PANEL 1. Scene in office, as Louise clears up her desk. Mark faces her.

PANEL 2. Louise, hands outward, looking at the reader, as if her thoughts in the previous panel were just proven true by what Mark has said.

PANEL 3. Louise, ready to leave office. Mark sits on desk and smiles at her as if he has just thought of a wonderful idea.

PANEL 4. Louise alone, suddenly looking interested and excited, expecting Mark to ask her for a date.

PANEL 5. Mark lights his pipe, expressionless, as if he has changed his mind. Louise seems plenty angry.

PANEL 6. Door slams shut as Mark looks at it, slightly surprised and bewildered.

editor of that magazine must be careful not to buy Hedy scripts which call for many characters in each panel and for many only shots.

It's the editor's task to make sure that the scripts he buys are perfectly suited for the artist to whom they are given, and also to insure that the artist interprets the writer's script exactly as the writer intended it.

Of course, there are some artists who write their *own* scripts, but they are in the minority. The average artist, even though he may be capable of writing his own script because of his long-standing familiarity with the character he draws, would still prefer to have a writer write the script for him so that he can concentrate entirely upon the drawing.

Therefore, you, as a writer, should acquaint yourself with the style of artwork which is used in the script you are interested in writing. And then slant your story in such a way so that particular style of artwork will blend in perfectly with your story. The writers who concentrate on such details are the ones who attain top recognition and top rates in the phenomenal comics field.

Now then, here you are, a fairly accomplished writer interested in trying your hand at the comics. What type of writing is your forte? Is it adventure, teenage humor, fan-

DIALOGUE SAMPLE

PANEL 1. Louise: (thought) He *never* notices *me*! All he ever thinks of is the *Blonde Phantom*!

Mark: Gosh, if I could only find where the *Blonde Phantom* lives! We could have a night of it together!

PANEL 2. Louise: See what I mean?

PANEL 3. Louise: Well, everything's finished for today, Mark! See you in the morning!

Mark: Say, wait a minute, Louise! How would you like to ...?

PANEL 4. Louise: *Huh*? Yes, what is it, Mark?

PANEL 5. Mark: Well, I ... er ... never mind! It wasn't important! Good night, Louise!

Louise: (thought) That's what I call a quick brush-off, you ... you ...

PANEL 6. Balloon from Louise: *Good night*!

Mark: Huh? Now what's she so mad about?

Sound effect: SLAM!

tasy, true crime? Let's assume you prefer teenage humor and you have decided to cast your lot with Timely Comics. The next step is to write to the editor and get a list of the teenage magazines he edits and, if possible, his story needs. After receiving the list of magazines he sends you, head for the nearest newsstand and look them over. Select the one which appeals most to you and for which you think your style is best suited.

But up till this point, your preliminary work is just beginning. You've now got to read every copy of this magazine you can lay your hands on. Suppose *Georgie* is the magazine you selected. Get old copies of *Georgie*, get current copies of *Georgie* and leave an order for future copies. Read that strip until you can feel you've known Georgie personally for years and can anticipate what each Georgie story will be about after reading the first page. Live with Georgie for days—get the *Georgie formula* down pat—and then—

Send some synopses of *Georgie* stories to the editor. Make them the same type of stories which had been appearing in all the *Georgies* you read. *Not* the same *plot*, just the same *type* of story.

Should your synopses click, you'll get an order for a *Georgie* story from the editor. He will tell you how many panels to write per page, how many pages in length to make the story, and any other relevant information.

Now it's up to you. If you write a perfectly satisfactory story (and there's no reason not to, if you've studied the magazines long and carefully enough) there's an excellent chance you'll be asked to do more stories on the same character—and later on, perhaps, additional stories for still other characters. For once you're "in," there are many assignments which can come your way.

So, those of you writers who are itching to crack new markets have a market waiting for you which is just made to order. It may seem a little complicated, but the rewards are well worth any time you may spend learning the comic style. I'm sure you won't regret spending the time—*I* didn't!

VOLUME XXXVI JULY 1955 NO. 8

TV's Sacred Cows

ROD SERLING

When one thinks of "legends of literature," TV writers rarely come to mind. But in the case of **ROD SERLING**, one has to make an exception. In 1954, Fredric Wertham published S*eduction of the Innocent*, attacking the comic book industry for its alleged corruption of America's youth. The U.S. Senate began an investigation into the effects of televised violence—at a time when more than half of American homes owned a television. Anxiety was high. Creators walked on eggshells. And behind the scenes, one man was figuring out a way to overcome such obstacles. But it didn't happen overnight. Four years after writing the piece that follows, Serling created *The Twilight Zone*, changing television—and writing for television—forever.

The initial problem in TV scripting is not in technique, not always in dialogue, and only briefly in learning the time sense. The high hurdle in this mass media is the awareness of touchy subject matter, sensitive areas of thought and conflict—the taboos that label a plot "controversial."

In television the following can happen—and did! The program *Studio One* changed the name of a Kipling story well known as "The Light That Failed" to a more innocuous title not so suggestive of bad bulbs. The reason? *Studio One* is sponsored by Westinghouse, whose stock in trade is electricity.

On *Kraft Theater* the name of a lead character was feverishly altered because "Borden" had certain connotations of cheese and this particular program, naturally, is sponsored by Kraft.

I cite these two cases as an indication of the subtle problems the writer needs to explore before putting keys to paper, if he's writing for television, to what vast depths of care he must go for fear of trodding on a sensitive toe or plucking too enthusiastically on the teat of a sacred cow.

A Field Full of Cows

Who and what are these sacred cows? First of all, there is a set of rather rigid taboos that most programs have mimeographed on a special sheet. They read and not necessarily in order of importance: sex, infidelity, fantasy, suicide, political controversy, racial or religious controversy, and sanguine violence.

Upon reading through these thematic pariahs, the writer sometimes wonders exactly how one can create a "conflict" with restrictions in so many areas.

Actually, there still remains an assortment of plots which may be based on sex, politics, violence, or what have you. Though you are limited in a horizontal sense—you can still write vertically. Look for depth in a single idea and a single set of characters—even if your choice of incidents is to some degree governed by a mimeographed sheet.

Your problem insofar as "touchiness" is concerned carries over into another area. Assume you've chosen an acceptable premise for conflict. This story involves neither illicit love, illegitimate babies, nor a homicide that must be shown on camera.

Elephants and Donkeys Too

Here come the hurdles and sometimes they assume a mountain-like quality. If you write about a politician, scrap it unsubmitted if your character says any single line which might link him to a definite existing party. This follows even if your character's words are no more controversial than a general discussion of a week's rainfall.

If a Democrat happened to have mentioned getting wet in the news recently—your story or at least, that line, is out! At no time may a character even remotely resemble either Republican or Democrat.

For no matter if your man is saint or louse, you'll have one of the major parties yelling for your scalp. You've no ideas the difficulties involved in this restriction. In a political story, you naturally must insert certain political talk and attitudes.

You find yourself looking skyward trying to find an issue which really isn't an issue at all. You search for a conflict which must never have been a conflict—at least not in the past one hundred years. You go down the line of current social, economic, and political issues and find that each one has been identified with a specific party.

If your character smiles when he says "Labor"—the writer is writing Democratic propaganda. If your character smiles when he says "Tariff"—you're an apologist for the G.O.P.

Sacred Professions and Ideas

The areas of "relative touchiness" are many. If you write of lawyers—make them honest. If you deal with ministers—they must literally be men of God. *Kraft Theater* did a show a couple of years ago where the part of a minister was portrayed in a not altogether sympathetic manner. The reaction was violent, quick, and frightening. If you tell the story of an Army officer on a field-grade level (Major on up), God help you if your man is a coward, a bully, or an incompetent jerk. If you discuss by chance (the brave ones amongst you) a politician—keep him on a local or at least regional level. No congressman is allowed even a temporal lapse of conscience.

Leave people for a bit and look at simple ideas. Mercy killing is out. Fratricide is taboo. Segregation is totally inadmissible. Communism is generally frowned on even when lambasted. Few shows actually say "The Soviet Union." Instead you sort of circle the rim with words like "Reds," "Iron Curtain," or "Commie." And it follows that no other actual foreign government can be permanently internationally scarred by using its real name if one of its native sons happens to be a bastard.

Doctors are among the most protected of the sacred cows. No hint of professional skullduggery is permitted a character with an M.D. Normally, murder trials provide fruitful fields for plotters. But the Dr. Sam case will be left alone by television because there just ain't no such thing as a bad medico—take television's word for it.

The Reasons for Sanctity

Summed up, here's the problem. The basic assumption is that the audience makes a mental connection between a character—and comparable real-life characters. They carry the step further by mental progression that makes each drama character a representative of the whole. Hence—a crooked lawyer means that all lawyers are crooked. A drunken doctor points an accusing (and shaking) finger at the entire profession. A bad Major General is merely a projection of the whole lousy officer corps. An unsympathetic minister makes it apparent that ministers, priests, and rabbis are a heartless bunch.

Now, to accept this basic assumption is to accept the fact that the vast audience of viewers have IQ's in negative figures. This is obvious nonsense. Viewers vary in their intelligence just as much as lawyers, doctors, Army officers, and what have you.

A malcontent from Brassier Falls, South Dakota, threatens never again to buy soap because the *Lux Video Theater* showed a dumb farmer. He is a farmer and he's not dumb. What's the idea? Identification. The farmer sees a dumb farmer in a story and draws the inference that the program is saying that all farmers are dumb. The agency reads this guy's letter and draws an inference that every farmer who saw the show was injured by it.

Fireside Theater once did a live adaptation of Shirley Jackson's wonderful short story, "The Lottery." In its television treatment, it was made a simple and yet gripping story of the poison of prejudice. There was a raft of mail—mostly violently negative with a recurring theme—"You guys mean to tell us that this goes on in the U.S.A?" This was *Fireside Theater*'s last venture into a deep and meaningful conflict.

Studio One produced a Reginald Rose story called "Thunder on Sycamore Street." It was good, solid, tough, and honest reporting of mob violence. Some town in the West mailed a petition to the producer accusing him of foreign and Communist ideology. The basic tenet of this show was no more and no less than a few lines in the preamble to the Constitution. And the producer, Felix Jackson, mailed a copy of this document to the frantic characters who were protesting. But it went into the record.

Avoiding the Cows

Do you skip television as a market? I don't. I keep trying. Some of my stuff gets produced even when there's really no cut-and-dried knowledge of what the reaction will be.

I've learned now that if you're dealing in a theme that invites misunderstanding—to write it in a qualifying way. I supplement it with dialogue of some inference that I am not using symbols. I show that I am dealing with one specific group in one specific situation.

I wrote once before in *WD* that a writer's best bet in preparation for TV writing was to watch TV shows. This still holds. See what the various series are doing, the themes they're attacking, the relative direction of the attack—flank or frontal. Then use these as guideposts.

There'll be times very likely that you'll run afoul of certain principles you've held dear and important. You'll find yourself dealing with a problem that calls for a solution you, yourself, don't believe. What you do about it is your business. I generally just try to stay away from any theme that forces me to compromise.

My advice is that if you've got burning feelings in certain directions—don't write plays about them for television. Save this earnestness for novels or legitimate plays.

I'm positive that television, with all its little fears and apprehensions, still provides an important and legitimate art form wherein a man can write an honest and sometimes important piece of prose.

So don't try to slaughter the sacred cows. Just head for another pasture.

VOLUME XLIV JANUARY 1963 NO. 2

Controversy: Sharpest Sword of the Paperback Novelist

HARLAN ELLISON

As the title of the following piece might imply, **HARLAN ELLISON** can, at times, be controversial. Controversy and excellence, however, very often go hand in hand. *The Washington Post* describes Ellison as "one of the great living American short story writers," which may actually be damning him with faint praise. To say that Ellison is one of the world's greatest living writers, period, is closer to the truth. Respected equally for his award-winning contributions to television, film, and literature, Ellison illustrates some of the characteristics that make his work so memorable in "Controversy." At the time he wrote this piece, Ellison was twenty-seven. He had already published more than five hundred short stories and articles, as well as ten novels and story collections. Clearly, it was just the beginning.

Just for openers, here's the basic situation for a paperback novel's plot. Use it if you want to. At the moment, I'm hooked up on projects, can't get around to it, and I offer it free and clear (with perhaps just an acknowledging note). I use it here just to define our terms, so we both know what I mean when I speak about "controversy" as a potent weapon. Here, then, a basic situation:

James Hoffa, erstwhile Czar of America, has recently announced that he will elect the President of the United States in the next campaign. Mr.

Hoffa, whether we care to admit it or not, has become a frighteningly powerful figure on the American scene, without the accompanying sense of humility or sense of duty that makes such a power an asset, rather than a threat. Let us imagine a nameless government agency has come to the same conclusion, and, all considerations of morality or fair play be damned, has decided the only way to insure the "common good" is to secretly employ a pistolero who will assassinate the Labor Czar. In the book, for obvious reasons, we don't call him Jimmy Hoffa. We call him Wally Horn or Phil Newell or Nicholas Green or, if we want to say a little something about the Contemporary Scene, and resuscitate the modern suspense novel in even the slightest particular, we say *dammit* and call the Labor Czar Jimmy Hoffa, making certain not to do anything in the book that will get the legal counsel of the Teamsters Union piqued. So ...

Our nameless government agency runs all the qualifications for the Perfect Assassin through the Univac scene, and comes up with such pretties as (a) he must be a crack shot, (b) he must have had military experience and not be incapable of taking another life, (c) he must be in some area of work that would reasonably allow him to get close to the Labor Czar, he must be (d) intelligent, (e) imaginative and inventive, (f) highly moral, as well as honest and (g) bearer of a pure-fire hatred of Hoffa and the sort of corruption he typifies. Add to this staggering list of qualifications the additional factor of Hoffa's not having already blacklisted the intended assassin, and the Univac logically comes up with only one candidate, George Gillespie, a minor official in a Tucson truckers' local; a WWII veteran, ex-sharpshooter, and Ranger, Gillespie has been a prime force in eliminating corruption in his union, and has on several small occasions expressed his virulent loathing for Hoffa-ism.

In a situation similar to the U-2 incident and its subsequent denial of existence by the White House, a sub rosa representative of the Nameless

Agency inveigles Gillespie into taking on the job, assuring him that if he's caught before the fact, he will most likely turn up eaten by worms or acid, and if caught after the fact he may well be prosecuted for murder in the first. Morality, a sense of the impending doom of Hoffa's mere existence, and covert threats, Hoffa-based, on Gillespie's wife and son if he doesn't let the Tucson local wheel-deal as the Teamsters prefer, impel Gillespie to take on the impossible chore of killing a national figure. Through devious machinations instigated by the Nameless Agency in the Teamsters' own home territory, Gillespie gets invited as the representative from his local to a big union conference. There, he saves Hoffa's life in a fake assassination staged by the Nameless Agency. Hoffa takes a liking to Gillespie and respects his brand of outspoken defiance. He feels Gillespie is a man to trust and begins to seek his company. Gillespie gets tight with Hoffa and finds the man is a dedicated despot, that Hoffa no more thinks of himself as a vandal and a blackmailer of nations than Hitler thought of himself as a murderer and psychopath.

This, incidentally, is one of the minor messages of the plot: No man considers himself a criminal; no man can conceive of himself as a doer of evil; the mind is generally incapable of such realities and would rather condemn the society or the powers-that-be as persecutors and too dull-witted to understand the essential good of the acts. And when you find a man incapable of understanding the depth of depravity of his own acts, then how can you, in all good conscience, kill him? He then becomes an object of pity, a figure in need of help.

These are Gillespie's thoughts, finally, and what he does to resolve his situation makes for the bulk and conclusion of the novel. Finis.

(If you call the Labor Czar by a fictitious name, you can employ such lovely character-delineating incidents as Gillespie falling for the Czar's daughter, becoming an adulterer, and thus having yet *another* reason to feel guiltier than the man he's supposed to knock off; Gillespie learning of all the inside rottenness of the union; Gillespie being himself corrupted. There's a veritable Niagara of material in the basic idea, I suspect, for the paperback novelist prepared to stand behind a "hot" idea—the beat being in subject matter as well as treatment. One might even call it, uh, *controversial*.)

Or how about a political satire titled "The Day They Kidnapped Caroline Kennedy"? (Local agents of the FBI who would like the ground-plan of such an operation, to take place during JFK's vacation to West Palm Beach, are advised to seek out this author, not the editors of *WD*.) Or how does a racial tensions novel of the hatred between the Afroamerican (Negro, to you) and the Puerto Rican strike you? Have you ever considered an outspoken treatment of the upper-middle-class Jewish set in cities like Detroit, Pittsburgh, or Cleveland, something titled, perhaps, "The Red Velvet Ghetto," in which the shallowness of their existence is contemplated as a reaction to centuries of enforced emotional isolationism? Have you ever wondered what goes through the heads of a white woman and a colored man as they walk through a group of jeering adolescents, the more subtle ramifications of an interracial marriage?

Has anybody ever written a definitive novel about narcotics addition among doctors? The real face of evil in our times as mirrored by the corruption in police departments? The frightening bestiality of American youth as depicted by their dress, speech, reading and rutting habits, and most of all by the perversion of The Twist? What about a book that says life in Yankeeland today is a combination of frustration, conformity, the Time of the Clipster, and idle hero-worship? Has anybody considered a novel of the poor little *schnorer* who runs a one-arm grocery being squashed by the chain market all neon and white porcelain? Ever considered a character study of a Jayne Mansfield-type, illustrating what wrongness in our society elevates such a parody of womanhood to the level of a goddess?

These might loosely be termed "controversial" topics. That is, they depart in lesser or greater degree from the normally accepted ideas of what a contemporary novel may say. They are the same sort of material from which men like Sinclair Lewis, Budd Schulberg, D.H. Lawrence, Henry Miller, and Nelson Algren have drawn books that shook up their times. These books aren't being written today.

In their place we have *Peyton Place*, which relied on a publicist's dreams of social ostracism in a New England town to gain notoriety. We have *The Chapman Report*, which toyed with Everyman's prurient interest in sex surveys. We have half-baked pastiches and pastel vignettes on lukewarm topics from men and women who have gotten as close to their subject matter as Beverly Aadland might get to sainthood. The whys and why nots of social conduct that have forced this dearth of stimulating subject matter on the American reading public are not my province here (though my anger at them manages to creep in occasionally). I'm chiefly concerned with the pride in craft and common sense, dollar-oriented, that should convince even the most tepid of hacks to try and *say something*, to yell, and get the message across. To partially fulfill the obligations of the writer: to mirror his times and point up with insight what the man in the street may know, but never have put into coherent conceptual shape. All considerations of responsibility and stature and pride and cultural value aside, there is *money*, *honey*, in writing a book that deals with an explosive topic.

Now that we've established what "controversial" means—and a word, just a bit later, on the distinct difference between "controversial" and "sensational"—let me try and show by example how guts can be a good moneymaker.

(Don't let me con you, gentle reader: I'm not particularly concerned with whether or not you make a dime off your writing, but if I can persuade a few more writers to talk about the important things, then my flummery in disguising the Crusade under commercial terms will have been worth it. The end, the means, etc.)

Initially, it stands to reason that of the two or three hundred paperbacks released in a thirty-day period by the fifteen major paperback houses (this does not include the "prestige" outfits such as Anchor, New Directions, Oxford University Press, Meridian, et. al.), there is going to be a pressing need from release period to release period for topical books. They've got all the Westerns, detective operas, science fiction, and nurse novels they can handle, but people who will do contemporary-themed books are scarce. This, of course, is in the paperback original market. Hardcover is another gig entirely, not our concern here.

So ... the release schedule is there, publishers want to capture as much of the glutted paperback market, *per book*, as they can. Now you tell me: Is your entry, dealing with an exposé of the dance studio racket, going to attract more interest than a straight shoot-'em-up private-eye saga, or is the average, run-of-the-slushpile script going to make the jaded editor click his heels and shout "Eureka"? You tell me.

The book with a daring slant continues to accrue benefits even after it is bought; in small ways, exciting ways. The editorial staff finds itself getting enthused about it, telling each other it has much stuff ... and then you get a better cover on the book, sharper promotional copy, a warmer publicity treatment, and the next time you hit their office with a script the residue electricity still flickers and they cannot help but offer you a highly sympathetic reading, apart from the intrinsic worth of the new book. On the stands, the book is consequently a lot more distinctive, more appealing, and if the gods so will it, the book gets bought. An everyday novel may get its share of reviews (though the criminal attitude of most book reviewers that an original paperback is less worthy of comment than hardcover hampers it from the start, but the controversial tome *compels* the reviewer to take heed). Thus is built the reputation.

And even as impressive as the foregoing may seem—from experience I can vouch for its factuality, incidentally—it is nothing by comparison with the major benefits of having written a book with intestinal fortitude; benefits that include:

- A personal statement by *you*, the writer, of a segment of your times, of the world around you, and hence, a more violent involvement with your craft and with yourself, and with the world you write about.
- A "growing" in talent and craftsmanship, from having dealt with larger topics and having come to grips with them in whatever the depth your ability has allowed.
- The finding of a more secure place for yourself in the world of the writer, where self-identification and strength of conviction are more important and valid than sales.
- The beginnings of a corpus of material from which ideas for future works will come. No one ever has a *single* writing idea, spin-offs are frequent, and in a contemporary subject of some pith and moment, the chances of branch ideas are multiplied enormously.
- Lasting value. Not only a tendency for such books to go back and back and back to press for second and third printings, but a habit of controversial novels to snowball in popularity. Word-of-mouth works for them, and long after its initial on-sale period, the book can still be found readily, and you'll continue to make money on it.

As to the *nature* of controversy, I have found it to be dichotomous in that it is both ludicrously simple and immensely complex. While controversial matter can be as uncomplicated a subject as birth control or the John Birch nuts, it can also be as subtle and elusive as a new trend in art criticism or (as I found in a recent article by William Burdick in *Harper's*) a brief recounting of the personal hardships of the Australian aborigine in the outback.

Controversy is at one and the same time like necking with a girl and discovering the key to quantum mechanics. The former, because once you've learned the nature of the game, and the ever-changing rules, you never forget. You can be a hundred and nine years old, but you recognize it when it confronts you. The latter, because it always has some new mystery, some new facet that demands exploration, an elasticity of the intellect, and a freshness of approach to unravel.

Caution, however. Too often, sensationalism is confused with controversy. There have been many recent paperbacks (and, in fact, one entire paperback line has predicated itself upon persiflage topics of momentary interest) that have dealt sensationally with topics too important to have been given such short shrift. For the bad writer, for the hack, for the dilettante, the "hot" topic is great grist. It covers his flaws. It provides a ready basis for sale, apart from how good the execution may be. And in the hands of such corrupters of the craft, the subject that has meat and meaning becomes just another vehicle for trite characterizations, bad ethics, soggy morality, and cliché situations.

Handled with perception, honesty (the importance of honesty cannot be stressed too much!), and vigor, an idea of extraordinary significance can be a consuming project for the writer and a distinct contribution to the mainstream of contemporary fiction. Another caution, of less importance, but still worth mentioning: Don't try to set out to write the Great American Novel. It's been written. Twice.

(For purists, *Huckleberry Finn* and *Moby-Dick* are my choices for TGAN. Miller's *Tropic of Capricorn* comes high on the list of runners-up, but then, so does Walter Tevis's *The Hustler*, which is an exemplary model of what is meant by a controversial subject. Aspiring novelists would do well to explore all four of these books, not so much for style or direction as for the vividness of approach to some pretty ordinary topics that resulted without exception in unquestionably controversial novels.)

The trap into which all writers have, will, or should fall into, of writing The Great American Watchamacallit, is such an uncluttered and inviting one that from time to time I'm sure even the greatest have to pull themselves up short by the shift key to remind themselves that it is *story* first that they should write. If it happens that the Great Somethingorother gets written in the bargain that's peachy-keen, but primarily the purpose is to tell the story, portray a facet of life as truthfully and individually as possible, and leave the hamming to the poor unfortunates in Venice West or Greenwich Village back streets.

(Not to belabor the point, but just to give a few more examples of "hot" topics, sample the wonder of "Tell Me a Riddle," by Tillie Olsen, first published in *New World Writing*, and reprinted in the Martha Foley *Best American Short Stories: 1961*, or, for want of a book that contains as many offbeat themes, my own recent collection, *Gentleman Junkie & Other Stories of the Hung-Up Generation*.)

I've already mentioned the supplementary benefits a novel of controversial ideas accrues. But

Can You

JOURNEY INTO ANOTHER WORLD

yet remain in this one?

ALL of the intelligence of the universe is not centered on this small globe—the earth. Do you know that there are invisible forces and powers beyond this world that can—and do—influence you tremendously? If you could not see or hear, your present world would shrink greatly. Do you also know that you can do the opposite—extend your consciousness so that you can become a citizen of the universe? Stop being earth-bound! Let the Rosicrucian teachings unfold to you how your mind can annihilate space and cause you to experience a oneness with the Infinite and all of its worlds. Experience Cosmic Harmony!

Write for the fascinating FREE book, "The Mastery of Life." Address: Scribe V.Z.U.

TRUTHS AGELESS AS TIME

The Rosicrucians

SAN JOSE (AMORC.) CALIFORNIA

there is one, touched on earlier herein, that has deeper roots than even the publishing industry cares to admit. In the case of reviews in newspapers, book sections, magazines, et. al., a "hot topic" novel (and by now you must realize my use of that phrase is more an indication of a dearth of appropriate words to label such diverse kinds of books, than a reference to such paperbacks as *Sin Girls on a Holiday* or *My Lust Is Crimson*, which are also termed "hot" in the trade) draws attention. The ridiculous snob attitude of almost 90 percent of the legitimate book reviewers in this country, as regards paperbacks, is indeed a shameful thing.

Generally, they ignore paperback originals totally. If they somehow or somewhere feel a twinge of guilt, they lump a handful of currently released "classics" into a 2" x 1" column ghetto imaginatively titled "Current Paperbacks" or "Lower-Priced Editions." These reviews generally read like this:

For Whom the Bell Tolls, Ernest Hemingway (Zygote Books): a reprint of the late Master's study of men and love during war.

She, H. Rider Haggard (Blatt Novels): one of the more peculiar adventure novels of this English author's career.

The Brothers Karamazov, Fyodor Dostoyevsky (Ivymoss Editions): another reissue of the perennial favorite concerning interfamily tensions in pre-Stalinist Russia. Good!

The foregoing may seem just a trifle satirical until you realize the immensity of the average book review section's pomposity. They will devote column after column to the most worthless current novel "making a splash" but will not even deign to notice a brilliant tour de force, if it's between paper covers.

My favorite, and most personally terrifying, experience with one of the underlings who put together these monuments to mediocrity happened while I was editing a paperback line in Chicago. We had sent out our first two titles to some three hundred newspapers and periodicals, with hopes that perhaps a quarter of them would manage to slip a review into print. One of these books was highly reviewed in *Esquire*, *The New York Times*, two dozen other magazines and newspapers, and was picked by the *Chicago Tribune* (a paper that does *not* sell paperbacks short) as one of the one hundred best paperbacks of the year.

But concerning this book we received a letter from a young lady on one of the larger Southwestern dailies, who informed us—with straight face and great pride in her stand—that she could not be bothered reviewing the book because "the type is too small, and I don't like the quality of the paper." So help me God.

I was appalled. For days, I was too stunned to reply. Finally, the fury seethed through and I dashed her off a note in very bad taste (that surely killed our line of books for review in that paper, for all time to come) that concluded:

> It has always been my misguided impression that a book reviewer's job is to consider the content of a book, rather than the esthetic pleasures to be gained from savoring type styles and the tactile jollies of cream-skin papers. However, your comments have shown me the light, and if we ever issue any Giant Golden Books with big big big letters for remedial reading purposes, we will certainly send you something you can review.

All of this flummery is included not to discourage you, but to make you aware of a continuing chuckleheaded policy on the part of most "serious lit'ry reviewers" that can be more readily circumvented by producing a book that has some guts to it ... in effect, a book that they *cannot* ignore. The recent series of Ballantine paperbacks on contemporary themes (*The Unamericans*, *Articles of Dissent*, *Sartre on Cuba*, etc.), all with strong moral and emotional tones, have received wide mainstream attention. They were too important to pass off as *just another cheap paperback*.

The past ten years have seen a revolution in the reading habits of the American public. For many years, other countries have had a publishing industry that took into consideration the sad but inescapable fact that most people would rather spend their money on faster cars, shinier appliances, and faster, shinier women than on anything as dull and pointless as a book. So they have had paperbacks in one form or another that were so inexpensive the Mass Reader could buy them without hurting his pocket too much. But only in the past ten years has this been so in Yankeeland.

Now we have available to The Common Man in Our Time more and better reading matter than at any other time in our history. He can educate himself from a single well-stocked newsstand, or he can indulge his basest pruriences, from another equally-as-well-stocked stand. He can trace the important messages of every writer from Aristophanes to James Baldwin without accumulating a library that in days past would have been possible only for a *grandee*.

The unfortunates of the situation—lack of recognition by reviewers, a bastard-child attitude by much of the uninformed public, lurid covers, overcrowded racks, a torrential flood of authentic garbage-in-book-format, hard selling, shallowness as a median—all pass into unimportance before the possibilities now open to the writer.

You can say very nearly *anything* you want to say in a paperback. Publishers *want* to take chances on books that will draw a clamor and some legitimate publicity. They *want* to publish controversial books. That their reasons are mercenary and yours may be lofty should not deter you. The businessman and the creator have been forced to walk hand in hand for too long for us to suddenly get uppity. Consider them self-interested patrons of the arts if you must, but *write* those gutty books.

We're abiding in a time when the world is going more than just a little mad. We live in a world where phoniness and corruption and false ideals seem more and more to be the accepted norms. In some very positive ways, the future rests in the hands of the novelist, the man who sees his world, sees what is right and wrong with it, and is not afraid to speak out about it.

No one changes the world overnight.

But a controversial paperback has a longer on-sale date than just overnight.

It's your world and your responsibility. All it takes is a little guts and a lot of talent. If you've got the credentials, the guts, and the talent, there's a great deal of money, a great deal of prestige, and most important, an unbelievable amount of pride and satisfaction waiting for you.

We're all waiting to read your book.

VOLUME LIV NOVEMBER 1973 NO. 12

The Horror Writer Market and the Ten Bears

A TRUE STORY BY STEPHEN KING

STEPHEN KING was born on September 21, 1947. Like most writers born to the craft, he began writing early—by his own estimate, at approximately six or seven years of age. It's not surprising, then, that his writing style was so fully developed by the time he wrote this particular article. He was already a veteran short story writer (his first being published in 1967), and one can immediately recognize the unique voice that would soon become his trademark.

The year after *Writer's Digest* readers saw this piece, King would publish his first novel, *Carrie.* Its success was a harbinger of things to come, with every subsequent King novel attaining best-seller status.

In the nearly forty years since, King has attained extraordinary financial success as well as critical acclaim, including six Bram Stoker Awards, six Horror Guild Awards, the Horror Writer's Association's Lifetime Achievement Award, one Hugo Award, one Nebula, one O. Henry Award, three World Fantasy Awards, and one Quill Award for sportswriting. King is also the 2003 recipient of The National Book Foundation's Medal for Distinguished Contribution to American Letters.

At parties, people usually approach the writer of horror fiction with a mixture of wonder and trepidation. They look carefully into your eyes to make sure there's no overt bloodlust in them, and then ask the inevitable question: "I really liked your last story ... where do you get your ideas?"

That question is common to any writer who works in a specialized genre, whether it's mystery, crime, Western, or science fiction. But it's delivered in different tones for different fields. It's directed to the mystery writer with real admiration, the way you'd ask a magician how he sawed the lady in half. It's directed to the science fiction writer with honest respect for a fellow who is so farseeing and visionary. But it is addressed to the horror writer with a sense of fascinated puzzlement—the way a lady reporter might ask mild-mannered Henri Landru how it feels to do away with all those wives. Most of us, you see, look and seem (and *are*) perfectly ordinary. We don't drown houseguests in the bathtub, torture the children, or sacrifice the cat at midnight inside of a pentagram. There are no locked closets or screams from the cellar. Robert Bloch, author of *Psycho*, looks like a moderately successful used car salesman. Ray Bradbury bears an uncomfortable resemblance to Charles M. Schulz, creator of *Peanuts*. And the writer generally acknowledged to be the greatest master of the horror tale in the twentieth century, H.P. Lovecraft, looked like nothing so much as a slightly overworked accountant.

So where do the ideas—the *salable* ideas—come from? They come from my nightmares. Not the night-time variety, as a rule, but the ones that hide just beyond the doorway that separates the conscious from the unconscious. A good assumption to begin with is what scares you will scare someone else. A psychologist would call these nightmares phobias, but I think there's a better word for our purposes.

Joseph Stefano, who wrote the screenplay for *Psycho* and who produced a mid-1960s television series called *The Outer Limits*, calls these fears "bears." It's a good term for the aspiring writer of horror fiction to use, because it gets across the idea that general phobias have to be focused on concrete plot ideas before you can hope to scare the reader—and that's the name of the game. So before we go any further, let's take a look at a few bears—ones we're all familiar with. You may want to rearrange some of the items on my list, or throw out a few and add some of the skeletons in your own closet. But for purposes of discussion, here is my own top ten.

1. Fear of the dark
2. Fear of squishy things
3. Fear of deformity
4. Fear of snakes
5. Fear of rats
6. Fear of closed-in places
7. Fear of insects (especially spiders, flies, beetles)
8. Fear of death
9. Fear of others (paranoia)
10. Fear *for* someone else

The bears can be combined, too. I took a #1 and #10 and wrote a story called "The Boogeyman," which sold to *Cavalier* magazine. For me, fear of the dark has always focused on a childhood fear: the awful Thing which hides in the closet when you're small, or sometimes curls up under the bed, waiting for you to stick a foot out under the covers. As an adult looking back on those feelings (not that we ever conquer them completely—all those of you out there who don't have a bedroom lamp within reach of your hand please stand up), it seemed to me that the most frightening thing about them was the fact that grown-ups don't understand it very well—they forget how it is. Mother comes in, turns on the light, smiles, opens the closet (the Thing is hiding behind your clothes, well out of sight—it's sly) and says, "See, dear? There's nothing to be afraid of." And as soon as she's gone, the Thing crawls back out of the closet and begins to leap and gibber in the shadows again. I wrote a story about a man who finds out that his three children, who have all died of seemingly natural causes, have been frightened to death by the boogeyman—who is a very real, very frightening monster. The story takes a childhood fear and saddles an adult with it; puts him back into that dreamlike world of childhood where the monsters *don't* go away when you change the channel, but crawl out and hide under the bed.

About two years ago I decided that the scariest things going would be rats—great big #5s, breeding in the darkness under a deserted textile mill. In this case, I began with the bear and built the plot (including the deserted mill) to fit it. The story climaxed with the main character being overwhelmed by these giant rats in the dark and enclosed subcellar of the mill (slyly hedging my main bet by working in a generous dose of #1 and #6). I felt sorry for the poor guy—the thought of being overrun by giant rats frankly made my blood run cold—but I made 250 dollars on the sale and managed to take one of my own pet fears for a walk in the sun at the same time. One of the nice things about working in this field is that, instead of paying a shrink to help you get rid of your fears, a magazine will pay you for doing the same thing.

George Langlahan, a Canadian author, wrote a novelette called *The Fly*, using a #7 bear, made a sale to *Playboy*, and has since seen his bear made into three movies—*The Fly*, *The Return of the Fly*, and *The Curse of the Fly*. The late John W. Campbell wrote a cracking good horror story in the early 1950s called "Who Goes There?" using a #2 bear which turns out to be a sort of walking vegetable from another planet. The story was turned into a classic horror movie called *The Thing*. Hollywood has always understood the principle of working from the bear out—surrounding a basic fear with a plot, rather than the other way around. Edgar Allan Poe wrote the same way, and suggested again and again in his literary essays that the only way to write a short story was to begin with the effect and then work your way out.

The would-be writer of horror stories may be tempted to stop right here and say: That's a lousy list of bears, fella. There isn't a werewolf or a vampire to be had. True enough. Not even an escaped mummy hunting for tanna leaves. My humble advice is to leave these bears to their well-deserved rest. They've been done to death. There are undoubtedly a few twists left in the Old Guard, but not many. Even the endlessly proliferating comics market is turning away from them in favor of more contemporary subjects—but more on that later.

Another caution in order at this point: Don't think that because you have selected a scary bear, the rest of the story will be a snap. It won't be. Horror isn't a hack market now, and never was. The genre is one of the most delicate known to man, and it must be handled with great care and more than a little love. Some of the greatest authors of all time have tried their hands at things that go bump in the night, including Shakespeare, Chaucer, Hawthorne ("My Kinsman, Major Molinaux" is a particularly terrifying story, featuring a #9 bear), Poe, Henry James, William Faulkner (*A Rose for Emily*), and a score of others.

So where is the market today? For straight fiction, it's mainly in the men's magazines. But the writer who feels he can approach *Playboy* or *Cavalier* or *Penthouse* or *Adam* with a 1930s-style blood-pulp-and-sex meller is going to find the market has progressed beyond that to a reasonable point of sophistication—good for the professional who wants to work seriously in the genre, bad for the amateur who thinks he can mix a couple of sea monsters with an Atlantic City beauty contest and come up with a few hundred bucks. And so, before a listing of some possible markets, a few practical hints on selling horror to the men's magazines.

1. Don't feel obligated to add sex to your story if there isn't a sex angle there to begin with. We've both been to the corner drugstore and know that pinups are a stock in trade, along with articles that deal with the sex life of the American male. But a fair proportion of the fiction steers clear

of women entirely, dealing with "escape" subjects instead: survival situations, science fiction, crime, suspense ... and horror.

2. Read the market. To be perfectly blunt, your chances of selling a story to a men's magazine you haven't read is probably no more than 2 percent, even if your story is another "The Lottery." Get rid of the idea that all men's magazines are the same. Find out who is buying stories from 2,000 to 4,000 words, who is buying out-and-out fantasy, who has a penchant for psychological horror, who is publishing good stories by people you never heard of.

3. Take a hard, critical look at your own story and try to decide if it's better, worse, or about equal to the fiction being published in the magazine you're considering. The realization that your brainchild may not be up to *Playboy*'s standards may be a bitter pill, but it's better than wasting postage in a lost cause—especially when you could be selling your story to another editor.

4. Throw away Poe and Lovecraft before you start. If you just screamed in agony, wait a minute and let me expand a little on this one. If you're interested in the horror story to begin with, you were (and possibly still are) an avid reader of Edgar Allen Poe and Howard Philips Lovecraft. Both of these fine writers were rococo stylists, weaving words into almost Byzantine patterns. Both wrote some excellent short-short stories ("The Tell-Tale Heart" by Poe can be read in ten minutes, and Lovecraft's "In the Tomb" is not much longer—yet the effect of both stories is never forgotten), but both did their finest work in longer form. *The men's magazines don't buy novelettes*. The average length of accepted fiction is 2,500 to 4,000 words. Neither will they buy much, if any, fiction written in the styles of Poe or Lovecraft. In spite of the antique charm both hold for modern readers, most editors regard the

style as outdated and bankrupt. If you're still screaming and cradling your wounded manuscripts, I'm sorry. I'm only telling the truth. If it's Poe or Lovecraft, send it to a fanzine and be content with your contributor's copies.

A great many writers begin with the mistaken notion that "the Lovecraft style" is essential to success in the field. Those who feel this way no doubt pick up the idea by reading the numerous Lovecraft-oriented anthologies on sale. But anthologies are not magazines, and while the idea is no small tribute to H.P.L.'s influence on the field, it's simply not so. If you're looking for alternatives (ones that are adaptable to the men's magazine format), I'd recommend John Collier, Richard Matheson, Robert Bloch (who began as a Lovecraft imitator and has made a successful switch to a more modern style), and Harlan Ellison. All of these writers have short story anthologies on the market, and a volume of each makes a wonderful exercise book for the beginner.

5. When your story is ready for rewrite, cut it to the bone. Get rid of every ounce of excess fat. This is going to hurt; revising a story down to the bare essentials is always a little like murdering children, but it must be done. If the first draft runs 4,000 words, your second should go about 3,000. If the first is around 3,000, you can still probably get down to about 2,500 by tightening up the nuts and bolts. The object here isn't to shorten for the sake of shortening but to speed up the pace and make the story fly along.

Almost all of the men's magazines are excellent markets for the beginning horror freelancer. They need lots of material, and most of them could care less if you're an unknown. If your story is good, and if you pick the right market, you can make a sale. Below [on page 200] is a listing of *some* possible men's magazine markets. Check your *Writer's Market* for further details on other markets.

I have a particular warmth for *Cavalier*, because they published my own first marketable horror stories. Both Doug Allen and Nye Willden are warm and helpful, and if your story is good, they'll publish it. They report in four to six weeks and pay from two to three hundred dollars depending on length and number of stories published. The best length is around 4,000 words.

Escapade is another good market to try. They have upgraded their fiction considerably over the last year and are willing to pay top dollar for quality stories. *Adam* and *Knight* are the flagship magazines of a whole line of publications, including the *Adam Bedside Reader* and a new slick SF magazine, *Vertex*. Your story will be considered for publication in any and all publications. *Adam* has been one of the most consistent publishers of science fiction/horror, and like *Cavalier*, they pay more to authors who consistently submit salable material. Three thousand words is a good length here. If your story has sex interest and is still quality, I'd say send it to *Adam* first.

Best for Men and *Rascal* is another chain outfit. Shorter fiction sells well here: 2,500 words is about average. Sex interest is preferred, but still not necessary if the story holds up without it.

Penthouse, *Playboy*, and *Oui* are all quality markets, and all pay well—well enough to attract "name" authors much of the time. But all three accept freelance material on occasion. Probably the most useful thing I can say about the three of them is don't bypass them if you think your story is really top-drawer stuff. Start at the top. You may find a thousand-dollar check from *Playboy* waiting for you in the mailbox some morning—or four hundred dollars from *Penthouse*.

There is another market for the horror freelancer that should be discussed before sending you back to your typewriter, and that is the rapidly proliferating comic magazine market. Most of these are a good deal like

Cavalier
Dugent Publishing Corp.
236 East 46th Street
New York, NY 10017
Douglas Allen, Editor
Nye Willden, Associate Editor

Escapade
See Magazines, Inc.
53 East 54th Street, Suite 4B
New York, NY 10022
P.J. Emerson, Editor

Adam, Knight, and *Vertex*
8060 Melrose Avenue
Los Angeles, CA 90046
Don Pfeil, Editor

Best for Men, Men's Digest, Rascal
2715 N. Pulaski Road
Chicago, IL 60639
Frank Sorren, Editor

Sir!
21 West 26th Street
New York, NY 10010
Everett Meyers, Editor

Oui
919 North Michigan Avenue
Chicago, IL 60611
Jon Carroll, Editor

Penthouse
Dugent Publishing Corp.
1560 Broadway
New York, NY 10036
James Goode, Editor

Playboy
919 North Michigan Avenue
Chicago, IL 60611
Robert Macauley, Fiction Editor

the DC line of comic books that was published in the 1950s. At that time, they were called "the new trend" comic books.

The "new, new trend" magazines aren't in the comic racks with *Superman* and *Batman*, as a rule. You'll find them with the standard magazines, and in standard magazine size. A black-and-white comic panel accompanies each advancing scene.

I can hear the purists in the audience starting to grumble right now—what has all that blood-and-guts claptrap got to do with me? I'm a *writer*, not a lousy comic book scenarist.

Well, the purists rarely make enough money to pay overdue library fines in the freelancing business, but if you're still not convinced, at least take the time to look at a few of the new wave comic magazines before passing them up. They rarely reach the plateau of *Art*, but they're far from trash. The artwork is often superb, and while the writing is more often just competent than really good, it is rarely as awful as that churned out in some of the other specialized markets. And the magazines have their own fanatic horde of the faithful—fans that often know more about the arcane lore of terror than the writer himself. In a recent issue of *Creepy*, a college student took a writer severely to task for putting a witch-burning into his story of the Salem witchcraft hysteria of the 1660s. No Salem "witch" was burned, the reader quite rightfully pointed out.

Again, reading the market is essential. Go out to your local newsstand and pick up a dozen or so at a swipe. Your chances for success without reading the market first is zero. Your second step should be a query letter, which also serves as a note of introduction. Mention any sales you have made in the horror field to other markets.

The editor will probably ask you to submit several "summary" stories. A summary should run no more than 300 words, and you can include anywhere from one to a dozen in a package. You may get a go-ahead on all of them, only two or three, or (sadly) none at all.

Following a go-ahead, the story must be expanded so it will fill six, seven, or eight pages in the final magazine copy, and it must be written in TV script form so that the assigned artist can collaborate.

The same rules that apply to the men's fiction markets go down here. Sex is okay if it isn't overplayed; there is no comics' code to regulate magazine-size comic periodicals. But keep it tasteful and leave it out altogether if it doesn't play a central part in the story. Avoid all the tired old bears; leave them for the staff writers to rehash.

Below are some address and magazine titles for the comic market. As you can see, they're all chain publications:

WARREN PUBLISHING COMPANY
145 East 32nd Street
New York, NY 10016
James Warren, Editor
W.B. DuBay, Managing Editor

MAGAZINES PUBLISHED:
Creepy
Eerie
Vampirella

SKYWALD PUBLISHING CORPORATION
18 East 41st Street
New York, NY 10017
Alan Hewitson, Editor

MAGAZINES PUBLISHED:
Psycho
Nightmare
Scream

MARVEL COMIC GROUP
575 Madison Avenue
New York, NY 10022
Roy Thomas, Editor

MAGAZINES PUBLISHED:
Tales of the Zombie
Dracula Lives!
Monsters Unleashed
Vampire Tales

EERIE PUBLICATIONS, INC.
222 Park Avenue South
New York, NY 10003
Carl Burgos, Editor

MAGAZINES PUBLISHED:
Weird
Horror Tales
Terror Tales
Witches' Tales
Tales from the Tomb
Tales of Voodoo

The Warren Publications are the most open to freelance inquiries and contributions; they were first in the field and still publish the best material.

They use from fifteen to eighteen stories per month (to get an idea how good the form can be when it's working, see "Dead Man's Race" in *Creepy* #54, story by Jack Butterworth and art by Martin Salvador). Second choice for good horror material would be the Marvel Comics Group magazines, which are an offshoot of the more conventional and tremendously successful Marvel comic books, such as *Spider-man* and *Incredible Hulk*.

Skywald is fairly new to the trade, and at this writing they seem the most vital—constantly moving ahead, breaking new ground, and using consistently innovative stories. Be warned, however, that the freelancer is in strong competition here with a "bullpen staff."

There are also a few strictly horror magazines on the market, mostly holdovers from the old pulp days, but they are generally in the reprint business and payment on original ranges from twenty-five to a hundred dollars.

Americans have always loved a good horror story, and in these days when everyone is mourning the "death" of short magazine fiction, it's good to know that, in this field at least, the beast is still alive and kicking. And snarling. And drooling ...

VOLUME LV DECEMBER 1974 NO. 1

The Zen Writer

RAY BRADBURY

Some describe the sensation as being "in flow." Athletes call it "the zone." By any turn of phrase, it's that mental state under which a person operates at his or her peak, producing the highest quality work possible, without … well … working at it. In "The Zen Writer," **RAY BRADBURY** treats readers to a brief explanation of how such genius happens. And he would know. In addition to his numerous awards and international acclaim for such works as *Fahrenheit 451* and *Something Wicked This Way Comes*, he has also been awarded a star on the Hollywood Walk of Fame, the National Book Foundation's Medal for Distinguished Contribution to American Letters and The National Medal of Arts, the highest award given to an artist by the U.S. Government. Bradbury eventually adapted the essay from which this excerpt was originally drawn into the title piece for his classic book, *Zen in the Art of Writing*.

The old sideshow Medicine Men who traveled about our country used calliope, drum, and Blackfoot Indian to insure open-mouthed attention. I hope I will be forgiven for using Zen in much the same way, at least here at the start.

For, in the end, you may discover I'm not joking after all. But, let us grow serious in stages.

What words shall I whip forth painted in red letters ten feet tall?

WORK.

That's the first one.

RELAXATION.

That's the second. Followed by two final ones:

DON'T THINK!

Well, now, what have these words to do with Zen Buddhism? What do they have to do with writing? With me? But, most especially, with you?

First off, let's take a long look at that faintly repellent word WORK. It is, above all, the word about which your career will revolve for a lifetime. Beginning now, you should become not its slave, which is too mean a term, but its partner. Once you are really a co-sharer of existence with your work, that word will lose its repellent aspects.

Let me stop here a moment to ask some questions. Why is it that in a society with a Puritan heritage we have such completely ambivalent feelings about work? We feel guilty, do we not, if not busy? But we feel somewhat soiled, on the other hand, if we sweat over-much?

I can only suggest that we often indulge in make-work, in false business, to keep from being bored. Or, worse still, we conceive the idea of working for money. The money becomes the object, the target, the end-all and be-all. Thus work, being important only as a means to that end, degenerates into boredom. Can we wonder then that we hate it so?

Simultaneously, others have fostered the notion among the more self-conscious literary that quill, some parchment, an idle hour in midday, a soupçon of ink daintily tapped on paper will suffice, given inspiration's whiff. Said inspiration's being, all too often, the latest issue of *The Kenyon Review* or some other literary quarterly. A few words an hour, a few etched paragraphs per day and—voila! We are the Creator! Or better still, Joyce, Kafka, Sartre!

Nothing could be further from true creativity. Nothing could be more destructive than the two above attitudes.

Why?

Because both are a form of lying.

It is a lie to write in such a way as to be rewarded by money in the commercial market.

It is a lie to write in such a way as to be rewarded by fame offered you by some snobbish quasi-literary group in the intellectual gazettes.

Do I have to tell you how filled to the brim the literary quarterlies are with young lads and lasses kidding themselves they are creating when all they are doing is imitating the scrolls and flourishes of Virginia Woolf, William Faulkner, or Jack Kerouac?

Do I have to tell you how filled to the brim are our women's magazines and other mass-circulation publications with yet other lads and lasses kidding themselves they are creating when they are only imitating Clarence Buddington Kelland, Anya Seton, or Sax Rohmer?

The avant-garde liar kids himself he will be remembered for his pedantic lie.

The commercial liar, too, on his own level, kids himself that while he *is* slanting, it is only because the world is tilted; *everyone* walks like that!

Now, I would like to believe that everyone reading this article is not interested in those two forms of lying. Each of you, curious about creativity, wants to make contact with that thing in yourself that is truly original. You want fame and fortune, yes, but only as rewards for work well and truly done. Notoriety and a fat bank balance must come after everything else is finished and done. That means that they cannot even be considered while you are at the typewriter. The man who considers them lies one of the two ways, to please a tiny audience that can only beat an Idea insensible and then to death, or a large audience that wouldn't know an Idea if it came up and bit them.

We hear a lot about slanting for the commercial market, but not enough about slanting for the literary cliques. Both approaches, in the final analysis, are unhappy ways for a writer.

What is the greatest reward a writer can have? Isn't it that way when someone rushes up to you, his face bursting with honestly, his eyes afire with admiration and cries, "That new story of yours was fine, really wonderful!"

Then and only then is writing worthwhile.

Quite suddenly the pomposities of the intellectual faddists fade to dust. Suddenly, the agreeable monies collected from the fat-advertising magazines are unimportant.

The most callous of commercial writers loves that moment.

The most artificial of literary writers lives for that moment.

And God in his wisdom often provides that moment for the most money-grubbing of hacks or the most attention-grabbing of literateurs.

For there comes a time in the day's occupations when old Money Writer falls so in love with an idea that he begins to gallop, steam, pant, rave, and write from the heart, in spite of himself.

So, too, the man with the quill pen is suddenly taken with fevers, gives up purple ink for pure hot perspiration. Then he tatters quills by the dozen, and hours later, emerges ruinous from the bed of creation looking as if he had channeled an avalanche through his house.

Now, you ask, what transpired? What caused these two almost compulsive liars to start telling the truth?

Let me haul out my signs again.

WORK.

It's quite obvious that both men were working.

And work itself, a fter awhile, takes on a rhythm. The mechanical begins to fall away. The body begins to take over. The guard goes down. What happens then?

RELAXATION.

And then the men are happily following my last advice:

DON'T THINK!

Which results in more relaxation and more unthinkingness and greater creativity.

Now that I have you thoroughly confused, let me pause to hear your own dismayed cry.

Impossible! you say. How can you work and relax? How can you create and not be a nervous wreck?

It can be done. It is done, every day of every week of every year. Athletes do it. Painters do it. Mountain climbers do it.

Even I can do it.

And if I can do it, as you are probably hissing now, through clenched teeth, you can do it, too!

All right, let's line up the signs again. We could put them in any order, really. RELAXATION or DON'T THINK could come first or simultaneously, followed by WORK.

But, for convenience let's do it this way, with a fourth developmental sign added:

WORK.

RELAXATION.

DON'T THINK.

FURTHER RELAXATION.

Shall we analyze word number one?

WORK.

You have been working, haven't you?

Or do you plan some sort of schedule for yourself starting as soon as you put down this article?

What kind of schedule?

Something like this: one thousand or two thousand words every day for the next twenty years. At the start, you might shoot for one short story a week, fifty-two stories a year, for five years. You will have to write and put away or burn a lot of material before you are comfortable in this medium. You might as well start now and get the necessary work done.

For I believe that eventually quantity will make for quality.

How so?

Quantity gives experience. From experience alone can quality come.

All arts, big and small, are the elimination of waste motion in favor of the concise declaration.

The artist learns what to leave out. His greatest art will often be what he does not say, what he leaves out, his ability to state simply with clear emotion, the way he wants to go.

The artist must work so hard, so long, that a brain develops and lives, all of itself, in his fingers. By work, by quantitative experience, man releases himself from obligation to anything but the task at hand.

The writer must let his fingers run out the story of his characters, who, being only human and full of strange dreams and obsessions, are only too glad to run.

Isn't it obvious by now that the more we talk of work, the closer we come to relaxation?

Tenseness results from not knowing or giving up trying to know. Work, giving us experience, results in new confidence and eventually in relaxation. The type of dynamic relaxation again, as in sculpting, where the sculptor does not consciously have to tell his fingers what to do. The surgeon does not tell his scalpel what to do. Nor does the athlete advise his body. Suddenly, a natural rhythm is achieved. The body thinks for itself.

So again the three signs. Put them together any way you wish. WORK. RELAXATION. DON'T THINK. Once separated out. Now, all three together in a process. For if one works, one finally relaxes and stops thinking. True creation occurs then and only then.

But work, without right thinking, is almost useless. I repeat myself, but, the writer who wants to tap the larger truth in himself must reject the temptations of Joyce or Camus or Tennessee Williams, as exhibited in the literary reviews. He must forget the money waiting for him in mass circulation. He must ask himself, "What do I really think of the world, what do I love, fear, hate?" and begin to pour this on the paper.

Then, through the emotions, working steadily, over a long period of time, his writing will clarify; he will relax because he thinks right and he will think even righter because he relaxes. The two will become interchangeable. At last he will begin to see himself. At night, the very phosphorescence of his insides will throw long shadows on the wall. At last the surge, the agreeable blending of work, not thinking, and relaxation will be like the blood in one's body, flowing because it has to flow, moving because it must move, from the heart.

What are we trying to uncover in this flow? The one person irreplaceable to the world, of which there is no duplicate. *You.* As there was only one Shakespeare, Molière, Dr. Johnson, so you are that precious commodity, the individual man, the man we all democratically proclaim, but who, so often, gets lost, or loses himself, in the shuffle.

How does one get lost?

Through incorrect aims, as I have said. Through wanting literary fame too quickly. From wanting money too soon. If only we could remember, fame and money are gifts given us only *after* we have gifted the world with our best, our lonely, our individual truths. Now we must build our better mousetrap, heedless if a path is being beaten to our door.

Let the world burn through you. Throw the prism light, white hot, on paper. Make your own individual spectroscopic reading.

Why aren't more "creative" stories written and sold in our time, in any time? Mainly, I believe, because many writers don't even know about this way of working which I have discussed here. We are so used to the dichotomy of "literary" as opposed to "commercial" writing that we haven't labeled or considered the Middle Way, the way to the creative process that is best for everyone and most conducive to producing stories that are agreeable to snobs and hacks alike. As usual we have solved our problem, or thought we solved it, by cramming everything in two boxes with two names. Anything that doesn't fit in one box or another doesn't fit anywhere. So long as we continue to do and think this way, our writers will continue to truss and bind themselves. The High Road, the Happy Way, lies between.

The time will come when your characters will write your stories for you, when your emotions, free of literary cant and commercial bias, will blast the page and tell the truth.

Remember: *Plot* is no more than footprints left in the snow *after* your characters have run by on their way to incredible destinations. *Plot* is observed after the fact rather than before. It cannot precede action. It is the chart that remains when an action is through. That is all *Plot* ever should be. It is human desire let run, running, and reaching a goal. It cannot be mechanical. It can only be dynamic.

So, stand aside, forget targets, let the characters, your fingers, body, blood, and heart *do*.

Contemplate not your navel then, but your subconscious with what Wordsworth called "a wise passiveness." You need to go to Zen for the answer to your problems. Zen, like all philosophies, followed but in the tracks of men who learned from instinct what was good for them. Every wood-turner, every sculptor worth his marble, every ballerina, practices what Zen teaches without having heard the word in all their lives.

Now, have I sounded like a cultist of some sort? A yogi feeding on kumquats, grape nuts, and almonds here beneath the banyan tree? Let me assure you I speak of all these things only because they have worked for me for eighteen years. And I think they might work for you. The true test is in the doing.

Be pragmatic, then. If you're not happy with the way your writing has gone, you might give it a try.

If you do, I think you might easily find a new definition for WORK.

And the word is LOVE.

VOLUME LXI SEPTEMBER 1980 NO. 10

To Make a Short Story Long . . .

ORSON SCOTT CARD

One of **ORSON SCOTT CARD**'s earliest works, the child-rearing guide titled *Listen, Mom and Dad* (1978), did little to indicate the legendary status he would attain in the fields of science fiction and fantasy. It was only a year prior that Card had begun to publish short fiction with some regularity. One of these pieces, appearing in the August 1977 issue of *Analog Science Fiction & Fact*, was titled "Ender's Game" (which Card eventually revised into the 1985 Hugo and Nebula Award-winning novel of the same name). It was from these humble beginnings that Card began to carve his legend. The article that follows captures the author at a period shortly after his own successful transition from writing short stories to novels.

In the Munich Olympics in 1936, the Germans were very clever. They didn't let the equestrians from other nations see the course the horses would have to race. At one point in the course, after the normal obstacles that all the horses easily coped with, there was a fence. And beyond the fence was a strip of water dozens of yards across, far too wide for any horse to jump.

When the non-German equestrians reached that obstacle, they all tried to jump, of course, and floundered. But the German rider, knowing all about it, had his horse daintily step over the fence and walk gently through the water with perfect form.

It was cheating. But it's the kind of thing many of us face when we try to switch from writing short stories to writing novels. We're used to coping with three thousand or even ten thousand words. But suddenly there yawns before us a huge expanse of words—one hundred thousand or more. And when we try to leap over it as we would with a story, we end up with a soaking, as often as not.

Six months after I got my first check for a short story sale, I took stock of my earnings. I had sold a total of four stories in that time, for which I had been paid a total of 980 dollars. This was still 20 dollars less than my monthly salary at my magazine editing job.

It didn't look like I would be able to go freelance very soon, not on short story sales alone. If I wanted to be a full-time writer, I was going to have to write a novel.

So I sat down at the typewriter and began writing. I was confident. After all, what was a novel, if not a short story that had more things happen before the end? So, page by page, my first novel flowed from my typewriter. It was a science fiction epic that spanned a thousand years and dealt with the lives of twenty characters.

And it only lasted for 120 pages.

I began to suspect there was more to writing a novel than just "having more things happen."

Longer Is Shorter

Most of us who write fiction begin with short stories. There are several practical reasons for this: Short stories look easier to write. If you write a bad one that never sells, you have lost only twenty pages' work, not three hundred. And—perhaps the most common reason of all—short stories are what your college creative writing teacher wanted to see, and now you're in the habit.

How do you make the leap from short stories to novels? That intimidating stack of blank pages you have to fill is enough to frighten off most would-be novelists. But if you're one of the rare ones who is determined to go ahead, there are some things you can do to help yourself over the hurdle.

How do I know the arcana of switching to the novel form? I learned from experience. I wrote some bad novels. And each one's flaws taught me how to write the next one better.

That first novel—that 120-page thousand-year epic. I knew something was terribly wrong with it. So I took it to a friend, a fine editor who had been criticizing my short stories for me. He read it; he returned it to me silently.

"Well?" I asked.

"Um," he said. "Sure is long."

Long? A hundred and twenty pages? "The problem is it's too short."

"No," he insisted. "The problem is it's too long. It's absolutely boring. From page three on, I could hardly get through it."

The novel began like any of my short stories. I jumped into the main character's problem with both feet and tried to make him personally interesting. It worked fine.

But on page three, I started really getting into the plot. I introduced two more characters and moved my protagonist into a life-and-death struggle. By page five, he had resolved that problem and was off on another adventure. By page ten, he had saved the world. By page thirty, he had saved another world.

I wasn't writing a novel at all. I was writing a plot outline. I was so keenly aware of how much story line I had to cover that I had raced ahead and not paused to give the reader time to absorb anything.

Short stories are designed to deliver their impact in as few pages as possible. A tremendous amount is left out, and a good short story writer learns to include only the most essential information—only what he needs to create mood, get the facts across, and prepare the reader for the climax.

But novels have more space, more time. When a reader sits down with a book, he is committing several hours of his life to reading it. He will stay with you for much more peripheral material; he expects, in return, that you will provide him with a fuller experience than he could possibly get from a short story.

In my first draft of my first novel, I had written *history*—a bare retelling of events.

When I set out to write the second draft, I knew I had to write biography—a detailed exposition of what my characters thought and said and did, and what in their past made them act that way.

My second draft was more than three hundred pages long, and included only half the plot of the first draft. But it was a much better book. That is, it could be read by a person who actually stayed awake without liberal doses of NoDoz.

My friend read it again and came back much happier. "It still isn't very good, but at least it's *shorter* this time."

Don't Get Buried in Plot

One of the things that fooled me on that first draft was the idea that if a novel is ten times the length of a short story, it must have ten times the plot. But that is rarely the case.

Think of John Fowles's novel *Daniel Martin*—629 pages of always excellent, often brilliant prose. Yet the plot, the actual, essential plot, could have been expressed in a forty-page novelette. I suspect it would be a mediocre story at best, but it could easily be done, because not that much happens on the direct plot line. Reduced to its absurd minimum, *Daniel Martin* is the story of a financially successful screenwriter who returns to England at the request of a dying friend with whom he feuded years ago. The friend's wife was the woman the screenwriter really loved and wanted to marry back in their days at Oxford; the dying friend reveals that he knew his wife had an affair with the screenwriter and wants the two of them to get together after his death. Having delivered his message, the friend kills himself, and the screenwriter and the woman he once loved do indeed fall in love again, much to their own surprise.

Sounds like a melodramatic little story, doesn't it? And it might have turned out that way—except that stories and novels are not just devices for recounting plot.

When I first plotted that first novel of mine, I was thinking of a short story as a sort of thread through time, a few events long; I thought of a novel as simply a longer thread to fill up the pages. My metaphor was all wrong, however. Writing is not just one-dimensional.

So when you sit down to plot your novel, don't try to come up with ten times the number of events you usually put in a story. You will usually want more events than in a story, of course, but you should still leave yourself plenty of leisure to explore from character to character, from thought to thought, from detail to detail. A novel need not cover a thousand years or forty-eight characters or the Renaissance in Italy; you have the freedom to use the novel form to write about a single life or a single year or a single incident. Despite the deceptively simple plot of *Daniel Martin*, or perhaps because of it, Fowles was able to take his readers by surprise, bringing us to love the seemingly jaded and shallow narrator as he reluctantly showed us his true self a layer at a time.

Gulps and Swallows

My first novel went through several more drafts, and I thought I had finally found a system for coping with its length. I was a short story writer, wasn't

I? So why not cut up the plot into five or six novelettes? They would all lead to a climax at the end, and yet I would be on familiar ground, writing thirty or forty pages in each section, just like a story.

Well, it worked—and it didn't. I sold the novel, and people even bought copies of it and read it, and some liked it. But the critics didn't, and much as it pains me to say, they are fundamentally right. Because that little trick of cutting the novel up into short stories simply doesn't work.

A novel isn't a half-dozen short stories with the same characters. The seams invariably show. Why? Because a novel must have integrity. The novel, no matter how dense and wide-ranging it might be, must have a single cumulative effect to please the reader. Every minor climax must point toward the book's final climax, must promise still better things to come.

But in my first novel (all right, I'll name it: *Hot Sleep*), instead of a series of minor climaxes leading toward the final climax of the book, I had six completely unrelated climaxes. In the first short story, my protagonist, as a child, faces a terrible dilemma that shapes his whole future. But when I start the second story, years have passed and those earlier events are not very important anymore—it's hard to see any real effect they might have on the events of the rest of the novel. And at the end of the second story, all but one of the major characters lose their memories in a disaster in space, and to all intents and purposes the third part of the book is another entirely new beginning. All the reader's emotional investment is gone, and he has to begin all over again. No wonder some readers got impatient!

In a way, however, my instinct was correct. You can't write a novel all at once, any more than you can swallow a whale in one gulp. You do have to break it up into smaller chunks. But those smaller chunks aren't good old familiar short stories. Novels aren't built out of short stories.

They're built out of scenes.

Lights! Camera! Action! Cut!

Think of the way a movie works. A new setting is almost always introduced with an establishing shot, showing the audience what characters are present and where they are. Almost every time the film skips from one place to another without actually following the character there, the audience is given some time to get its bearings.

Then, as the film progresses, the camera cuts from one point of view to another, or follows as the characters travel from one place to another. The camera is able to focus on a particular thing that a character is looking at—or that the character is unaware of. But all through a single action, the camera keeps our attention tightly focused on the important matters. Then, when that scene ends, there is another establishing shot; another line of action begins.

As you see the story unwind on the screen, you aren't really aware that between each new setting there are really many scenes, small bits of action leading to a single, small climax or revelation. After all, neither novelists nor filmmak-

HOLLYWOOD GHOST

at large! Ready to help with your writing—and selling—problems. I'll tell you if a script (screen, TV, magazine, novel) is salable, and if not how to revise it: $1 per thousand words. Or I'll do it over. Ask me about my kind of ghosting!

DOROTHY DOYLE

1129-25th St. **Santa Monica, Calif.**

CALLING ALL WRITERS!!!

In November I announced that I might be able to take on a few more authors for any professional collaboration. If you are in earnest about writing send for my FREE booklet, *The Road to Writing That Pays*, and I'll tell you how to get THE TWELVE PILLARS OF WRITING WISDOM, which constitute the basis of my original, exclusive, and highly successful system.

TO WRITERS OF JUVENILE FICTION. Here is news! I have taken on one of my most successful students to head my juvenile department. Now you may have the sympathetic guidance of a writer who, four years ago, was right where you are now, who, since then, has had four books published by Dutton and four by Oxford University Press, who is now under contract for two books a year and who got $500 for a story in Ladies' Home Journal which is now being dramatized. All done under my careful coaching.

So, whether you want to do adult or juvenile fiction, write me. My booklet *The Road to Writing That Pays* is FREE. Merely state whether you are writing adult or juvenile fiction.

SCAMMON LOCKWOOD

102 E. 22nd St. **New York, N. Y.**

ers show everything that happens. Tremendous amounts of detail are skipped over, left out—hinted at, perhaps, but never shown. All of the action is compressed into the events that are shown. While a filmmaker must compress everything into two hours or so, a novelist has a great deal more freedom. Within reasonable limits, you can include all the pertinent information, and the reader will be right there with you.

Like a filmmaker, however, you must present that information carefully. You can't just list the events and motives and speeches of the characters—that's history. Bad history, in fact. Instead, you present the information dramatically, through characters who have understandable desires and who are carrying out understandable actions, and with a structure that helps the reader notice and understand and feel what you want him to.

And the structure you use is composed of hundreds of different scenes, of varying lengths and varying degrees of importance, each one a single continuing action.

A single, continuing action may be, for instance, a sword fight that begins with an insult at a party and continues all over the palace until one man finally gasps with a sword in his chest and the hero, panting, watches his enemy die.

A single, continuing action may be a man standing a the window of an apartment in a tall building, looking out over a city watching a helicopter land, regretting his decision not to be aboard it.

A single, continuing action may be a journey across the United States, summarized by telling, in two paragraphs, the routine of a single day of travel; that summary is extended to cover all the days of travel.

Each such scene is a unit, designed to have its own effect on the reader; when the scene ends, the reader knows something more—and feels something more.

How is that different from writing a short story? Ideally, a short story is an indivisible unit—every sentence in it points toward the single climax that fulfills the entire work. One moment in the story controls all the rest. But in a novel, that single climax is replaced by many smaller climaxes, by many side trips or pauses to explore. If you keep shaping everything to point to that one climax, your reader will get sick of it after a hundred pages or so. It will feel monotonous. To keep the reader entertained (i.e., to keep him reading) you must give him many small moments of fulfillment along the way, brief rewards that promise something bigger later.

How does this work in a particular novel? Let's go through chapter twenty-seven of a recent bestseller, Stephen King's *The Stand*. After each scene number, the number of paragraphs in the scene appears in parentheses, followed by a synopsis of the scene.

1. (4) Protagonists Larry and Rita have noticed that the electricity is beginning to go off, and the smell of the decaying bodies is terrible; Larry is afraid New York will soon be unlivable.
2. (2) Flashback: They found the body of a man they had been aware of, murdered. It affected Rita deeply.
3. (20) Dialogue: Larry and Rita eat breakfast, and Larry makes the decision to leave.
4. (8) Rita suddenly rushes to the bathroom, vomits. She is fast becoming unable to cope with the disaster.
5. (3) Flashback: Rita is not as strong as Larry had thought at first.
6. (1) Larry wonders if he can take care of her.
7. (13) Dialogue: She decides to go with him, even as he comes to resent her more because of her weakness.

At this point, King takes a larger break. There is a line space, and suddenly we are with Larry and Rita as they walk along the streets of New York. In those first seven scenes, there is a definite sense of building toward a single climax, the moment in scene seven where Larry catches himself hating her. King writes: "Then he felt the familiar surge of self-contempt and wondered what the hell could be the matter with him."

" 'I'm sorry,' he said. 'I'm an insensitive bastard.' "

It is a pivotal moment for Larry; it is the reason why he takes responsibility for her even though he hates the thought of taking her along. It explains his motive. It also sets us up for later tension in later scenes, and finally, in a small way, it leads us to the climax of the novel.

Yet each of the small scenes leading to that climax had a closure all its own. Scene one closes with Larry's dark dream of a black thing that wants him. Scene two closes with the observation that seeing the dead man had made a powerful change in Rita. Scene three ends with a startling change—after a peaceful conversation, Rita suddenly has an expression on her face that scares Larry. Scene eight ends with the starling revelation that Rita is pathetically eager to do whatever she thinks Larry wants her to do. And so on.

Every scene advances the reader toward the minor climax in the seventh scene. Each scene conveys the necessary information and then closes in a way that increases the tension, the reader's expectation of a climax. And the scenes vary—first are exposition in the author's voice, then a flashback in Larry's mind, then dialogue between Larry and Rita, then physical action as Rita rushes to the bathroom to vomit, then flashback, then reflection, and then dialogue again.

It is as if King had cut from camera to camera, showing us the continuing action from different points of view, revealing bits of information that together built to a whole—the superscene that ends with the line space. And the chapter is composed of five superscenes of varying length that, together, tell a complete episode. The chapter as a whole cements Larry and Rita together in our minds, despite the tension between them. We end up understanding and liking both. They have managed to get out of New York alive, but we know their adventures are just beginning.

Cliffhangers

These are the gulps you can use to down a whole novel. You never sit down to write three hundred or five hundred or one thousand pages. You sit down to write a series of scenes that create a superscene with its own minor climax; you then add superscenes together to create the climax that completes the chapter.

Yet, while each closure, each minor climax, each chapter climax is fulfilling to the reader, none of them is *completely* fulfilling. Inherent in every climax is the promise of more tension and greater fulfillment later. In its crudest form, this is the cliffhanger technique—putting the protagonist into an awkward dilemma and then leaving him hanging there while the reader waits to buy the next day's installment. Such obvious tricks irritate most readers; but the technique, in more subtle form, is essential to creating a novel as a whole. After all, what is a novel if not the writer's attempt to involve the reader emotionally in a dilemma and keep him involved until its resolution? In your short stories, you could hold off until your single climax because the reader would stay with you for such a brief time; but in a novel, the reader's patience is not infinite.

Of course, I seriously doubt that Stephen King sat down and planned out each of those seven scenes. I wonder if he even outlined chapter by chapter. The selection of what scenes to present is art; it is felt, not intellectualized. For me, most of those decisions are unconscious. It feels right to include this scene; it feels right to interrupt the action here for a flashback that reveals important information; it feels right to describe this particular setting in loving detail.

You *can* consciously plan, however, to keep yourself aware of the possibilities open to you, so that you use all your tools. You can concentrate on the scenes and superscenes at hand, instead of letting the climax of the novel, hundreds of pages away, distract you from what you are creating now.

And, while you aren't writing short stories anymore, you *have* cut that whale of a novel into pieces small enough that you, like the reader, can forget about the hundreds of pages ahead and concentrate on only the few pages ahead and concentrate on only the few pages needed to reach the climax of this particular scene.

As a friend of mine once said, "I'd a lot rather fight two tons of tiny lizards than a two-ton fire-breathing dragon."

The Second Will Be Better Than the First

Novels and short stories are different art forms. They have a lot more in common than do, say, novels and paintings, or even short stories and poems. Yet you are crippling yourself if you try to write a novel under the impression that it's just more of the same thing you have been doing with short stories.

Even if you keep in mind all the things I have pointed out, you will probably find new mistakes or problems I haven't mentioned. After all, there were some things I did *right* in my first novels that you might do wrong. And undoubtedly there are some things I'm *still* doing wrong that I haven't caught yet—and therefore can't warn you about.

Each novel you write, however, will make the next one easier. I'm not talking about mere confidence, either, though finishing one novel will certainly make the next one seem less intimidating. Whether or not you notice what you're learning, you are learning. When I was an eight year old, first throwing a ball at a basketball hoop, I missed time and time again. But gradually I began to be able to hit the backboard every time, and eventually I got good enough to have the ball come somewhere near the basket on every shot. Though I'm still a miserable basketball player, I did unconsciously learn and improve. In writing novels, of course, each shot takes a long time, and you aren't able to see so easily whether you missed or not. But your brain is still plugging along, learning to become comfortable with the form.

Too comfortable, sometimes. I studied Spanish for eight years and was pretty good at it—but then I lived in Brazil for two years, and spoke Portuguese the whole time. Those languages are so similar that by the end of those two years, I literally could not speak Spanish at all—Portuguese had taken over.

I find a similar thing happening to me now. With four novels under my belt, I find it increasingly hard to use that similar but still different "language" of short stories. I keep forgetting that I don't have hundreds of pages to work with; and my most recent thrity-page story finally ended at 130 pages, and even at that I felt that I had left out two-thirds of what should have been in it. In other words, my short story came out as a novel whether I wanted it to or not.

Anybody have any advice on how a novelist can learn to write short stories?

Writer's Digest

PART III

Pieces of History

February

VOLUME I DECEMBER 1920 NO. 1

The Day of the Writer

HARVEY HALE

Reading the piece that follows, it takes one a moment to realize that it was written during the silent film era—seven years, in fact, before the premiere of *The Jazz Singer*, the first feature to utilize recorded dialogue and singing. And yet, as HARVEY HALE points out, even without sound, writers were vitally important to the filmmaking process. Existing works of literature, from which films could be adapted, were becoming scarce and too expensive to purchase. Original stories were needed—fast! Even with dialogue limited to the occasional title card, plots still needed to be crafted, characters fleshed out, themes defined. The world was hungry for films, which meant that writers were in demand. More so, in fact, than ever before.

These are days of great opportunity for the man or woman who can think clearly and who knows how to evolve original ideas and weave them into photoplay plots. Everywhere we turn, we meet the same demand on the part of motion picture producers, scenario editors, and actors.

"Give us plays, original ones," they cry.

Never before was opportunity so great for the unknown writer. If you can write; if you can work out good, clear-cut action plots; if you have that quality of perseverance which glories in the ultimate triumph over repeated disappointments—then get into the game of writing for the moving pictures. You don't have to be known. You will be if you make good.

It is an entrancing business—a creative world—and the reward for living therein, loyally, painstakingly, and studiously is fame and fortune. Fame, much larger than ever before known by writers of photoplays or scenarios; fortune, beyond the wildest dreams of the successful writers of the three- and five-reelers of a few years ago.

This is the day of the screenwriter, and the reason for his popularity among producers and scenario editors is the very real dearth of good, original scenario material. A few years ago, scenarios and synopses brought authors nominal fees—twenty-five and fifty dollars—and occasionally one hundred or three hundred dollars was received for an exceptionally good story. Today—we have it on high authority—any photoplay story that is worth producing at all, is worth five hundred to one thousand dollars and more.

It is the old law of supply and demand working in the film industry. We have seen the industry grow to stupendous proportions. Producers first vied with one another in the making of elaborate and costly pictures. Then they were bidding higher and higher for the services of players. Those were the days of the actors.

Conditions such as these, which caused many thinking people to shake their heads in anticipation of the financial rocks for which the film industry seemed to be heading, have been adjusted. But producers of photoplays still face a serious problem that can be solved only by the writing people of the country.

On the one hand, the producer faces the great American public, educated to appreciate originality and fine workmanship in film plays, and constantly demanding more. On the other hand, he sees the available supply of literary classics, the work of novelists and magazine writers, rapidly becoming exhausted and their purchase price mounting ever higher. The handful of trained scenario writers on the staffs of the producing companies are not able to cope with the situation. The producer must turn for help to the unknown, in the hope of discovering fresh ideas, new methods of storytelling, different action and atmosphere.

But let those of us who would write for screen productions be sane in our approach to this work. Let us not deceive ourselves into believing that success in this business can be attained at a single bound.

Let us face the facts. It is not possible for *anyone* to become a successful photoplaywright. No one can guarantee that *you* will be successful in your work, extravagant statements of some correspondence schools to the contrary. Remember that success cannot be bought with money in this profession. The purchase price is study, consistent hard work, and perseverance to overcome all obstacles.

Study, dream, write. That is the recipe for success. Good textbooks, dictionaries, encyclopedias may be obtained with little effort and at small cost. Think of the characters and situations you want to make up your story. Visualize the scenes and then work them out carefully so that your thoughts are expressed in certain, crisp language. Do not waste words. Write action, not description, and don't forget to *work*.

VOLUME II SEPTEMBER 1921 NO. 10

The Girl Reporter

ALLIEÑE S. DE CHANT

The following article was written only one year after American women gained the right to vote. And though it would be many years—decades, in fact—before any real sense of equality could be acknowledged, *Writer's Digest* was on hand to address the exciting new opportunities for women in the field of journalism. Written by **ALLIEÑE S. DE CHANT**, the piece is quaint—even patronizing at times—but overflowing with energy and enthusiasm, vividly capturing the romantic notion of being a reporter in an era when all things seemed possible and "girls" could do anything—maybe even better than boys.

"To be or not be a reporter" is the question that puzzles the mind of an ever-increasing number of young girls who have the "itch" to write and are ready and prepared to step out on the bottom rung of the ladder to begin the climb to journalistic success.

What does the "Fourth Estate" hold for the girl reporter? What are the qualifications? What are the mental and material returns and compensations? How is a story handled? These are some of the many questions she has in her wide-awake mind. By answering them, from personal experience dearly but happily earned on a small-town daily and a metropolitan sheet of no mean reputation, perhaps we may help her make *the* decision.

How important is the "Fourth Estate"? Edmund Burke once said: "There are three estates (the nobility, clergy, and people) in Parliament, but in the reporters' gallery yonder there sits a fourth estate more important than they all."

What is news? "Big news is anything of public interest that is new," says an authority.

Who is a journalist? "He who preaches the gospel of humanity."

Is it worthwhile to become a journalist? Yes. "To be in touch with the thought and happenings of the world gives opportunity for interpretation of life to the broader public of the magazine and the published volume." Or, "to have the fascination of doing things; of being in the forefront of the world's activities, is to be a reporter."

What are a reporter's requirements? "Her laboratory manual of literature," says Christopher Morley, "equals close, constant, vivid, and compassionate gazing at the ways of mankind."

She must have eyes to see, skill to write, and a heart to feel. That is the best definition we know. She must have a nose for news, the itch to write; a knowledge of human nature; a knowledge of the English language. She must be a woman of good habits, of well-groomed appearance, of pleasing personality, and of high character. She must possess patience and not a little ingenuity. She must know her subject; think clearly and deeply; write understandable English. She must read widely and know the big facts of the world and its doings. According to Morley, she must use "swift, lively, accurate observation."

She must be willing to work hard, to endure long hours, and to take caustic criticism with a smile and a grim determination not to make the same mistake twice. She must have literary taste and a keen ambition to get ahead. She must learn to write accurately without revision and think ahead of her typewriter. She must learn the value of making acquaintances—of cultivating people who can furnish an item—and she must learn the art of managing the conversation.

And above all, she needs a saving sense of humor!

Charles E. Van Loan's advice to a cub reporter is couched in these words: "Facts, my boy, facts! When I send you out to ask a man a question I want the answer and nothing less. Nothing more, either. I don't care what kind of pants the man had, if any, or whether he pulled 'em over his knees when he sat down. Never mind saying he met the reporter with a bright smile and a warm handclap. The thing I want is the answer to the question. Facts, bare facts, that's what we want here, young man!"

"Successful newsgetting is the art of knowing where Hell will break through next and having a man there," says J.B. McCullagh of the *St. Louis Globe Democrat*. The greatest assignment ever given to any reporter was couched in but four terse words uttered by James Gordon Bennett, of the *New York Herald*, to Henry M. Stanley: "Go and find Livingstone!" The reporter went and found him and opened Africa to the world.

How shall news be secured? First of all, the girl reporter needs a notebook, an Eversharp pencil. When she "corners" her prospect for a story, she must secure answers to five simple questions, i.e. "Who? What? Why? When? Where?" When she has obtained those, she may be sure she has her story covered. Take a fire, for example: She must find out its origin, the time and the place, number of people killed or hurt, number of firemen injured, loss, insurance. She must find out whether the owner intends to rebuild or not. Then, too, she must get a picture in her mind of how the fire grew and spread. After she has her story, she, in her "write-up," must learn how to tell the story in the first paragraph. Readers, nowadays, rarely read beyond the first paragraph or two. Some get no farther than the headlines.

Or, to take the story of a wedding to be used in the society column: She must learn the names of the bride and bridegroom, the time and place of the wedding, the name of the officiating clergyman, and the name of the man who gave the bride away. Details as to the bride's costume are also necessary, together with those of the bridal party. Stress is also placed on the setting and on the reception that followed. The destination of the wedding journey is also reported together with the name of the town or city where the newly wedded couple will reside.

Women are given suffrage stories to "cover," so-called "sob stuff," and assignments having to do with women or children. They are rarely assigned fires, wrecks, murders, and the like, unless it is to get the "sob stuff" angle. "You wouldn't expect a woman," remarked one city editor, "to climb the spar of a burning building to get the 'inside' of a big story of a fire, in time for the last edition, nor would I assign her to the story of a murder where it would be necessary for her to use fistic methods to make her way through the mob." Be that as it may—the girl reporter who can, in the vernacular, "deliver the goods," can get the best assignments and the getting of them is well worth the effort!

Her best field lies in "human interest" stories about young folks, old folks, middle-sized folks, children—heart stories that tell of ambition, of success, of triumph—perhaps of abject failure—stories of which the reader can say: "That's real! That's true! That inspires me!"

The girl reporter can get that "heart" twist to her stories if she "has eyes to see, the skill to write, and the heart to feel" and life for her can never be dull, ambition is always ready to climb one rung higher, and the good she can do is immeasurable! Her success cannot be measured by the yardstick of the pay envelope, which contains from twelve to twenty dolloars on up to forty-five dollars or a salaried job for an experienced newsgatherer, city editor, or feature writer.

Journalism offers a wide field for the girls of tomorrow—that Fourth Estate, "more important than they all," and as the girl reporter measures up to her job and realizes her high ambitions, so will the opinions of thousands be molded and shaped for cleaner living, deeper thinking, more spiritual and more loving doing! Have you the "itch" to write, the eyes to see, and the heart to feel? Then write!

VOLUME III APRIL 1922 NO. 5

When You Write for the Screen

JEANNIE MACPHERSON

Just as it had for novelists and short story writers, *Writer's Digest* made a point of providing writers for the film industry with the information they needed to succeed. In the 1920s, the public's hunger for films was so great, in fact, that a large portion of the magazine's content focused upon just those issues: developing "photoplays," moving to Hollywood, getting paid, etc. In the 1922 piece that follows, **JEANNIE MACPHERSON**, special scenario writer for Cecil B. DeMille Productions, shares some invaluable thoughts on what a good screen treatment should—and should not—include.

The motion picture is the universal entertainment. It appeals to all ages, classes, and both sexes.

Remember that fact in writing for the screen.

Universality of appeal is the quality which every screen story must have. It must, in theory at least, hold out the promise of entertainment and a genuine thought for every individual who is a potential spectator.

The screenwriter plays to an audience unheard of before the advent of the motion picture. Where the stage playwright or the novelist reaches hundreds of thousands at the most, the photoplay reaches millions. Approximately nine million people see motion pictures every day in the United

States alone. And the United States is but a small part of the potential audience on any one picture.

Keep those facts in mind in writing scenarios. It is a fact never forgotten by the professional writer. The latter reckons that a thought worthy of screen production must reach all the world or it is but a partial success. That's why the professional writer selects the theme with extreme care and elaborates it with even more attention to the details.

Stories—the product of untrained writers—reach my desk every day, that have been written without this fundamental fact in mind. By the very selection of their subject the writers automatically exclude a large proportion of their potential audience. Here a story attacks the Negro problem in a manner offensive to the South; another attempts to deal with the subject of organized labor in a way that would offend every member of a labor union.

Other writers make the mistake of writing about subjects which are beyond the understanding of the average spectator. I do not mean that these stories are too good for the public, on the contrary, they are not nearly good enough. And one of the reasons that they are not good enough for production is the fact that they are of such a restricted appeal. They require specialized knowledge which all the world does not possess. Thereby they automatically cut off a large portion of the public from the enjoyment of that picture.

The ideal screen story might be said to be one which would appeal to the college professor and the ditchdigger equally; to the society woman and the servant girl.

To achieve such an ideal is a task that is monumental in itself. But to even approximate such an ideal, it is necessary that every effort be made to select a theme with the widest possible note of appeal. Don't antagonize the college professor or the ditchdigger, the society woman or the servant girl by the very subject matter of your story.

The truly great screenplays have been built around stories with that note of universal appeal. Great acting, perfect direction, excellent photography, and scenic work all play their part. But if the story lacks the universal note, the other qualities are sheer waste.

One frequently hears the plea that "the story was too good for the public." The implication is that the story or the finished picture went over the heads of the audience.

This is absolute nonsense. There is no such thing as a picture that is "too good for the public." The reason pictures fail is because they are not good enough for the public. That same public is the hardest critic in the world. It refuses to be fooled. Advertising and publicity cannot make it like that which is unworthy of it.

The real reason for each and every failure in the world of drama is that the play is faulty. No other reason really counts. And in the world of the photoplay, one of the surest ways to fall short of the mark set by the public is to write for a restricted audience.

Insofar as possible, avoid the type of subject matter that goes beyond the understanding of the average individual. Not all of us are captured by Arab raiders in the Sahara desert. But we can all understand being captured and we can feel vicariously the emotions of the captive.

It has been my experience that the most successful photoplays have been written around everyday matters. Problems of married life offer a subject for the scenario writer that, while it is exceedingly dangerous to work with, meets with the widest possible sympathy and understanding from the public. That's because all of us have a thorough working knowledge of marriage. We may not all be married, but we have friends, relatives, and acquaintances who are. And we can see in the picture psychology and emotional reactions with which we are all familiar.

That doesn't mean that matrimonial problem plays are the only ones that the public approves of nor does it mean that every amateur writer should immediately turn his or her attention to a story on this subject. It merely illustrates the point of universality, which is the basis of every successful screen story.

VOLUME III OCTOBER 1922 NO. 11

This Thing Called Censorship

SMITH C. MCGREGOR

Just as some are compelled to create, others are compelled to suppress. For whatever reason—be it personal philosophy, religion, political agenda, or moral imperative—there have always been special interest groups and highly motivated individuals who take it upon themselves to try and limit those things that we can see, read, or think. And in 1922, things were no different, with writers, as is often the case, being the target. Here, **SMITH C. MCGREGOR** demonstrates the timeless need to have writers think freely.

It is not new, this thing called censorship. Ever since the invention of motion pictures there have been efforts to impose official control on this medium of expression, and the present agitation for a board of Federal censors is but a logical development of a propaganda that has been carried on for years. In fact, some cities and a few states have censored the photoplays shown in their territory for a number of years, the state of Pennsylvania being an example.

Many people of influence honestly believe that censorship is the only way to better the motion picture industry. They have listened to the arguments of those who might profit by the censorship system until their own common sense has been warped and turned aside. Of course, any fair-minded person will admit that some productions deserve to be censored and otherwise controlled. But shall we deliberately sacrifice the majority, and the good they are doing, in order that a small minority may also be destroyed?

Censorship promises much. We are told that it will elevate the moral standards of the motion picture and otherwise benefit all who come in contact with it. That is certainly a noble aim, one in which every writer is interested, and which deserves their unfaltering support—if censorship can really do the things claimed for it.

But can it? Why is it that the years of control in Pennsylvania and other states where it is in use cannot show a single instance of these promises becoming realities? It is because censorship and the principles it represents are directly opposed to the best interests of the masses.

Censorship is ever based on the principle of the few judging for the majority. The photoplay art is essentially intended for the masses, which accounts for its remarkable growth. But let us cast aside this question of the right of the few to decide for the multitude; let us consider the actual making of a photoplay and the effect Federal control would have on the methods that have so far given America and the world a new art.

More and more reform advocates are urging that control be imposed on the writers of screen stories, as such a course would make it unnecessary to cut expensive scenes from a finished production. Not even a reformer would expect a great artist to turn out masterpieces with only a limited number of brushes and colors, yet the writer is expected to turn dictated rules into the highest art!

Delve into the far corners of the world and seek out those things that have come down through the ages possessing the elusive something we call art, and the one great fact that stands out above all others is that the masterpieces were conceived by those who refused to set a limit for their creative powers. As a writer, your supply shop is the delicate something within you that we define as the imagination, and once you limit the heights to which it can go, you have stopped its growth toward perfection.

This thing called censorship is not invincible. That great legitimate weapon of a free people, Public Opinion, has not yet been called upon to express the true will of the masses. Every literary worker has a task to do if the art of creative writing is to be secured for future generations. Think! Encourage others to do their own thinking! A nation that does its own thinking will not consent to the censoring of its favorite entertainment.

VOLUME XXIII FEBRUARY 1942 NO. 3

Censorship

OFFICE OF CENSORSHIP

December 7th, 1941. The Japanese launch their attack on Pearl Harbor. Four days later, Hitler declares war on the United States. Shortly thereafter, the following article ran in *Writer's Digest* magazine, per the request of the **OFFICE OF CENSORSHIP** in Washington, D.C. But unlike the censorship issues detailed in the previous article, this was a plea for discretion, requesting the compliance of all media to restrict what they revealed about American and/or Allied military operations, as well as how and when they revealed it. In this case, at least, this self-imposed censorship was easy to ask for — and comply with. Clearly, it was not freedom of speech that was in danger, but freedom, period.

It is essential that certain basic facts be understood from the beginning.

The first of these facts is that the outcome of the war is a matter of vital personal concern to the future of every American citizen. The second is that the security of our armed forces and even of our homes and our liberties will be weakened in greater or less degree by every disclosure of information which will help the enemy.

If every member of every news staff and contributing writer will keep these two facts constantly in mind, and then will follow the dictates of common sense, he will be able to answer for himself many of the questions which might otherwise trouble him. A maximum of accomplishment will be attained if editors will ask themselves with respect to any given detail, "Is this information I would like to have if I were the enemy?" and then act accordingly.

The result of such a process will hardly represent "business as usual" on the news desks of the country. On the contrary, it will mean some sacrifice of the journalistic enterprise of ordinary times. But it will not mean a news or editorial blackout. It is the hope and expectation of the Office of Censorship that the column of American publications will remain the freest in the world, and will tell the story of our national successes and shortcomings accurately and in much detail.

Here is a summary covering specified problems.

All of the requests in this summary are modified by a proviso that the information listed may properly be published when authorized by appropriate authority. News on all of these subjects will become available from government sources; but in war, timeliness is an important factor, and the government unquestionably is in the best position to decide when disclosure is timely.

The specific information which newspapers and magazines are asked not to publish *except when such information is made available officially by appropriate authority* falls into the following classes:

Troops

The general character and movements of U. S. Army units, within or without the continental limits of the United States—their location; identity or exact composition; equipment or strength; their destination, routes and schedules; their assembly for embarkation, prospective embarkation, or actual embarkation. Any such information regarding the troops of friendly nations on American soil.

The request as regards location and general character does *not* apply to troops in training camps in continental United States, nor to units assigned to domestic police duty.

Ships

The location, movements, and identity of naval and merchant vessels of the United States in any waters, and of other nations opposing the Axis powers, in American waters; the port and time of arrival or prospective arrival of any such vessels, or the port from which they leave; the nature of cargoes of such vessels; the location of enemy naval or merchant vessels in or near American waters; the assembly, departure, or arrival of transports or convoys; the existence of mine fields or other harbor defense; secret orders or other secret instructions regarding lights, buoys, and other guides to navigators; the number, size, character, and location of ships in construction, or advance information as to the date of launchings or commissionings; the physical set-up or technical details of shipyards.

Planes

The disposition, movements, and strength of Army or Navy air units.

Fortifications

The location of forts and other fortifications; the location of coast defense emplacements, or antiaircraft guns; their nature and number; location of bomb shelters; location of camouflaged objects.

Production

Specific information about war contracts, such as the exact type of production, production schedules, dates of delivery, or progress of production; estimated supplies of strategic and critical materials available; or nationwide "round-ups" of locally published procurement data except when such composite information is officially approved for publication.

Specific information about the location of, or other information about, sites and factories already in existence, which would aid saboteurs in gaining access to them; information other than that readily gained through observation by the general public, disclosing the location of sites and factories yet to be established, or the nature of their production.

Any information about new or secret military designs, or new factory designs for war production.

Weather

Weather forecasts, other than officially issued by the Weather Bureau, to lie within a radius of 150 miles from the point of publication.

Consolidated temperature tables covering more than twenty stations, in any one publication.

Special forecasts issued by the Weather Bureau warning of unusual conditions, or news stories warning the public of dangerous roads or streets, within 150 miles of the point of publication, are all acceptable for publication.

Photographs and Maps

Photographs conveying the information specified in the above summary, unless officially approved for publication.

Detailed maps or photographs disclosing location of munition dumps or other restricted Army or Navy areas.

This has no reference to maps showing the general theater of war, or large-scale zones of action, movements of contending forces on a large scale, or maps showing the general ebb and flow of battle lines.

Special care should be exercised in the publication of aerial photos presumable of nonmilitary significance, which might reveal military or other information helpful to the enemy; also care should be exercised in publishing casualty photos so as not to reveal unit identifications through collar ornaments, etc. Special attention is directed to the section of this summary covering information about damage to military objectives.

General

Casualty Lists: There is no objection to publication of information about casualties from a newspaper's local field, obtained from nearest of kin, but it is requested that in such cases, specific military and naval units, and exact locations, be not mentioned.

Information disclosing the new location of national archives, art treasures, and so on, which have been moved for safe-keeping.

Information about damage to military and naval objectives, including docks, railroads, or commercial airports, resulting from enemy action.

The spread of rumors in such a way that they will be accepted as facts will render aid and comfort to the enemy. It is suggested that enemy claims of ship sinkings, or of other damage to our forces, be weighed carefully and the source clearly identified, if published.

Information about the transportation of munitions or other war materials, including oil tank cars and trains.

Information about the movement of the President of the United States, or of official military or diplomatic missions of the United States or of any other nation opposing the Axis powers—routes, schedules, or destination, within or without the continental limits of the United States; movements of ranking army or naval officers and staffs on official business; movements of other individual or units under special orders of the Army, Navy, or State Department.

Interviews with men on leave, columns and so on, are included in the above requests, both as to text and illustration.

If information should be made available anywhere which seems to come from doubtful authority, or to be in conflict with the general aims of these requests; or if special restrictions requested locally or otherwise by various authorities seem unreasonable or out of harmony with this summary, it is recommended that the question be submitted at once to the Office of Censorship.

In addition, if any newspaper, magazine, or writer handling news or special articles desires clarification or advice as to what disclosures might or might not aid the enemy, the Office of Censorship will co-operate gladly. Such inquiries should be addressed to the Office of Censorship, Washington.

VOLUME XXIII AUGUST 1942 NO. 9

Our Job

OFFICE OF FACTS AND FIGURES

Nine months after America entered World War II, the OFFICE OF FACTS AND FIGURES provided *Writer's Digest* with the following information—a plea, of sorts, to writers everywhere. And for those wondering what they could do to help beat back the Axis powers, preserve American liberties, and, finally, win the war, it provided answers. Today, many would see such a request as ludicrous, unlikely to be upheld by all but a few. Clearly, however, this particular time—and this particular enemy—demanded a level of unity we've rarely experienced before or since.

There are six basic themes that point the way toward a better public understanding of the war. Practially anything that is written falls under the heading of one of the six points made by President Roosevelt on January 6, 1942, in his State of the Union address to the nation.

The six themes are:

1. The Issues—What are we fighting for ... why we fight.
2. The Enemy—The nature of our adversaries ... whom we fight.
3. The United Nations—Our brothers-in-arms ... why we need them.
4. Word and Production—The war at home ... how each of us can fight.
5. Sacrifice—What we must give up to win the war.
6. The Fighting Forces—The job of our fighting men at the front.

At various times it is wise to emphasize one of them more than others. For example, when enemy propagandists attempt to becloud the issues of the war with false rumors about peace offensives or independent action by one of the United Nations allies, stories in the magazines which vividly define the true issues and the real position of our allies can be enormously helpful. Similarly, when restrictions are imposed upon civilian life, it becomes extremely useful for the magazines to lend their support by editorial exposition and dramatization of the sacrifices every American must make for victory.

Recognizing space limitations, one or two themes may be given priority as editorial possibilities at specific times. The Magazine Division will be glad to advise from time to time what subjects will be important six to ten weeks ahead.

Approaches

(Some suggestions for developing the themes)

1.THE ISSUES

(a) Play up stories (fiction and nonfiction) which show that we are fighting for survival as a nation, that the actual existence of the U.S.A. depends on victory.

(b) Seek out and feature dramatic examples of what the words "freedom" and "slavery" mean wherever they are found and, conversely, what it is like to live without freedom of speech and religion, freedom from want and fear.

2.THE ENEMY

(a) Expose the scheme for world domination originated within the Nazi party many years ago.

(b) Show the fatal effects of appeasement when dealing with would-be world dictators.

(c) Discourage overconfidence on the part of Americans; the United States never has lost a war, but neither has Japan.

(d) Counteract also the American tendency to be "scared" in spurts; to settle into "living-as-usual" after momentary outbursts of anger or alarm.

(e) Combat defeatism by showing the real and powerful weapons which work toward ultimate victory of the United Nations.

(f) Squelch the rumor factories' output by emphasizing, again and again, that accepting rumors for facts leads to being a "stooge" for Hitler.

3. THE UNITED NATIONS

(a) Glorify the old American adage "In unity there is strength"—Ben Franklin's philosophy that "we must hang together or most assuredly we shall hang separately."

(b) Show that the union of free peoples is fundamentally stronger than its enemies in population, armed forces, raw material, production capacity, wealth, and—important—justice and idealism.

(c) Oppose the Axis technique of "divide and conquer" with stories and articles showing the invincibility of all the twenty-six United Nations in opposing this world strategy.

(d) Make your readers understand the aspirations and philosophies of the other United Nations, no matter how different historically, socially and economically; show their relation to the things for which this country stands. Understanding cements friendship.

(e) Awaken appreciation and admiration for the feats of heroism of our allies—the accomplishments of the Chinese, the Russian, the British people in the face of superior strength, and the stubborn resistance of the conquered peoples, who carry on even to this day.

(f) Label the Axis's unity-destroying lies, especially about England and Russia, for what they are.
(g) Build confidence by showing the terrific sea-spanning tasks of joint military control, lend-lease, etc.
(h) Extend the knowledge of the public about our Latin-American neighbors, show how important a friendly Latin-America is to a successful war.

4. WORK AND PRODUCTION

(a) Point out the progress of war production (only as released through official channels, for obvious reasons).
(b) Show the importance of the war worker.
(c) Relate each civilian to the war program—show how everybody can contribute by working harder at his or her own job.
(d) Dramatize the meaning of time in the execution of the production program.
(f) Emphasize the need for speedy conversion of all factories and idle machinery into war factories and war machinery.
(g) Play up information which shows production goals can be attained.

5. SACRIFICE

(a) Make "going without" a voluntary national practice by showing how it helps win the war.
(b) Define luxury as anything which is not really needed and prepare consumers for giving it up.
(c) Educate everybody to continued systematic purchases of war bonds and stamps.
(d) Explain the anti-inflation campaign and its reward for the average citizen.

(e) War on hoarding.

(f) Show that sacrifices are everybody's contribution, and every effort is being made to distribute them as evenly as possible.

6. THE FIGHTING FORCES

(a) Exalt in dignified terms the mortal realities of war, the heroic sacrifice of individual soldiers and sailors who have been willing to die that their country might live.

(b) Dramatize the work of all branches of the armed services, particularly the vital functions of convoy and supply, which often are neglected.

(c) Keep American mothers and fathers informed of local activities of men in camps and naval stations.

(d) Emphasize the reasons for unified command of the war on a world-wide scale, so that readers identify not only our commander but those who command United Nations troops and ships all over the world.

[Editor's Note: Following are some of the themes on which to base fiction and fact features for October publications.]

NURSE RECRUITING (nursing as part of our fighting job) is now and will continue to be a worthwhile story. They Government's Sub-Committee on Nursing says *fifty-five thousand young women are needed as student-nurses* during 1942-1943; sixty-five thousand will be needed for 1943-1944. For your information, there has been *nothing like an adequate response so far*. The Army and Navy will take ten thousand graduate nurses this year. Their loss means many more student-nurses are needed, for after the first six months of training, *three trainees can replace two graduate nurses*. Stories which stress the humanitarian aspects of nursing, the adventure which comes at the end of training, both in overseas wartime service and in the tremendous reconstruction period which must follow, and the rewards of nursing as a profession would help get the recruits. Here the sacrifice motive might be used; for nursing requires personal sacrifice just as soldiering does, and is as essential. But there are positive rewards. Nursing offers new opportunities in the fields of psychiatry and mental hygiene, in public health, and nutrition (particularly in South America). The institutional nursing, nursing education, and public health fields already offer salaries from 2,500 to 6,000 dollars a year and higher. For further facts about nursing, see the Nursing Information Bureau, 1790 Broadway, New York City.

GIRLS FOR WASHINGTON JOBS (the war at home). Conditions in the Capital have been presented in such an unfavorable light to date that a serious situation is developing regarding the filling of future needs for stenographers and clerks in the war agencies. The Civil Service Commission already has encountered family reluctance to send girls who could be useful to Washington, yet about twenty-five thousand more clerks and stenographers are needed for the next six

The pen is, and always will be, mightier than the sword. The sword runs through one man and he is dead. The sword cleaves a book in half, and the separate parts are burned to white ashes, but the idea in the book spreads forever more. Had Voltaire never written a line, there might well have been no French Revolution, no American Revolution.

Had Hitler been a brute without an idea, instead of a brute with a brutish idea, *Mein Kampf* would never have been written, and the Germans would not have an idea, an ideal, if you please, for which to fight. The Russians gain their fortitude, their raison d'etre from *Das Kapital.*

An idea, a theme, or an ideal dignifies and sanctifies a war. Without it men do not fight. They merely kill and quit.

To coalesce the press into presenting a harmonious idea front, the Government of the United States offers this confidential memo to editors, writers, and literary agents. We applaud heartily this intelligent summary of editorial requirements for general magazines in this war.

Additional copies of this issue of *Writer's Digest* are available gratis to editors who desire to send copies to their contributors.

months of 1942! Although it is true the city of Washington is crowded, *there are still rooms to be had*, and more are to be made available by fall; girls coming to the city do have an exciting, engrossing time; are in no moral danger greater than that of any other large city; they enjoy being "in on" things; and they find satisfaction in the knowledge they, too, are *helping* to *win the war*.

Suggestion: Perhaps this theme can best be played up in fiction stories.

LABOR STORIES. Intelligence reports reveal that laboring men and women in certain sections of the country have vague forebodings as to their future security. Much of this is connected with fear of inflation and distrust of management. Regulations seeking to eliminate profiteering (especially the new Price Adjustment Boards of the Army, and Navy Departments and Maritime Commission, which return sums to the Government on large contracts) could help mitigate these forebodings. The simpler the stories are, with all facts reduced to dramatic and homely example, the more good they do.

THE UNITED PEOPLES (our brothers-in-arms and why we need them) should receive continuing attention. This can be done in hundreds of ways. There is a story along these lines to suit all types of magazines. Too much cannot be done to bring to the attention of every man, woman, and child that this is a war between two philosophies of life, a free world vs. a slave world. *Reiteration of the fact that twenty-seven nations are battling—together— for the four freedoms* is the only way to combat Axis lies; i.e., Germany's about the existence of super-men, Japan's about a white man's or a colored people's world.

Articles about leaders of the United Nations, the heroism of men fighting with us, the unity of interests of enlightened people wherever they exist, are positive weapons against the enemy's technique of "divide and conquer." Understanding our allies and our Latin-American neighbors strengthens the ties among us. *The magazines can play a large part in increasing this understanding.*

POST-WAR PLANNING can be encouraged with the publication of provocative articles on what the world must be like after we have won this war. Wars are fought more fervently if the "whys" are understood by all the fighters and their families; peace may be discussed in more realistic terms. Vice President Wallace's speech, "The Price of Free World Victory," of May 8, 1942, before the Free World Association in New York City, copies of which may be obtained from the Office of Facts and Figures, is recommended as a source of inspirational material for magazines. People are beginning to realize now that, *though we won World War I, we lost the peace*—by not striving wholeheartedly "to create a world where there could be freedom from want for all peoples," as Vice President Wallace has said. It is advised that discussions of actual boundary lines of countries be avoided, but all phases of the free world which must follow the next peace be discussed—not only by national leaders, scientists, but by busines men, housewives, artists—by everybody seeking to insure freedom from fear and want in the future.

PART IV
Interviews

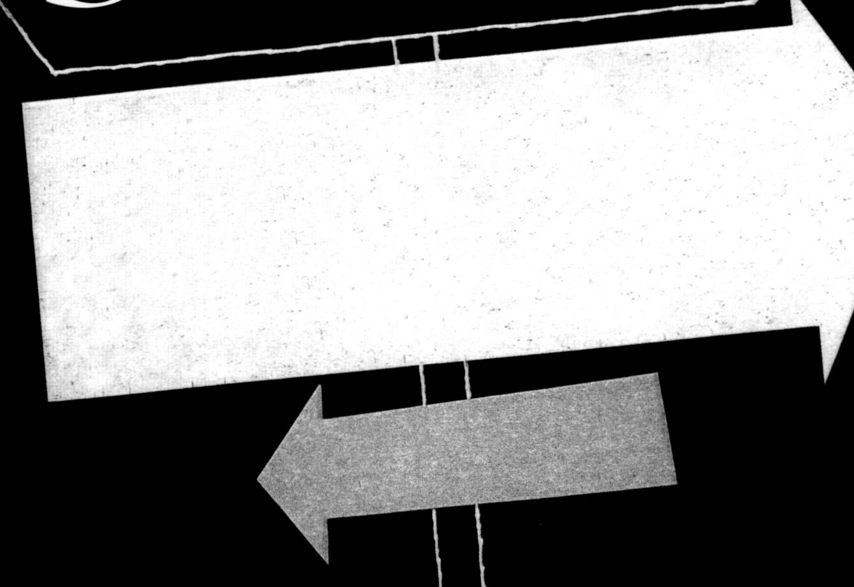

VOLUME VII JANUARY 1926 NO. 2

Carl Sandburg Talks on Poetry and Children's Stories

INTERVIEW BY HENRY HARRISON

Though perhaps known best for winning two Pulitzer Prizes, one for poetry (*The Complete Poems of Carl Sandburg,* 1950) and the other for biography (*Abraham Lincoln: The War Years,* 1939), CARL SANDBURG was a master of nearly every form of writing. A successful journalist, film reviewer, historian, political activist, and novelist, the following interview finds him contemplating the nature of poetry and children's books in early 1926 (his much beloved *Rootabaga Stories* had come out six years earlier). That same year, Sandburg would publish his first Lincoln biography (a two-volume set titled *Abraham Lincoln: The Prairie Years*). It received an overwhelmingly positive reception, encouraging Sandburg to continue his efforts, which culminated in the 1939 Pulitzer noted above.

We were seated at the dining table: Carl Sandburg, Mrs. Sandburg, the little Sandburgs and I. We spoke of this and of that while Carl partook of beer—real beer, by the way. That's one of the things I shall remember Elmhurst, Illinois, for—Carl Sandburg's beer. And, apropos, I ought to mention the excellent grape-juice preparation I imbibed so cordially. But this, I fear, is supposed to be an interview, not a treatise on the quality of beverages. So let me go.

"Only the other day," said Mr. Sandburg in the course of our chat, "a young man asked me to read some of his poems and criticize them for him. I told him right there and then that all the criticism in the world will not keep him from being a poet. If he wants to be a poet, nothing will prevent him. It is up to him, not to any critic of his." And Mr. Sandburg proceeded to nibble another peanut.

After our beakers of beer were absorbed, and the table was cleared, and Mrs. Sandburg and the little Sandburgs left the room, I began to fire my queries at mine host.

"How did you become a poet?" I asked, and Mr. Sandburg gave me this answer: "I never sent the manuscript of a first book of poetry to a publisher. I had a number of free verse pieces that had been printed fugitively in magazines, but I didn't think there was really an audience for these pieces."

I asked Mr. Sandburg what he thought of free verse.

"It's the oldest and the earliest of the forms," he replied. "Free verse is inevitable, as inevitable as rain. It is like feathers on a duck. Life isn't natural without it. In some ages it has been written, in others it has been spoken. But it must always exist."

"What do you think of the poetry magazines?" I asked.

"The more the better," answered Mr. Sandburg. "I consider them a remarkable phenomenon. There's *Poetry, A Magazine of Verse, The Lyric West, The Southwest Review, All's Well, The Measure,* and others. One might wish that the youth of former epochs might be so well represented."

Of the poetry of the future, Mr. Sandburg jested. "It may connect with the radio. But it is too difficult to answer that question seriously. One might run into a thousand different hazards."

I asked mine host his say on rhyme and rhythm. "I'm afraid you'll have to let that go," he replied. I asked him what he thought of blank verse. "You'll have to let that go, too," he answered. And so blank verse must take a blank reply.

"What country do you think has produced the best poets?" I inquired.

Mr. Sandburg answered: "I wouldn't trade any particular group for Whitman, Emerson, Thoreau, and Poe. Also, you might mention Melville for his *Moby-Dick* is a poem. It's as sure a poem as the Book of Job is a poem."

I was quite surprised when mine host informed me that he didn't know whether or not our modern poets are better than those of yesterday. Surely, I thought, Carl Sandburg would acknowledge the present-day group much superior to the bygone batch. But Mr. Sandburg didn't know. "I'd have to go into a long discussion concerning that," he added.

"Who do you think is our best poet?" I continued.

"As soon as I'm told who is the best ball player," retorted the poet, "I'll tell you who is our best poet. I can say, however, that I have enjoyed and admired Robert Frost, Edgar Lee Masters, Edna Millay, and Dorothy Dudley, a New York woman who has written prose that is actual poetry."

Mr. Sandburg took himself to the couch hard-by, and rested himself. He had been playing with a ball against the wall while answering some of my questions.

"What do you think of inspirational poetry and of manufactured verse?" I interrogated.

Mr. Sandburg chuckled. "You write the answer," he ordered. "I'll trust you to write the correct answer." "Why so?" I asked. "Well, I like the way in which you put the question." Now I dare not take the role of answer-man.

"What are your ideas on poetry?" I asked him. The poet in this poet refused to answer. "That's too sweeping and broad a question," he said. "I could write a book on that." (To queries Mr. Sandburg did not answer, he could write a book about.)

"Well, what do you think constitutes good poetry?" I followed up.

"That's also too general," he replied. "But I suggest that you quote my definition on poetry. Really, I could have written a book about the definition alone."

Here you have his definition:

1 Poetry is a projection across silence of cadences arranged to break that silence with definite intentions of echoes, syllables, wavelengths.

2 *Poetry is an art practised with the terribly plastic material of human language.*

3 Poetry is the report of a *nuance* between two moments, when people say, "Listen!" and "Did you see it? Did you hear it? What was it?"

4 *Poetry is the tracing of the trajectories of a finite sound to the infinite points of its echoes.*

5 Poetry is the sequence of dots and dashes, spelling depths, crypts, and cross-lights, and moon wisps.

6 *Poetry is a puppet show, where riders of skyrockets and divers of sea fathoms gossip about the sixth sense and the fourth dimension.*

7 Poetry is a plan for a slit in the face of a bronze-fountain goat the path of fresh drinking water.

8 *Poetry is the slipknot tightened around a time-beat of one thought, two thoughts, and a last interweaving thought there is not yet a number for.*

9 Poetry is an echo asking a shadow dancer to be a partner.

10 *Poetry is the journal of a sea animal living on land wanting to fly the air.*

11 Poetry is a series of explanations of life, fading off into horizons too swift for explanation.

12 *Poetry is a fossil rock-print of a fin and a wing, with an illegible oath between.*

13 Poetry is an exhibit of one pendulum connecting with other and unseen pendulums inside and outside the one seen.

14 *Poetry is a sky dark with a wild-duck migration.*

15 Poetry is a search for syllable to shoot at the barriers of the unknown and the unknowable.

16 *Poetry is any page from a sketchbook of outlines of a doorknob with thumbprints of dust, blood, dreams.*

17 Poetry is a type-font design for an alphabet of fun, hate, love, death.

18 *Poetry is the cipher key to the five mystical wishes packed in a hollow silver bullet fed to a flying fish.*

19 Poetry is a theorem of a yellow-silk handkerchief knotted with riddles, sealed in a balloon tied to the tail of a kite flying in a white wind against a blue sky in spring.

20 *Poetry is a dance music measuring buck-and-wing follies along with the gravest and stateliest dead-marches.*

21 Poetry is a silver of the moon lost in the belly of a golden frog.

22 *Poetry is a mock of a cry at finding a million dollars and a mock of a laugh at losing it.*

23 Poetry is the silence and speech between a wet struggling root of a flower and a sunlit blossom of that flower.

24 *Poetry is the harnessing of the paradox of earth cradling life and then entombing it.*

25 Poetry is the opening and closing of a door, leaving those who look through to guess about what is seen during a moment.

26 *Poetry is a fresh morning spiderweb telling a story of moonlit hours, of weaving and waiting during a night.*

27 Poetry is a statement of a series of equations, with numbers and symbols changing like the changes of mirrors, pools, skies, the only never-changing sign being the sign of infinity.

28 *Poetry is a pack-sack of invisible keepsakes.*

29 Poetry is a section of river-fog and moving boat-lights, delivered between bridges and whistles, so one says, "Oh!" and another, "How?"

30 *Poetry is a kinetic arrangement of static syllables.*

31 Poetry is the arithmetic of the easiest way and the primrose path, matched up with foam-flanked horses, bloody knuckles, and bones, on the hard ways to the stars.

32 *Poetry is the shuffling of boxes of illusions buckled with a strap of facts.*

33 Poetry is an enumeration of birds, bees, babies, butterflies, bugs, bambinos, baba-yagas, and bipeds, beating their way up bewildering bastions.

34 *Poetry is a phantom script telling how rainbows are made and why they go away.*

35 Poetry is the establishment of a metaphorical link between white butterfly wings and the scraps of torn-up love letters.

36 *Poetry is the achievement of the synthesis of hyacinths and biscuits.*

37 Poetry is the mystic, sensuous mathematics of fire, smokestacks, waffles, pansies, people, and purple sunsets.

38 *Poetry is the capture of a picture, a song, or a flair, in a deliberate prism of words.*

"What do you think of poetry courses?" I asked mine host.

"I wouldn't give an offhand opinion," he replied. "I could write a book about that." What books Carl Sandburg could write!

"Of sex relationships as far as poets are concerned?" I continued.

"The poets haven't solved that any more than the soldier, the sailors, or the railroad men," he answered. "Or the traveling salesmen," I suggested. "Or the traveling salesmen," he echoed.

I asked: "Is the poet born, not made?"

"In the same sense that racehorses are not made," he answered, "and prizefighters—and prize egg-laying hens."

"You agree, then, with Amy Lowell when she said that the poet must learn his trade like the cabinetmaker his?" I asked.

"Yes, I do," Mr. Sandburg declared. "Writing is a trade just as bricklaying is."

From poetry I proceeded to the delicate art of writing stories for children. Mr. Sandburg was intolerant of those who dismissed children's stories because they were essentially children's stories. The Chicago poet asserted: "There's supposed to be a separate state of idiocy and low intelligence among children that prevents grown-ups from reading children's stories, unless in an endurance test. Many stories for children should be absorbed by adults."

Mr. Sandburg believes that his *Rootabaga Stories* are far more consequential than his poems. "I'm sure of their simplicity and of their finality," he maintained in allusion to his stories. "I'm pretty sure that the bulk of my verse will—." "Fade away?" I suggested. "Yes, fade away," he said, "and two or three of my *Rootabaga Stories* will remain two thousand years from now."

Mine host admires Hans Christian Andersen. He feels that Master Hans is more important than Keats, at least, as far as Carl Sandburg himself is concerned. He also enjoys Kipling, Grimm, and "then an immense range of fold tales and myths of all nations." Mr. Sandburg, incidentally, believes that "most children are better than what is handed them."

"What should make a children's story?" I asked.

"That runs partly into negatives," Mr. Sandburg answered. "The sorry feature of the bulk of children's stories is that they magnify the glory of princes and princesses, dukes and duchesses, marquises and marquises, kings and queens, sultans and viziers. They glorify those who neither fight nor work."

"But they also glorify generals and soldiers," I suggested, loathing war.

"Yes, but at least soldiers take chances. They fight, anyway," he retaliated.

The inspiration of children's stories is no simple matter, as many free-lance authors doubtless know too well. Writing stories for kiddies is arduous as far as plot and style are concerned.

"Loafing with children will provide you with the inspiration," advised Mr. Sandburg. "You must enjoy the play of their minds. You will find material in them when they are whimsical and contemplative. Searching the child who is still alive is another way of getting inspiration. The oldest of people who are really alive, and who were children once, will furnish you with matter. People who have to deal with children, and who once had no childhood themselves—that is deplorable."

We spoke of other matters—movies, aspirations, vagabonding, and more. And then I bade au revoir to this famous poet, this man who has been a mild-wagon driver, a porter in a barber shop, a scene-shifter, a trucker at brick kilns, a pottery workman, and all before he was seventeen! Carl Sandburg has washed dishes in hotels, has pitched wheat in Kansas, has been a painter (not the kind that is associated with art galleries); has been a soldier—in other words, everything to make him—shall I say fit to be?—the poet.

VOLUME X OCTOBER 1929 NO. 11

Shaw, the Dictator

INTERVIEW BY JUDGE HENRY NEIL

To refer to someone as a "force of nature" is very near to naming them **GEORGE BERNARD SHAW**. Shaw, born July 26, 1856, landed on the literary landscape like a giant, sending out shockwaves with every step he took. Driven by supreme, unwavering confidence in both his opinions and intellect, Shaw left his mark upon nearly every form of writing popular in the early twentieth century, from political pamphlets and books to plays and films. He is the only person to have won both a Nobel Prize (1925, for Literature) and an Oscar (1938, for adapting his own play, *Pygmalion*, into a screenplay). The essay that follows details a meeting between Shaw and the author at a period right between those two incredible achievements.

My introduction to Shaw took place the day after I arrived on my first visit to England. Shaw was residing at his country home at Ayot, St. Lawrence, in the beautiful county of Hetford. Eager to meet the world-celebrated writer with whom I had corresponded for years, I gladly took advantage of his invitation to call.

Shaw's telegram closed by saying that I would be met at the railroad station, and almost before I had alighted from the train a tall man stood beside me, grabbed my bag, and intimated that the car was waiting. We drove through country lanes at such a speed that I momentarily expected to be precipitated from the machine. Conversation, even fragmentary, was out of the question. Not until we stopped, with a grind of brakes, at a gate set in a wooden fence, was I able to collect my scattered wits and wonder why the face of the driver seemed vaguely familiar.

Without giving me time to put my thoughts into words the chauffeur sprang from the car, again seized my bag, and opened the gate for me. He then rapidly preceded me along the garden path, flung open the house door, and stalked ahead of me into a sitting room. On a sofa lay a lady.

"My dear," said Shaw, "this is Judge Henry Neil."

So this was Shaw! I gazed at him in astonishment. He laughed, his eyes twinkling humorously.

"Evidently the Judge expected to see a gaunt red-bearded Irishman, flourishing a shillalah!" he said, and then I knew why, although the features had seemed familiar to me, I couldn't "place" the driver of the car. I had always pictured my host as the possessor of a brilliant red beard and had forgotten the passing of time and its natural whitening effect on beards.

After dinner Shaw took me for a walk over his estate. As we passed the village church he told me that the house in which he lived was the parson's house but that as he could not afford to live in it he rented it to Shaw and himself lived in a couple of rooms in a cottage in the village.

Shaw's quick, decisive manner was very forcibly exemplified by his mode of greeting me, and his driving of the car is indicative of the man's character. Terseness, rapidity, absolute confidence in himself, and super-courage of his opinions have made Shaw a veritable dictator in his own sphere, literature. His fearless writings are read and quoted more universally than those of any other living author. Six days out of seven, Shaw occupies space on the front page of newspapers, printed in every civilized country and in many languages. Any scrap of news that can be gleaned about him is flashed from one side of the globe to the other.

It has been my good fortune to spend many hours in intimate talk with Shaw, to draw his opinion on almost all subjects. His viewpoints are always illuminative, often startlingly original, but never, even when he is most radically opposed to the other man's opinion, does Shaw lose his temper or his sense of humor.

Like all of his countrymen, Shaw is a born fighter; his pen is mightier than the swords of tens of thousands.

More than half a century ago, the then young, poor, and unknown author had already determined the principles that were to guide him through his stormy literary career, and all the sarcasm and derision that has been hurled at him has never caused him to swerve from those principles.

Shaw has never aimed at popularity. There have been many times in his life when he was the most unpopular writer in Great Britain, yet he has amassed wealth from the sale of his books and royalties on his plays. He has two beautiful homes, replete with every comfort and containing costly works of art, to which those who desire to see him must crave admittance. But, once having gained an entrance to the genius' sanctum, Shaw proves himself the perfect host, solicitous for his guest's physical well being. He may, however, if he is in the mood, provide a positive grilling by way of mental entertainment!

To discuss any subject with Shaw is like taking part in a fencing match with the world's champion

SHAW AS A YOUNG MAN

As a young man, George Bernard Shaw had four novels sent back to him, express collect, before he had his fifth novel accepted. At present, his dramamtic comedies are in high favor throughout the world. The Shavian method of writing is brilliant, thought-provoking wit, interspersed with direct speeches in which the actor practically addresses the audience.

Born in Dublin, 1856, Shaw stands today as the world's most famous writer-teacher. Some of his plays are *Candida, Arms and the Man, Man and Superman*, and a collection, *Plays, Pleasant and Unpleasant.*

as one's opponent, and using electrically charged rapiers as weapons. His brilliant and lightning-like thrusts of satire keep one's brain in a state of scintillation.

Shaw is a patient and sympathetic listener, but apt to make metaphorical mincemeat of opinions antagonistic to his own, preserving, at the same time, a perfectly friendly attitude toward his converser.

Shaw professes to be a pacifist; his attitude during the World War was such as to cause him to be ostracized as an unworthy citizen. Yet, in practice, he is an ever-ready fighter, and the hotter the battle (of words) the happier he is. He loves to goad and infuriate those who try to prick holes in his philosophy, but in no solitary instance has any person succeeded in ruffling is equanimity or in causing him to break his record for persistent good humor.

On the subject of charity, Shaw has made many scathing indictments. "Why should I give money to help take care of the wrecks caused by Capitalism?" was the way he answered one request for subscription to charity. So I planned to test his principles, and proved that a soft heart may beat in the same body that harbors a brain of diamond-like brilliance and cutting propensities.

One night as Shaw and I came out of a theater, I invited him to visit some of my lady friends. "I know a dozen or more who live near here," I said, "and they will be expecting me."

Shaw was somewhat taken aback but, after a moment's hesitation, he replied, "All right. Let's go to see them."

It was a bitter cold night. I led Shaw to a street at the back of the theater where on many occasions I had talked with old women who spent their days gathering waste paper and at night slept in doorways, using bags stuffed with paper as mattresses.

I introduced Shaw to my friends, watching with interest to see how they would appeal to him. His face softened as he spoke to them in a kindly voice. At the end of each conversation he gave each one of the ladies a half-crown (sixty cents). Later I asked Shaw why, after his many attacks on charity, he had given money to destitute women.

He replied, "To please myself. It won't do them any good, but I get pleasure out of showing them that I have money to throw away. They will spend it on beer and be back tomorrow night to their outdoor lodgings, just as if I had not given it to them. You can't help people unless you maintain them in a higher standard of living for a long time, long enough for them to get accustomed to the change."

Shaw's voice had gradually assumed a dry, cutting tone, and he concluded with one the most bitter Shavian sarcasms I have ever heard him utter. "Charity," he said, "is a poisonous dressing on a malignant sore. I hate the poor and look forward eagerly to their extinction. If I were poor my relatives would have to support me to keep me out of the poorhouse, which means they would have a strong interest in my death. As I am rich enough to have some property, my children, if I had any, would be impatient for my funeral and the reading of my will."

Shaw advocates equality of income, but he does not obey the command, "Sell all that thou hast and distribute unto the poor." He knows that such a course of action would land him either in a prison or the poorhouse or possibly an insane asylum.

Shaw is a capitalist who preaches Socialims. He does not preach Christianity, yet he indulges in charity while "hating" the recipients of his alms.

Like all other dictators, Shaw has achieved his position by riding roughshod over his critics. Public opinion has never caused him to swerve from his hard-and-fast principles; his superb egotism renders him immune from fear.

"I am right. Everything I do and say and think is right. If others disagree with me that does not make me wrong. My brain is the finest brain in the world today; it produces the best books, the best attended plays—"

And these are indisputable facts. For months Shaw's severely criticized, yet widest-read book of the year, has been at the head of the list of non-fiction sellers. Everywhere in the United States and on the Continent, as well as in Great Britain and her colonies, the Dictator's books occupy the most prominent places in bookstores. In all large cities, a Shaw play runs. Last year, when I was in Berlin, I read printed statistics which proved that Shaw's plays are more popular than those of any other foreigner. They run for longer periods than average German plays and are equally well patronized.

Shaw is the fashion. One may dislike his works and plays but it would be unfashionable not to read the one and see the other. That Shaw will not permit his plays to be screened, although he has been offered fabulous prices by movie-picture directors, is another spectacular piece of dictatorium.

Shaw has literally carved his way to the unique position of Dictator of Literature which he occupies. He does not care one jot or tittle whether his readers or his audiences agree with him or not. His dictate is that what he writes shall be read and, willingly or not, the public obeys his mandate and will continue to do so just as long as Shaw chooses to dictate.

VOLUME XLV AUGUST 1964 NO. 9

Treasure Chest at the Bunny Den

INTERVIEW BY KIRK POLKING

When one thinks of best-selling authors and award-winning fiction, *Playboy*—for many of us—rarely comes to mind. And yet, *Playboy* is, and has been for decades, one of the most respected and widely distributed vehicles for contemporary literature. Founded in 1953 by **HUGH HEFNER**, *Playboy*'s reputation for quality fiction grew quickly with contributions from Joseph Heller, Ian Fleming, Margaret Atwood, John Updike, Joyce Carol Oates, Kurt Vonnegut, Norman Mailer, and countless others. The interview that follows details Hefner's personal interest in making the magazine as well-known for its fiction as its women. Consider, then, that the next time someone tells you they actually "read" *Playboy*, you'd be well advised to believe them.

KIRK POLKING, the interviewer, was the editor of *Writer's Digest* magazine from January 1964 through May 1973.

EDITOR'S NOTE: *Part of this interview has been edited for space.*

A little brass plate on the door to Hugh Hefner's apartment on Chicago's near North Side carries the message "*Si non oscillas, noli tintinnare*"—"if you don't swing, don't ring."

With this tone of sophisticated freewheeling and a ripe audience, the thirty-eight-year-old editor and publisher of *Playboy*, in ten years, has built a publishing phenomenon.

In 1952, there were only two publications that could be called "general magazines for men": *Esquire* and the now defunct *Gentry*. Hefner was a sixty-dollar-a-week circulation promotion man on *Esquire*. When *Esquire* moved from Chicago to New York, offering him eighty dollars a week to go along, Hefner held out for eighty-five dollars, lost, and stayed in Chicago. Nights and weekends, he'd been putting together a magazine of his own. "I was struck by the fact that while there was a multiplicity of magazines in many areas, this wasn't so in the general men's field. There were plenty of outdoor and men's adventure books, but really only *Esquire* for indoor sports and *it* was changing."

Hefner decided it was leaving an ignored market among young city males who would appreciate "the pleasures of an apartment, the sounds of hi-fi, the taste of a dry Martini"—and the plates of the famous nude photograph of Marilyn Monroe he was able to buy from a calendar manufacturer.

Searching for a way to personalize his magazine idea, Hefner hunted around for some kind of symbol. "I rejected the notion of having a man, because *Esquire* had Eski, so I started thinking in terms of an animal. The rabbit had a kind of sex connotation and putting him in a tuxedo at the same time gave him a touch of sophistication. I thought it would be a humorous and a charming symbol. Shakespeare suggested 'What's in a name?' I suspect there's a good deal in it. We came very close to calling the magazine *Stag Party*—the notion being that we could change the concept of stag party and it would be on the emphasis of entertainment for men. We almost went to press with that title on it and the rabbit at that point was going to be a stag. (That's where our feature 'Party Jokes' comes from because it was originally stag party jokes).

"Changing the title at the very last minute, almost at the moment we were on press, sounds as if it were a kind of haphazard operation to begin with, and in simple truth, it was. There are many things about *Playboy*, particularly in those beginning years, that should break every rule in the game, and we have no business sitting here talking today."

(Hefner sits "here," drinking a Pepsi-Cola and dragging on his pipe, in the conference room of the combination apartment-second office and bunny-dormitory that is the forty-two-room tax deduction he owns at 1340 N. State Parkway. He's thin, good-looking, with a relaxed easygoing manner, and still incredulous at the success of his idea.)

With six hundred dollars of his own money and six thousand dollars borrowed from others, Hefner put his first issue on the stands December, 1953. The response he got from a promotion letter he'd written in advance to newsstand wholesalers prompted him to raise his initial press run from 35,000 to 70,000 copies, "but since magazines are sold on a completely returnable basis," he points out, "I could very easily have oversold my product by mail and been sitting with a lot of egg on my face. Fortunately the magazine sold."

One year later, his print order was 175,000 copies; by April 1955 it was 350,000. Today, his net paid ABC circulation is 2,489,000.

Although the package in which it's offered is slicker and thicker today, the basic ingredients are still the same. Volume 1 had Marilyn Monroe, Max Shulman, Boccaccio, Milton Caniff, a Men's Shopping Section. The same mixture of nude Playmates-in-living-color, articles, fiction, ribald classics, columns on food, fashion, travel are in the current issues, buttressed with added departments such as The Playboy Panel, The Playboy Forum, The Playboy Interview.

Playboy and The Writer

The business that grossed twenty-five million dollars last year for Hugh Hefner has also been good for his writers. Fifteen hundred dollars is the base rate for an article or a piece of fiction and three thousand dollars is standard for a *lead* piece in either department. Hefner supplemented that this year with a new system of bonuses which gives a basic 250 dollars jump in pay for each succeeding story or article from a writer in the same year. (Then the next year, the writer's first piece is paid for at the *average* of what he earned the preceding year. The only hook is that to qualify for escalation pay, writers must give *Playboy* first refusal on anything they write.)

Hefner's editorial director and the man who deals most directly with writers is A.C. Spectorsky, a trim, fortyish-looking writer-editor who, before joining Hefner in 1956, had been successively literary editor of the Chicago *Sun*, Eastern story editor for Twentieth Century-Fox, and editor on *Living for Young Homemakers* and *Charm*, editor-in-chief of *Park East*, and a senior editor at NBC-TV. His *The Exurbanites* was a 1955 bestseller. It was Spectorsky who brought to the magazine his contacts with good writers and agents and helped develop the literary side of the book. While *Playboy*, like any other big newsstand book, seeks and gets the work of already established writers such as Malamud, Kerouac, Baldwin, Waugh, Huxley, Steinbeck, and others, it has also given a great many checks to non-big-name writers.

"We are concerned," says Hefner, "by the tendency among some magazines today to place less emphasis on the nonestablished, nonagency-represented newcomer. As far as I'm concerned, this is the future of writing. The short story form has been hurt badly enough, both by some strange things that have happened inside of it in the last thrity years, and by the good talent being drawn off into advertising and television, that I think it's beholden upon us and others in the field to do everything possible to motivate new people to sit down and write."

Fiction at Playboy

What *kind* of stories does *Playboy* want to see from talented new writers? "Fiction with a genuinely masculine point of view" says Spectorsky, "which has nothing to do with the common concept of the masculine point of view being hairy chest, outdoor, adventure; the 'How-I-Killed-the-Sabre-Tooth-Tiger' type of fiction. Our principal interest is in more urbane subject matter. Now there's a great amount of despair, failure, and even abnegation of manhood and female domination going on in much of the good fiction we read. We've printed some of this when it's especially excellent, but we've published all types of fiction. To show some of the various themes we've treated, let's look at our inventory. Here's a story by Ray Bradbury called 'Heavy-Set.' This is a powerful story about a thrity-year-old who has been kept in a sort of retarded childhood by an overprotective mother, and how he responds to a Halloween party which turns out to be more adult than he is ready for.

"We have a story called 'City of Light '64' by Herbert Gold, who is a *Playboy* regular—almost a *Playboy* discovery. It's about a former American expatriate's revisit to Paris where he tries to relive and fulfill his bittersweet memories of earlier years and his own developed maturity and sense of reality im-

THE *PLAYBOY* PHILOSOPHY

Since *Playboy*'s first appearance on the newsstands, magazine men, readers, ministers, and literary critics have called it everything from a peep show for sophomores of all ages to the voice of the rising generation. Hefner says, "Everybody else was telling me what we were standing for and I felt I'd rather be damned for the things I really believe than for somebody else's notion of what *Playboy* represents."

To describe what *Playboy* believes in, Hefner published an article in his December, 1962 issue on "The Playboy Philosophy." Sixteen installments and 120,000 words later he's still telling 'em.

"It isn't a matter of being pure pleasure-bent or Hedonists by any means. It is a matter really of objecting rather strenuously to the Puritan aspects in our American heritage in which you have a tendency to feel guilty about pleasure, quite literally—not only sex, but also even the accumulation of wealth. We are a beautiful, guilt-ridden society in which we think the material benefits are great, but there's something wrong with the

continued on next page

pinges on this, and he comes away from it a wiser man. By Dan Jenkins we have a story about a syndicated TV columnist who tries to bully Hollywood network brass into airing a show he's written, and gets blackmailed in turn. A hard-boiled, funny, tough Hollywood story.

"Ken Purdy, whom we feel great pride in because we think we were instrumental in his developing as a fine fiction writer as well as article writer, has a story called 'This Time Tomorrow' which is a suspense adventure yarn about a five-million-pound robbery in England, and it is typically Purdy, and in a way symptomatic of *Playboy*, in that this is a completely amoral story. We are not for the bad guys or the good guys. We're just fascinated by what they do."

As you can see, *Playboy* stories have a beginning, middle, and end. *Playboy*'s first reader, who reads all of the two hundred unsolicited manuscripts received each week, says, "Many of the fiction pieces we get are not really finished short stories but impressionistic shreds of prose which should be filed away until such times as the authors sharpen their own storytelling sense and more fully develop their fragments. The other most common reason for re-

fact that we think so. I think that's nonsense. I don't suggest living for today is the only answer. I suggest that the wise man lives for today and tomorrow. A phrase I have used often in the past is that a person should work hard and play hard, too. Life is more than simply a vale of tears and is to be enjoyed. You get one time around and if you don't make the most of it, you have no one to blame but yourself.

From his initial chapter in December, 1962, Hefner has expanded The Playboy Philosophy into a sometimes rambling, exhaustively annotated discussion of sex and public attitudes toward it down through the ages. Interwoven throughout is the *Playboy* view of today's "upbeat" generation's "new (a)moral maturity."

By chapter sixteen in 1964, Hefner had reached sodomy and the other "crimes against nature" and stated, "We will reserve the expression of our own concept of rational sexual morality for a later installment of this series."

As an editorial teaser, The Philosophy must be the longest on record.

jection is the writer's not being sufficiently familiar with *Playboy*'s editorial requirements. I keep receiving *Good Housekeeping* and *Argosy* rejects with irritating regularity. But my patience with beginners in the field is far from worn away and despite what many may accuse us of, each manuscript is *read* and sometimes read twice or more. There is always a chance that the next envelope I open will contain a marketable piece of writing."

"It's our feeling," adds Spectorsky, "that the viability of the magazine depends on developing new writers instead of just publishing standard ones. Finding them is extremely difficult and a tremendous amount of effort goes into it."

Are there often cases where either a big-name writer or an agent tries to foist off somebody's less-than-best-work?

"It's a very frequent occurrence and it's not only disappointing because you get a slight lift of the heart when you see a big name show up in the morning mail, but it is discouraging because it is a tacit expression of a kind of contempt for us. I think it hurts the writers and it hurts the agent and it hurts our feelings and I could name, but won't, some big-name writers who have diluted their value and reduced their pay scale by insisting that their agent sell everything that they write, and the agent starts with us and the other high-paying markets and then the stories wind up in *Playboy* imitators or worse. It's not good for anybody. It's bad for the consumer who sees a big name on the cover of a magazine and gets a lousy story. I think the road to ruin for a magazine is to try to exist on second-rate work by top-rank writers. The other discouraging thing for us about some important name writers, in addition to their sending us second-rate work, is when they reveal by the material they submit to us that they don't know what we want. They think, for example—well, it's for *Playboy*—it has to be sexy. I would say we almost lean over backward to balance the frisky, romantic, pictorial elements of the magazine with writing which deals with sex frankly and candidly and masculinely, but only when it is a legitimate element in the material, not dragged in by the heels.

"And we have no technical restrictions at all. We've had third-person and first-person stories, the story within a story type, shifting viewpoints and just about every other kind. If the style fits the material, that's grand. The one thing that we *do* insist on is *story* as such. We have no interest in vignettes—slices of life. Oh, we've printed them. I think we've printed everything, including stories by women. But not many. We ran a novelette by Françoise Sagan which was written from a feminine point of view and our readers loathed it. I think it was the least popular thing we've ever done. The thought behind running it was that this was a perfectly good story and that although it was told from a feminine point of view, she was, at that time, having such an impact on the young and disaffiliated of the world that our readers would be interested in what she had to say. And they weren't. They said that they had heard it before—that there was nothing new in it—that it was a pretty flimsy story compared to the kind of fiction we usually publish and that they thought that the only reason we did it was because of her name value, which was the last thing they would expect from *Playboy*. Were we going the route of other magazines? Well, they complained bitterly. It would be ridiculous for me to sit here and say we've never made a mistake. That one was a boner."

To the charge by some writers that *Playboy* has a stable of favorite writers, Spectorsky says: "Obviously, there are some writers who are in our groove more than others, but the continuing problem is not to select between favorites and non-favorites but to find good material. We have never not bought a story because we have too many."

Articles in Playboy

Nonfiction at *Playboy* must fill special requirements. "We use three to four nonfiction pieces in every issue and, perforce, can't deal with very timely material as news magazines can, or the way black and white magazines can.

Our production deadlines are tough in that way. We feel that in nonfiction, particularly, the interest of our readers must be a fairly compelling guide. There's no point in our buying a superb article on polio in summer camps or how to insure a house in the suburbs or how to be happy though married (except humorously). But there's no restriction in the sense that a subject is taboo for us because it's dangerous. We will deal with controversy in a way that would make other magazines absolutely scandalized because it would be a direct slap at their advertisers, for example. In that sense, we are more like *The New Yorker*. I think that, actually, we have bought more unknown writers in nonfiction than in fiction. "The Pious Pornographers," for example, by William Iversen, was published at a time when I think he would have been the first to say he was an unknown. I think that in ten years of publication, we've never had a more provocative, attention-compelling article. It was a devastating and witty analysis of the handling of sex in fiction and nonfiction in women's magazines and, as a matter of fact, we have "The Pious Pornographers Revisited," by William Iversen, coming up in September.

"T.K. Brown III typifies the once-unknown writer who found a congenial reception at *Playboy* for both fiction and nonfiction. The year after his first sale to us, he won our annual fiction award of one thousand dollars for the best story published in our pages in a year." (This is matched by a nonfiction award each year.)

"We also buy ideas," says Spectorsky, "when we feel that the writer probably can't pull off a full-length article. For these, we've paid everything from 50 to 250 dollars, depending on how well developed they are. In some cases, there's a border-line situation where the research is good and the idea's good but the writing doesn't make it, and then we buy the article as research and assign it to someone else. In that case, we'd be apt to pay more—as high as 750 dollars on occasion. We have a pretty small staff and they are pretty busy, so in these cases we try to assign it to a writer whose work we like, but who has run into a sort of dry spell on ideas. (As a matter of fact, half the nonfiction we print is from ideas generated in editorial meetings and suggested to writers.)

"We give the writer every encouragement. If an article which we have commissioned turns out to be short of the mark, and the author's sincere attempts to bring it up to snuff don't pay off, we'll pay a turn-down price of 250 to 500 dollars.

"Knowing how to write for us encompasses a great many things. We strongly believe that there is a deplorable tendency to associate serious subject matter with pompous writing. And we demand of nonfiction writers that they be lively and original writers. We want them to be capable of not only thorough research, but original creative thinking about the fruits of research. And we don't want them to short shrift the reader by taking a vast subject and treating it in a shallow or inadequate way. We would much rather limit the subject and have a better exposition in deeper form."

The Future of the Field

At the moment, *Playboy* is riding high with a healthy circulation (75 percent voluntary purchase at the newsstand) and the prospect of even more since World War II babies are now entering the *Playboy* age bracket. Although it has numerous imitators, no really strong second book has emerged to challenge its position the way *Look* followed *Life, Newsweek* followed *Time*, and *True, Argosy*.

Some of the books have editorial initiative; others are simply copy the bare skin sections of *Playboy*. Some are very slow pay (Volitant, publishers of *Man to Man, Mr. Magazine*, and *Sir* seem to be the worst offenders here) and some are barely scooting along financially.

As far as *Playboy* itself is concerned, beyond its own basic personality (see The *Playboy* Philosophy, page 275), Hefner thinks it is possible for the casual reader who may have been drawn into the book originally by the girls and jokes to "graduate" into the fiction and articles and get hooked on those and stay with him. "People usually talk about the girls," he says, "but obviously we didn't invent girls. We may have bent them in the middle and put staples in their navels, but they've been here a long time. The real reason for *Playboy*'s success is that there has been a tremendous shift in attitude between this and the last generation—it seems to me—a tremendous difference—and a great gulf in point of view exists between these two generations that are only twenty-three years apart. And the majority of the communications industry in all forms, until a very short time ago, was reflecting only this part of the population and has now begun to shift. We were the first magazine to give a voice to this new attitude and it is that, I think that makes the magazine successful. Obviously, we've got to continue to do that. Magazines are very much like people in many ways. It's possible to get middle-aged. It's possible to get hardening of the arteries, to get old and die. *Playboy*, in its essence, is a very contemporary book. If the staff that I have and if I, myself, do not remain contemporary and of the times in our point of view, then obviously we will be replaced in the future by somebody who is."

VOLUME LXVI NOVEMBER 1985 NO. 12

Vonnegut on Writing

INTERVIEW BY MICHAEL SCHUMACHER

Sadly, **KURT VONNEGUT**, best known for crafting extraordinary works of fiction that combined satire, science fiction, and biting social commentary, passed away on April 11th, 2007, four months prior to the publication of this book.

Vonnegut's life was often a sad, pessimistic one. His mother committed suicide on Mother's Day, 1944. That same year, Vonnegut was taken as a prisoner of war while serving in the U.S. Army. He survived the bombing of Dresden, which killed more than 130,000 German citizens, by taking shelter in a meat locker under a slaughterhouse (the basis of his classic *Slaughterhouse-Five*). After the bombing, the Germans put him to work disposing the bodies. Thirteen years later, his sister died of cancer. Clearly, such events weighed heavily on him. One year prior to granting the interview that follows, Vonnegut attempted suicide himself and penned Galapagos, a novel that examines the role our overdeveloped brains play in the perpetuation of human misery.

The interviewer, **MICHAEL SCHUMACHER**, was well known to *Writer's Digest* readers, having conducted interviews with the likes of Norman Mailer, Studs Terkel, Joyce Carol Oates (on page 300), and many others. In the years since, he has written biographies of Eric Clapton, Phil Ochs, Francis Ford Coppola, and Allen Ginsberg. His most recent work is *Mr. Basketball: George Mikan, the Minneapolis Lakers, and the Birth of the NBA.*

Jokes can be noble. Laughs are exactly as honorable as tears. Laughter and tears are both responses to frustration and exhaustion, to the futility of thinking and striving

anymore. I myself prefer to laugh, since there is less cleaning up to do afterward—and since I can start thinking and striving again that much sooner.

—*Kurt Vonnegut, from* Palm Sunday

From the beginning of his career as a novelist, Kurt Vonnegut has been deeply concerned with the way the human race has addressed its potential, and with the prices we have paid—in terms of lost faith, misplaced kindness, or even the escalation of cruelty—as we work our way along in time.

Like his precursor and model, Mark Twain, Vonnegut addresses these issues by making his readers laugh at their own stupidities or grit their teeth at the world's injustices. It is virtually impossible to read a Vonnegut novel without feeling exactly what Vonnegut wants you to feel, whether horror at the massive destruction and loss of lives at Dresden, Germany, near the end of World War II (*Slaughterhouse-Five*), desperation over the grim fate we face when confronting the ultimate in scientific and technological advancement (*Cat's Cradle*), or joy at watching an incredibly gentle and wealthy man, considered insane by his ladder-climbing peers, give away his kingdom to the salt of the earth (*God Bless You, Mr. Rosewater*). Compact and narrated in a style that seems simple, Vonnegut's books pack enormous emotional punches.

In October, Delacorte published *Galapagos*, Vonnegut's eleventh novel. (He has also written a play, a collection of short stories, and two miscellanies of nonfiction.) The story of a misbegotten cruise to the Galapagos Islands, the plot focuses on what happens when the ship's passengers are stranded and forced to face survival on an island six hundred miles from the mainland. With its allegorical overtones, it is a particularly strong statement about the way we have evolved, not as much physically as socially.

Vonnegut explains:

> The legend is that the Galapagos Islands were to Charles Darwin what the road to Damascus was to Saint Paul: Saint Paul became a Christian on his way to Damascus, and the legend—which isn't

> particularly true—is that Darwin caught on to the theory of evolution when he visited the Galapagos Islands.
>
> *Galapagos* is about human evolution—where we might go next, what kind of animals we are now, and how we're doing. We aren't really surviving very well, having evolved in the direction we've taken.

Vonnegut's own direction as a writer has itself been a curious sort of evolution. Raised in Indianapolis, he attended Cornell University with the idea of becoming a chemist, and he sought a master's degree in anthropology at the University of Chicago. Though he had written for high school and college newspapers, and had always entertained the notion of becoming a journalist, Vonnegut makes it sound as if his writing career came about more by process of elimination than by choice.

"She was a good writer," Vonnegut wrote in *Palm Sunday* about his mother, "but she had no talent for the vulgarity the slick magazines required. Fortunately, I was loaded with vulgarity, so, when I grew up, I was able to make her dream come true. Writing for *Collier's* and *The Saturday Evening Post* and *Cosmopolitan* and *Ladies' Home Journal* and so on was as easy as falling off a log for me."

Writing may have been easy for Vonnegut, but attaining his present level of success was not. After serving a brief stint as a public relations writer for General Electric (which gave him background for *Player Piano*, his first novel), Vonnegut moved his family to Barnstable, Massachusetts, and began to pursue a career as a fulltime writer. He admits today that raising six children on a freelancer's income was tough, occasionally grueling, with most of his income coming from selling short stories, book reviews and short nonfiction pieces to magazines and newspapers. His early novels were published as paperback originals, given lurid covers, and categorized as science fiction—hardly the promotion needed to produce bestsellers.

Vonnegut carried his bestselling idea in his head for twenty-five years before it reached fruition. As a scout during World War II, Vonnegut was captured by the Germans after the Battle of the Bulge and transported to Dresden as part of a menial labor force. When Americans firebombed and destroyed Dresden in 1944, Vonnegut's life was spared because he was imprisoned underground, literally in the cold storage of a slaughterhouse, while everything living or standing burned overhead. When the shelling had stopped, Vonnegut and his fellow prisoners were forced to burn the corpses of the victims.

This story and its impact on Vonnegut were told in *Slaughterhouse-Five*, a 1969 bestseller that was nominated for a National Book Award. (In the introduction to a special edition, Vonnegut commented on the success of the book: "One way or another, I got two or three dollars for every person killed. Some business I'm in.") Published at the height of the anti-war movement, *Slaughterhouse-Five* was afforded cult status on campuses across the country; ironically, the book is today one of the most frequently banned novels in America.

Success has neither spoiled nor jaded Kurt Vonnegut. His Manhattan home, in the shadow of the United Nations building, is modest. One of the building's four floors is used as a studio/office by Vonnegut's wife, Jill Krementz, the well-known photographer; the top floor contains Vonnegut's office, with the other stories serving as living quarters. The second floor, where we talked, seemed spacious with its high ceiling and sprawling stuffed furniture.

In his cardigan sweater and baggy pants, which accentuate his long, angular form, Vonnegut comes off more like a favorite uncle than a bestselling author. His body language indicates a relaxed man, even when he's speaking on topics he considers important or when he's fidgeting with this ever-present pack of Pall Malls. He is soft-spoken and pleasant, occasionally self-depreciatory and always candid. He smiles often, transforming an almost tired-looking face into one of boyish mirth, and he laughs easily, starting with a chuckle that works its way into an explosive, wheezing, coughing sputter brought on from years of chain-smoking. It didn't take long for me to realize that this combination of straight-from-the-hip speech and easy-going mannerism would be hard to translate into a question-and-answer interview: Words have a way of looking naked after they have been spoken and type-struck onto a blank sheet of paper.

So it goes.

WRITER'S DIGEST: In your *Paris Review* interview, you were talking about being a scout during World War II, and you mentioned that your job was "to go out and look for enemy stuff. Things got so bad that we were finally looking for our own stuff." Sounds like an interesting summation of your career.

VONNEGUT: What, that I've collapsed like the Battle of the Bulge? [Smiles.]

WD: No, I'm saying that writers, especially the ones just starting out, are always looking for "stuff" out there, and the successful ones seem to find it within themselves. Don't you think that writers are much like scouts?

VONNEGUT: It all depends. For instance, my son, Mark, is a writer, and he wrote because he had something very much on his mind. It was as though *he* had been attacked, rather than his looking for a place to attack. He was responding to a whack from life. A lot of people, particularly readers of writer's magazines, are looking for stuff to write about, because they want a job. They're out looking for any kind of idea, you know, that would get them into the profession, because they want this kind of job. They don't want a boss—they want to be free to travel and all that. So, yeah, they're like scouts looking for something—*anything*. But there are a lot of writers, my son included, who felt a necessity to respond to life and not necessarily start a new professional career at it. Mark's a pediatrician now, and he's very busy with long work hours and his family.

WD: How do you see yourself?

VONNEGUT: I've customarily responded to life as I've seen something that made me very much want to write about it—not that it made me very much want to get into the writing profession.

WD: You've said that you have to have an ax to grind—

VONNEGUT: Well, you've got to have something to write about. I've taught writing at Iowa, Harvard, and City College in New York. One big problem is that people don't have anything on their minds. They're not *concerned*—which isn't to say they need an ax to grind. Usually, a person with an ax to grind is a crank of some kind, or a partisan of some kind. So I reject the ax to grind. But you must be passionate about some aspect of life, because it's a high energy performance to create something the size of a book. It takes energy and concentration—not an ax to grind. You should have something on your mind. You should have opinions on things. You should *care* about things.

WD: In an essay on how to write with style, you said that caring was the main thing.

VONNEGUT: Yeah. English can be a fifth language, one way or the other. You can be quite eloquent at it. Of course, a lot of creative writing courses teach you how to counterfeit concern [laugh], how to counterfeit energy, sincerity and involvement. It's a little like going to modeling school to learn how to put on your make-up and always be beautiful [laughs]. People have succeeded going into the writing business as scouts, looking for any goddamned thing to write about and pretending concern for things they don't really care a hell of a lot about.

WD: In a way, young writers almost have to be concerned about fitting into slots, as far as publishing goes, rather than writing about something that may not sell. Publishers are less than enthusiastic about publishing first novels these days.

VONNEGUT: Well, I knew John Irving when he was younger, and his books were simply so compelling that they were published. I knew Gail Godwin. Both of them were students of mine at Iowa, and their stories were so compelling. They really didn't fit into any formula that Random House or Simon & Schuster or anyone else had in mind, but their books were so goddamned compelling that they were readable; they were exciting. Publishers would be perfectly willing to have formulas in mind, but nobody knows what the formulas are, except for a few flop books, like the ones Jackie Susann succeeded so well with, that other writers have succeeded with. That formula—I guess it was the Lyle Stuart formula—was to take whatever you had heard about a famous person, just rumors about them—Judy Garland, Frank Sinatra, anybody you've ever heard of—don't do any research on the person, and build a novel around the rumors. Change the names, of course [laughs]. And this seemed to be a formula for a hit. Or you can just talk about what it's like to be rich and go to Europe. One of the Lyle Stuart rules was that there ought to be at least five exotic cities in a book: Somebody chases somebody to Rome, then to Moscow, and then to Bangkok, or wherever. I mean, these books are a joke, in a way. Alfred Knopf, Random House, Scribner's, or whatever—they're certainly not looking for books like that; they're willing to let other people publish them, for God's sake, just as they're willing to let other people publish textbooks and so forth. I would say that younger writers are being discriminated against because publishers are putting less money into them then they used to, and publishers aren't as patient to let writers develop now; but one thing is that writers themselves have been faithless.

WD: In what way?

VONNEGUT: A young writer can be picked up by Scribner's, say, for a small advance, and Scribner's says: "This guy is really very good, or this woman is really very good—or will be. There's a lot wrong with his first book, but we'll publish the second one, which is pretty good. But Simon & Schuster, say, offers this writer $180,000 for his third book. So does he stay with Scribner's, who developed him? No, he leaves. So any publisher who's looking at a young writer who is saying, "Invest some money in me, I'm going to get better—any publisher in his right mind—knows that this person is going to jump immediately for a big raise. So publishers are wary of young writers, too, because they haven't been that faithful to the publishers who have invested money in them. America's a free-enterprise economy and so there are these business considerations, but I am persuaded that anybody who writes awfully well is going to be published because readers are going to like these books. The thing is to write compellingly and you're going to do very well. Robert Stone [author of *Dog Soldiers* and *A Flag for Sunrise*] certainly didn't conform to any formula; he was responding to the Vietnam War. He wasn't a scout; he was responding to something which has happened to the whole country.

WD: And this is what happened to you with the Dresden bombings?

VONNETGUT: Yes. In each case, it wasn't an ax to grind; it was a matter of reporting something that hadn't been discussed before. Plus, it was very interesting, too. Deeply absorbing. The function for Stone, for me, and for a lot of writers is, in part, journalistic: We do often deal with the issues of the day, rather than merely characters or static situations.

WD: Okay, let's say you care about something, such as you did with the firebombing of Dresden, and that you want to tell it in the best way possible, so readers are going to get exactly the way you feel about what happened. From there, you have so many different ways you can tell the story. You can tell it through black humor, or you can tell it straightforwardly, or in very flowery language ...

VONNEGUT: You can try them all. I mean, take your time, you've got all the time in the world. On that particular book, I suppose I got into it a hundred pages several times and the tone was wrong. It didn't sound right to me.

WD: What made you feel that your best method of writing was to write these fairly simple, declarative sentences, working in irony and humor as you did? How did you decide on that style?

VONNEGUT: Well, it's not something you can control very well, particularly if you've had an education. It's too visceral a matter. It's too intimate a matter, at least for somebody older than twenty-five, to be controllable. I think by then, the way you express yourself is bound right into your flesh and bones. I went to a wonderful high school—an elite high school—in Indianapolis. Such schools don't exist any more, because they're considered undemocratic. ... But, anyway, I went to a place called Shortridge, and the teachers I had were for straight, simple, forward writing. My intention was to become a journalist, and the high school had a daily paper. When I worked on that, it was simple, declarative sentences, saying as much as you knew, as quickly as possible, leaving yourself out of the story, and assaying no more than you really could be sure of. Philosophically, this appealed to me very much; telling anything beyond that seemed to me like lying. Speculation is very suspect. So I was trained that way in high school, appreciated it, and thought it was right.

Then I went to Cornell and worked on the *Cornell Sun*, which was a daily morning paper, a business separate from the university. Again, it was this straightforwardness. Whenever I was spoken to about bad writing, it was because of a lack of clarity or for saying something that obviously pretended to know something I had no right to know. That sort of thing. Ever since, I've found straightforwardness congenial, and it's made my books very short.

WD: How did you come upon these kind of sighs of resignation that have become your trademark: "So it goes," "Imagine that," "Hi, ho," etc.

VONNEGUT: Oh, you just try them. You're writing along, and all of a sudden you feel like saying it [smiles]. If it looks like a lousy idea, you can cross it out. I started doing it with *Slaughterhouse-Five*, every time anything died.

I had one death in the book, and I dismissed it with "So it goes." Then I tried the invention that any time anything died—including a bottle of champagne—I said, "So it goes," and I liked it. It seemed like a good idea. Again, it shortened the book—it didn't lengthen it. It was a comment on the finality of death and the inability to bring people back and the acknowledgement that we're all going to die someday and grieving probably doesn't help much, and so on. I could have had essays on those subjects; I could have gotten up to eight hundred pages with no trouble at all, with me ruminating on death. Another thing: It's very unlikely that I'd have any fresh ideas on death, since the subject has been discussed before [laughs]. After the death of somebody, people are ready to go to thousands of words before the action of the story starts up again.

WD: That sort of simple understatement had a hysterically funny effect.

VONNEGUT: If you write in the baroque mode, like Henry James ... it's so noisy. I mean, all these instruments playing, all at one time. It's difficult to stage surprises because nothing is going to stand out. So if you do keep it down, you'll hear one solo instrument when it cuts in. It's possible to stage a surprise. Also, if you're writing in the baroque manner—very complicated language and sentences and all that—jokes are going to be lost, because you can't time them. Jokes have to be quite naked to be understood. They have to be quite simple. There are gadgets for a joke to work—all parts have to be absolutely essential. You can't stray away from a joke to make an aside or anything else; you've got to go straight to the punch line as promptly as possible. So again, simplicity is essential. It's an important matter of style. In *Palm Sunday*, I said that the funniest joke in the world, if you tell it in King James English, comes out sounding like Charlton Heston [laughs].

WD: You grew up during the Golden Age of radio comedy. Those shows must have had quite an influence on your method of telling jokes.

VONNEGUT: They certainly did—and that was all based on sound, too. There was nothing to see along with the jokes. I consider Jack Benny one of the great men of our time, without question. And Stan Laurel, of Laurel and Hardy, too. Charlie Chaplin. Those people were geniuses, as great as anybody on the planet at that time. They knew how to construct jokes just exquisitely.

WD: And their humor often commented on serious topics.

VONNEGUT: Of course. Charlie Chaplin played Hitler. You cannot be funny, I think, if you're not dealing with serious matters. That's one reason I find Bob Hope not a great comedian, because there's nothing troubled in anything he says. In fact, he does not allude to unhappiness or the tragedy in a situation, and so forth. Laurel and Hardy sure as hell did. There was a great sadness in Benny, who was able to bring forth the Jewish tragedy without really mentioning it, just by his presence and manner. You can only be funny—unless you're Bob Hope, and you want to be funny in that superficial way—if you have matters of great importance on your mind.

WD: You're a person who makes people laugh, yet as a writer, you don't actually *hear* the laughter. Do you miss that? Is that the reason you go out on the lecture circuit and read you work?

VONNEGUT: I don't read the work; I lecture. If I read my work, nobody'd laugh. I lecture, I become sort of a vaudevillian. People do laugh. It's a very calculated performance. One problem with movies, incidentally, is that you can't pause for laughs. With any sort of live performance, if you really get the audience going, you can keep it going. When you start making jokes in the movies, the audience can still be laughing when you top the first joke, and they miss the topper. And when there's silence, they realize they've missed something. And they're stunned when you top it yet again: They're not in the mood for another joke, because they're still wondering what they missed. In theatre, you can get an audience going and mug like hell.

WD: I've seen that sort of thing happen in books, where a writer layers joke upon joke.

VONNEGUT: You can do that in a book, sure. You can pace yourself. The book has a certain advantage I hadn't thought of, which is instant replay, which virtually no other art form has.

WD: You come from Indiana, and that seems to be important in the development of your humor and point of view. Your characters all have decent, middleclass values that are being challenged by a terribly complex, uncaring society. Do you find that your having come from the Midwest has given you a different or unique outlook?

VONNEGUT: Well, I might have become ethnocentric if I had come from someplace closer to the center of gravity. If I arrived in the East believing that Indianapolis was the center of the universe, it was very quickly cleared up for me [laughs]. There are people—and I, in fact, am talking about my neighbors, these native New Yorkers—who do feel at the center of things. You've seen that cartoon of the New Yorker's view of the world: there's the East River, there's Jersey, and then you don't stop again until Los Angeles and San Francisco out there. No, socially, I haven't been in the position of being an explainer of things. I've been an outsider taking a look at it.

WD: How does that make your writing different from that of insiders?

VONNEGUT: If you're an outsider—if you're roaming the world as an outsider, wherever you go, you're a rootless person—then you are an explorer and you write as an explorer, as a journalist, as an ethnographer. You're probably going to do a pretty good job reporting what you see, in the sense of coming into a strange situation and gaining some insight into it. If you are already at home—as so many New Yorkers are, or Bostonians are—you become an exemplar. If I had been born in Boston, and still lived there, and was writing wonderful Bostonian novels, I would be an exemplar. I would write about what's best about Boston, and I would try to become better and better at that. As an Indianapolis person who left home, I'm a reporter everywhere, and I exemplify nothing except honest reporting. If you leave home, you become a reporter; if you stay home, you become an exemplar—particularly if you stay home in a town like San Francisco, Boston, New York, or Baltimore. Chicago writers are exemplars.

WD: Oh, yeah. People like Studs Terkel will always be associated with Chicago. Mike Royko *is* Chicago.

VONNEGUT: Well, he specializes in it and he's getting better at it all the time. For me to become better and better at being in Indianapolis all the time ... [laughs]. I had a friend who became the voice of the Indianapolis Speedway. Once a year he went on national TV, so he was the exemplar of Indianapolis.

WD: I wanted to ask you a few questions about your career and writing habits, so let's start at the beginning. At first glance, you appear to be one of those rare writers who quit a steady job to write fulltime because writing was the thing you did best. What convinced you that you could do that?

VONNEGUT: I was making more money on the weekend and in evenings than I was making working for General Electric.

WD: Still, writing fulltime is a tough, high-risk profession.

VONNEGUT: There's no question about it. It's an extremely high-risk situation. People are willing to take these extraordinary chances to become writers, musicians, or painters, and because of them, we have a culture. If this ever stops, our culture will die, because most of our culture, in fact, has been created by people that got paid nothing for it—people like Edgar Allan Poe, Vincent Van Gogh or Mozart. So, yes, it's a very foolish thing to do, notoriously foolish, but it seems human to attempt it anyway. William Kennedy, who's very hot now, experienced many, many bad years, but he kept at it. Nelson Algren [author of *A Walk on the Wild Side*] was a failure at the end of his life.

WD: So was James T. Farrell [of *Studs Lonigan* fame].

VONNEGUT: Yes. They were no longer able to make a living. So that's it, the nature of that particular game. If you can go to work for American Motors or Dodge or International Harvester in order to be secure instead of being a writer ...

WD: You'll never get the job done.

VONNEGUT: No, and then the factory goes under [laughs]. And you've lost everything. In the Soviet Union, of course, if they figure you're a writer, you don't have piecework anymore. You get some kind of salary. I don't know quite how it works, but you get a house, you get a car, you get all this, and you don't have to produce that much. They don't notice it, unless you don't produce anything. My son is a pediatrician, and this is essentially long hours and low pay because his patients, by definition, are just starting out in life and don't have much money, and the big bucks are with people in the last two weeks of their lives or in the intensive care units. ... So everything is a risk. A guy at American Motors can get his hands chopped off.

WD: When you were starting out, you were in an unenviable position because you were trying to support a family on income earned writing paperback originals and short stories. It must have been tough trying to keep things going.

VONNEGUT: Well, it really was. I mean, it's a young man's game, or a young woman's game, but you can survive as a writer on hustle: you get paid very little for each piece, but you write a lot of pieces. Christ, I did book reviews—I did anything. It was 85 dollars here, 110 dollars there—I was like Molly Bloom: "Yes I will, yes I will, yes." [Laughs.] Whatever anybody wanted done, I did it.

WD: Is that one of the reasons you don't write short stories now?

VONNEGUT: Oh they're very hard to do—they're much harder than a novel, I think, because they're far more artificial. Just to make a short story work, you have to misrepresent life. You've got to create a fist-like thing, a fist-like incident that's very clean and separate from the rest of life, like an egg, and there are not instances in real life, so you're going to misrepresent life. I think an ordinary person reading a well-made short story is delighted, because you play emotional tricks on people with plot and so forth. You create expectations and you satisfy them—and you're doing things to their body chemistry, really. The brain, as it processes the material, is sending signals to the nervous system, circulatory system, and all that. So special things are happening. It's a very entertaining thing for a writer to do—it's almost like doing crossword puzzles or something like that. It's a trick ... like writing a sonnet. It's hard to do, it *ca*n be done, and when you do it, it's amazing that you got away with it. A typical short story is somewhere between ten and twenty pages long. If you go to forty pages, you can treat life very truthfully.

WD: In the past, you've mentioned that you can't work with an outline. I wonder if we could talk about how you organize. Do you take a lot of notes? Do you spend a lot of time thinking out your novels?

VONNEGUT: It's like making a movie: All sorts of accidental things will happen after you've set up the cameras. So you get lucky. Something will happen at the edge of the set and perhaps you start to go with that; you get some footage of that. You come into it accidentally. You set the story in motion and as you're watching this thing begin, all these opportunities will show up. So, in order to exploit one thing or another, you may have to do research. You may have to find out more about Chinese immigrants, or you may have to find out about Halley's Comet, or whatever, where you didn't realize that you were going to have Chinese or Halley's Comet in the story. So you do research on that, and it implies more, and the deeper you get into the story, the more it implies, the more suggestions it makes on the plot. Toward the end, the ending becomes inevitable.

WD: But you do have specific things planned. You know that certain characters are going to do certain things.

VONNEGUT: I will pick a person, or a couple of people. ... When I started this book, I knew that these people were going to go to the Galapagos Islands. When they arrived in Ecuador, I was sure they were going to be in Guayaquil, in a hotel, and that they would be able to see the ship a half mile away at the waterfront. That much, I knew. After that, I also knew that hotels have managers and bellboys, and other people deliver news to the rooms—good news or bad news, whatever. There's also a cocktail lounge. Also, something's going to happen right away because the ship is going to sail right away. So you're not going to have people milling around the hotel, saying, "Do you want to see the cathedral?" or "Do you want to go home?" No. They've got to go on that ship, because the damn cruise cost them 1,500 dollars a head. So there's that much energy in the story, in the situation, to begin with.

WD: Plus you knew that they were going to be stranded on the island.

VONNEGUT: Maybe they wouldn't be. Maybe I'd strand them, and if it seemed like a bad idea, bring them back home again. It's only paper, you know. Yeah, I tried it and it worked, but I might have had all sorts of things happen.

WD: You once said that you wrote for an audience of one...

VONNEGUT: Everybody does.

WD: Who is that audience now?

VONNEGUT: I don't know. I think it's probably still my sister, who died a long time ago. I wouldn't have started that if a psychiatrist hadn't said it—not about me, but about all writers. I read this psychiatrist's study that said that every writer, in fact, writers for one person. If you don't do this, your work won't have the unity. The secret of artistic unity, I think, is to create for one person; anyone else who comes to it will sense this focus in the book.

WD: Who are you reading today? What do you find really exciting?

VONNEGUT: I read largely for social reasons now, because I know so many writers and I run into them and want to keep up with what they're doing. The exciting work that's going on in the country now is for the stage. There are some really exciting people, like Sam Shepard, writing for the stage. Novels are okay [laughs], but the high-energy stuff, *in my mind*, is happening on the stage.

WD: There was a period in your life when you were seriously considering writing plays.

VONNEGUT: Oh, I always wanted to, but there have been virtually no novelists who have written good plays, and also there have been virtually no playwrights who have written good novels. I think a young writer comes to a fork in the road very early and becomes one sort of a writer or the other. When I was young, there were a lot of very good playwrights, people like Tennessee Williams, and William Saroyan, and, God, I would get to New York to see whey they were doing. That sort of thing is happening now ... I envy those people. I'd rather be a playwright than a novelist now, because it seems to me that they're doing a lot more.

WD: One last question about the literary scene: Many writers of your generation seemed hell-bent on writing the so-called Great American Novel—almost to the point of making a competition out of it—yet three of the most popular novels in recent years—*Slaughterhouse-Five, Catch-22,* and *The World According to Garp*—were unassuming novels that chose to explore the human condition in a humorous way. I don't think anyone set out to the Great American Novel in these books, yet in many respects, they came damn close.

VONNEGUT: No, only confused nuts would set out to do this, to regard it as a competitive enterprise. Writing isn't that sort of business. That hotel in Paris—the Ritz—is now going to give a huge cash prize every year for what they say was the best novel in the whole world [laughs]. I suppose we should be perfectly content with *Moby-Dick* as the Great American Novel. We should let it go at that.

The trouble is, the country is too damn big. I mean, it's like writing the Great Asiatic Novel: You'd have to include the situation in Sri Lanka, India Gandhi—I don't know if the Russians are Asiatic or not, but we'd better include them [laughs]. The country is too goddamn big. A novel has to limit itself to the crew of a ship or a family; it's not a great way to process a huge number of people.

VOLUME XIII APRIL 1986 NO. 8

Joyce Carol Oates and the Hardest Part of Writing

INTERVIEW BY MICHAEL SCHUMACHER

By 1986, **JOYCE CAROL OATES** had proven herself to be a massively prolific, and often controversial, writer. Her novel, *Them*, a generational saga set in Detroit, won the 1970 National Book Award, while *Bellefleur*, published in 1980, sold more than one million copies. Moving between literary and genre fiction, poetry, plays, and nonfiction with equal grace and skill, Oates' writing seemed to know no boundaries of critical or popular success. Interviews with Oates were rare, making the one that follows something of a coup for *Writer's Digest*.

Joyce Carol Oates has come to typify the writer-as-artist. Shying away from interviews and public appearances, she prefers instead to work privately at her craft and teach her skills to others. Though the sheer bulk of her creative output seems to deny it, she revises her work tirelessly, rearranging words and passages—even titles of stories—to achieve their designed effects; on one occasion, she changed the entire ending of a novel between the time it was published in America and in England. Her idea of taking a break from the tension of writing novels is to write poetry or short stories.

When her first collection of short stories, *By the North Gate*, was published in 1963, few observers would have predicted that the quietly intense young woman from rural New York would develop into one of America's most prolific serious writers. Between then and now, Oates has published sixteen novels, twelve short story collections, five volumes of poetry and four books of literary essays, as well as plays and countless uncollected book reviews and short stories. *Prodigious* is an adjective often associated with her creative output, and her publishing history indicates the term is appropriate: At one point, she had three publishers—one handling her mainstream writings, another her poetry, and the third her experimental work. At age forty-six, Oates shows no sign of slowing down.

Reaction to her work has always been mixed, though generally favorable. As a college student, she submitted a short story to a *Mademoiselle* competition and won; in 1970, she won the National Book Award for *Them*, a novel set in Detroit, her home for six years in the mid 1960s. Her short stories are staples in the O. Henry and similar anthologies of award-winning pieces. Her work is studied on college campuses throughout the United States, in other literature and creative writing classes. One of her most recent novels, *Bellefleur*, sold more than a million copies and reached hardcover and paperback bestseller lists. She is a member of the American Academy of Arts and Letters.

Criticism of her work has mounted over the years, however; hostile reviewers dismiss her recent string of Gothic and romance genre novels as inappropriate or disappointing from a novelist who has proven herself so adept at contemporary themes. Her books have been assailed as too violent. Some critics have gone as far as to disapprove of the *number* of books she has written. It has been pointed out, to her displeasure, that she fails to "write like a woman"—whatever that means.

Though far from insensitive to critical reaction, positive *or* negative, she dismisses it with good humor: "I've never taken it very seriously, since for me the hard part of writing is the writing, not the critical response afterward. Conversely, the writer wishes that good, strong, positive reviews had the power to convince him or her that the writing is successful.

As John Updike has wryly said, we tend to believe the worst, and to think that the good reviews have simply been kind."

By all indications, Joyce Carol Oates is living a life rich enough for several people. In addition to her writing, she teaches at Princeton University, co-edits (with he husband, Raymond Smith) a literary quarterly, and publishes small-press books; for recreation, she enjoys cooking, jogging, bicycling, playing classical music on the piano, reading, and taking brief excursions to nearby New York City. She admits, though, that little of what she does takes her very far from her writing and, conversely, that almost everything she does is somewhat connected to her work.

"My life is a sort of double narrative," she says—"*my* life running alongside an interior/fictional life. The external life is often absorbing in itself, particularly here at Princeton, but the internal life is ultimately the one that endures. I do subordinate nearly everything else in life to my writing—that is, the thinking about the story at hand. But this may well be simply analogous to the degree of saturation in thought—of self or others or of various projects—common to all human beings."

"Telling stories, I discovered at the age of three or four, is a way of being told stories," she wrote in a *New York Times* essay. "One picture yields another; one set of words, another set of words. Like our dreams, the stories we tell are also the stories we are told." Born the daughter of a tool-and-die designer in the tiny town of Millersport in New York's Erie County, Oates recalls her rural upbringing as "a continual daily scramble for existence," frequently marred by her being bullied by older schoolmates. Storytelling became an important escape and she credits her paternal grandfather, a steelworker, as a great early influence. Not only did he delight her with stories, which she tried to emulate, but he bought her her first typewriter when she turned fourteen.

Her short stories appeared in small literary quarterlies while she pursued academic degrees in English, but when she read a publisher's ad seeking young writers, she set aside her academic life and began pursuing her writing fulltime. "After my first publication," she told *Publishers Weekly*, "I immersed myself in writing for twelve to sixteen hours a day. Writing became the core of my life."

When I ask if she could have done something other than write, she replies: "It seems to me in retrospect that I could not have done anything else, but the impulse to romanticize oneself is obviously dominant."

WRITER'S DIGEST: In a recent interview, you mentioned that you don't write for everybody, and that you don't expect everyone to read you. Who do you write for?

OATES: This is a difficult question to answer. I doubt that any *serious* writer thinks of an audience while he or she is writing. My primary area of challenge—or tension, or at times anxiety—is simply the work at hand, the next morning's provisionary and often endlessly revised and retyped scene. In structuring a novel, I have a quite detailed outline—even an "architectural" sort of design affixed to my wall—but as each chapter or scene is written, the whole design is altered. So I am in a constant state of tension while writing a first draft, as I am at the present time. Even the first draft is the consequence of what seems to be endless revisions of chapters, pages, even paragraphs. The primary focus of concentration is therefore the work at hand. To think of an audience—of anyone!—reading the material is virtually impossible. It's analogous to worrying about what you'll wear on the morning of March 10, 1988. One should live so long.

When the work is completed, however, one can make some sort of judgment, as editors and publishers do, about whether it is likely to be popular or no. I can't see my writing as ever being *popular*; much of it, to make even literal—not to mention emotional, psychological, or thematic—sense, has to be reread. When *Bellfleur* became a bestseller in both hardcover and paperback, no one was more surprised than I was, but I'm sure that many of the copies sold went unread or unfinished. For this, a writer does feel some slight guilt, I think, and hence my statement that I really *don't* see myself as writing for a very large audience.

WD: Over the years, you've addressed a number of critical attacks concerning the violence in your work, yet I can't help but wonder if there's a gender identification connected with the criticism: If Norman Mailer writes about a man finding the severed head of a woman, it's macho art-form; if you write a novel about a boy who murders his mother, or a novel about the assassination of a politician, critics question your motives. It's as if women are expected to be "civil" (in the Austen sense of the word) and controlled.

OATES: Yes, it's purely a sexist response, but I think it's beginning to diminish. In the past, it may well have seemed, even to responsible critics, that a woman's natural artform was needlework; hence, any deviation from this genteel activity was alarming. I did draw a good deal of angry abuse—"sickening," "loathsome," "disgusting," "mere trash"—and perhaps I still do. I've never taken it seriously.

WD: Did you read Mailer's *Tough Guys Don't Dance?* Though the book is contemporary, it seems familiar with much of what you were doing in *Mysteries of Winterthurn*. Both books seemed to be working to establish correlations and contrasts related to physical and psychological violence.

OATES: I haven't read Mailer's novel yet, but I would suspect that Mailer and I have many concerns or obsessions in common. However, the relationship between physical and psychological violence is one fairly generally explored, isn't it? I know I have been exploring it since my first published stories.

WD: About *Mysteries of Winterthurn*: You've said that book taught you a new way of writing. What did you mean by that?

OATES: The detective-mystery novel must be imagined both forward and backward. Unlike most novels—most serious novels, in any case—this peculiar and highly challenging genre demands absolute accuracy in terms of time, place, details, clues, etc. I realize, of course, that in conventional detective-mysteries the plot is all, or nearly all, but my concern was with writing a "double" novel in a sense, a novel of character and theme that nonetheless required the classic structure of the mystery. The novel I have written, however, is in fact an antidetective-mystery, a critique of the genre from the inside. As I grew to love the form, I grew to realize the strange nature of its restrictions and its many necessary exclusions—as in, for instance, a game of chess one must abide by the rules and take for granted that the world "beyond" the game board scarcely exists, in fact does *not* exist. Otherwise the game is jeopardized.

WD: That book, as well as the other period pieces you've written recently, not only recreated the times but was also authentic in duplicating the writing style of the day. How did you research this? Did you read a lot of nineteenth-century Gothic novels?

OATES: I've done a good deal of reading over the years, of course. But the nineteenth-century novel is immensely varied; what is meant by *Gothic*, in fact, is debatable. I read a number of novels by women writers of the mid and late nineteenth century. Susan Warner is the outstanding example. And etiquette books, handbooks on how to live—with such titles as *The Young Christian Wife and Mother*, which I discuss in *The Profane Art* in a long essay on stereotypical female images in Yeats, Lawrence, and Faulkner.

WD: You've worked in widely diverse styles in your stories and novels. The obvious question: Is style something that you can control, or do your stories dictate the way in which they are told?

OATES: It's a mysterious process. The character on the page determines the prose—its music, its rhythms, the range and limit of its vocabulary—yet, at the outset at least, I determine the character. It usually happens that the fictitious character, once released, acquires a life and will of his or her own, so the prose, too, acquires its own inexplicable fluidity. This is one of the reasons I write: to "hear" a voice not quite my own, yet summoned forth by way of my own.

WD: Your story collection *The Poisoned Kiss and Other Stories from the Portuguese* went as far as to name a fictional character as your "collaborator," giving the book a sort of visionary glow. Could you explain how that book came into being? Is this an example of what you mean when you say that writing is a transcendental function?

OATES: The appeal of writing—of any kind of *artistic* activity—is primarily the investigation of mystery. Somehow, by employing a deliberate speech-rhythm, or by unlocking it, one is able to follow a course into the psyche that reveals different facets of the self. *The Poisoned Kiss* is my journal of a sort of the most extreme experience of my own along these lines: Actually, I gave to the *voice* of the stories the adjective "Portuguese" because I knew only that it was foreign, yet not familiarly foreign. Beyond this, it is difficult to speak.

I should stress, though, that the voice of these tales was firmly joined to a fairly naturalistic setting by way of subsequent research and conversations with friends who knew Portugal well. And the tales were rigorously written and rewritten.

WD: Could you talk a little about revision? I understand that you spend a great deal of time reworking your novels and stories.

OATES: I revise endlessly, tirelessly—chapters, scenes, paragraphs ... I don't like to push forward with a story or novel unless it seems to me that the prose is strong enough to be permanent, even though I know very well that once the work is finished, I will want to rewrite it. The pleasure is the rewriting: The first sentence can't be written until the final sentence is written. This is a koan-like statement, and I don't mean to sound needlessly obscure or mysterious, but it's simply true. The completion of any work automatically necessitates its revisioning. The same is true with reading, of course—at least of a solid, serious, meticulously written work.

WD: How does a novice writer perfect revision skills?

OATES: Since we are all quite different, I can't presume to say. Rereading, with an objective eye, is a necessity—trying to see one's work as if it were the work of another, setting aside involvements of the ego. ... Revision is in itself a kind of artwork, a process of discipline and refinement that has to be experienced. It cannot really be taught. But my students are amazed and excited by what they learn by revising; they're usually very grateful that they are "strongly encouraged" to do so.

WD: Is it possible to revise too much? Can one be too much of a perfectionist—such as the painter who keeps adding brush strokes to a canvas until the original picture and is inspiration are painted over or altered beyond recognition?

OATES: Certainly. Some people think that, on some pages at least, *Ulysses* is over-polished, its slender narrative heavily burdened with various layers of significance, symbol-motifs, allusions. I am temperamentally hostile to the weighting down of a natural and spontaneous story with self-conscious Significance: To me, the hard part of writing *is* the story. The gifts of a Thomas Hardy, for instance, are far more remarkable than the gifts of a writer like Malcom Lowry, who so painfully and doggedly and willfully created a novel of symbols/ideas/Significance.

I admire Joyce immensely, of course; I've written a good deal about him. But he had the true Jesuitical mind—as he himself noted—plotting, calculating, outlining, dissecting: In *Portrait of the Artist as a Young Man*, Stephen experiences the "seven deadly sins" in a programmatic way, for instance; once one knows the key, the story seems willed, artificial, slightly tainted by the author's intention. It's ideal fiction for teaching, however.

WD: Where does your writing fit in?

OATES: Temperamentally, I may be more akin to Virginia Wolff, who worked very hard, as she noted in her diary, to achieve a surface of "fluidity, breathlessness, spontaneity." One wants the reader to read swiftly and with pleasure, perhaps even with some sense of suspense; one hardly wants the reader to pause and admire a symbol. In my genre novels, I had to use conspicuously big words since, to me, that is part of the quaint humor of nineteenth-century fiction—its humor and its power—but these are not my words, they are those of my narrators.

At the present time, I am writing a novel, set in the years 1947–1956, called *The Green Island*. My hope is to create a colloquial, fluid, swiftly moving prose that sounds, in places—when certain characters are on stage, for instance—rather rough, sheerly spontaneous. Yet I write and rewrite to achieve this "roughness." My prose tends to be more polished, to a degree, in its first state—at least more systematic and grammatical. To find the right voice for this novel, I have had to break down my own voice.

WD: You've drawn a distinction between ideal fiction for reading and ideal fiction for teaching. Have you, through your mainstream and experimental fiction, been seeking a compromise between the two?

OATES: Yes. I believe every writer wants to be read by as many people as possible—with the stress on *possible*. That is, one doesn't want at all to modify his or her standards; there is the hope that readers still make an effort, sympathize, try just a little harder, reread, reconsider—the effort that is routinely made with Modernists like Joyce and Yeats. Since I work so particularly hard on rewriting, and can do a dozen versions of an opening section after I've completed a novel to get it right or in harmony and proportion with the rest of the book, it would seem that my opening sections should be reread, too. Yet I doubt that many—any?—reviewers trouble to make the effort. However, I do keep trying. I must be incurably optimistic.

WD: Did you ever find yourself beginning a story or novel which was difficult or impossible to execute?

OATES: I have never begun a novel that hasn't been *impossible* for the first six or more weeks. Seriously! The outset of a novel is sheer hell and I dread beginning. But it must be done ... I've written one hundred pages or more to be thrown away in despair, but with the understanding that the pages had to be written in order that the first halfway-good page might come forth. When I tell my students this, they stare at me in pity and terror. When I tell them that my published work is perhaps one half of the total work I've done—counting apprentice work, for instance—they turn rather pale. They can't seem to imagine such effort and, in retrospect, I must confess that I can't, either. If I had to do it all over again, I'm not sure that I could.

WD: Much of your prose has a rhythmic and lyrical quality about it that approaches poetry. Do you consciously write for the mind's ear? Do you ever read passages aloud to hear what they sound like?

OATES: Absolutely, all the time. It's a practice I am totally dependent on, and have grown to love, though I don't usually read the passages out loud. *Silently out loud*, if that makes sense.

WD: Your use of ellipses, as well as your intermixing of short and long paragraphs on the same page, makes me wonder if you work to achieve a certain physical effect in your writing for the printed page. Are you looking for something physical?

OATES: Sometimes—certainly in my poetry and in some short stories. In *Childwold*, I had wanted varying spaces between the chapters to suggest varying "spaces" in the narrative and between characters, but my publisher didn't want to print the book that way.

WD: As it is, that was one of your most experimental major works. Your use of the second-person singular was one of your most interesting experiments in language. How did you come to choose that particular way of telling that story? Was it a difficult book to write?

OATES: *Childwold* was written first, almost in its entirety, in longhand. When I finally began typing it, I think it went rather smoothly. The *you* seemed necessary for Laney because, though Laney was not me/I, she lived through and saw numerous things that I experienced at one time or another. Her focus of consciousness seemed to demand the second-person singular, which I don't believe I have ever used since.

WD: I felt a Faulkner or Flannery O'Connor influence in that novel. Do you find yourself influenced by certain writers when you're working? Do you ever go back and reread one of the classics in an effort to capture a particular flavor or style?

OATES: My reading is so wide, varied, and more idiosyncratic that it is impossible for me to say anything specific or helpful. I was reading Faulkner, Dostoevsky, Thoreau, Hemingway, the Brontës, and many other classic writers in my early teens. These influences remain very deep, I'm sure. Only in my late teens and twenties did I read Lawrence, O'Connor, Thomas Mann, Kafka—yet these influences are still quite strong, pervasive. The curious thing, which I try to explain to my students, is that one can try very hard to be influenced but not succeed. Much of what we read is in a voice so alien to our own that there is no possibility of influence, though we might admire it a good deal. For instance, I admire Huxley, yet I could never have been influenced by him.

WD: Your books are filled with richly descriptive narrative passages. Do you keep notebooks or jot down ideas as you see them?

OATES: I do both, I suppose. For me, writing—and reading—are ways of *seeing*: I have a sharply visual imagination and love to see by way of words, and there are many writers (one might name Emily Brontë, Thomas Hardy, and D. H. Lawrence) whose visual imaginations are so powerful that one is immediately transported to an alien, but totally convincing world, by way of their prose. Oddly, merely viewing without the filter of words, as in a film, seems to me less satisfying. I get a good deal of happiness out of transcribing scenes in retrospect, by way of memory—evoking the formidable city of Detroit, for instance, in *Do With Me What You Will*, while at the time I was living in London, England, for a year; writing *Bellefleur*, set in the mountains of a region very much like upstate New York, while living in Princeton; and writing my current novel, *The Green Island*, with a Buffalo/Lockport, New York, location, again while living in Princeton. Conversely, I get no satisfaction out of writing about things immediately at hand; they don't interest me at all. Part of the motive for writing seems to me the act of conscious memory.

WD: A few questions about your writing habits: What is your daily schedule like?

OATES: I try to begin work around 8 A.M., stop at 1 P.M., begin again at 4 P.M., and work to perhaps 7 P.M. Sometimes, I will work in the evening—in longhand, not at my desk—but throughout the day I am *working* in my head so far as possible. This makes it sound rather constant and perhaps it is, but the activity is rather more exciting than tiring, at least when the story is moving along well. This schedule is an ideal day when I am not at the university or involved in other activities. Obviously, my two teaching days are radically different: I'm gone through the afternoon.

WD: Do you still work in longhand?

OATES: Yes. I'm very dependent on working in longhand. All my poetry and most of my novels are taken down in longhand first. It seems close to the voice, more intimate, less formal and artificial.

WD: In what way? Could you explain that further?

OATES: I don't think I can, really. Most poets write in longhand; even many of my students, who then turn to their word processors. I am not averse to using the typewriter, of course, at certain more pragmatic times.

WD: How do you feel about word processors? It would seem ideal for someone like you, who is usually involved in several projects as once.

OATES: I am not usually involved in several projects at once; in fact, when deep at work on a novel, I try to do very little else. My short story writing has sharply abated in recent years since I've been working on exceptionally long, complex novels.

The word processor isn't for me, since I am dependent on so many systematic, slow, deliberate rewritings. Often I retype a page that seems to me finally finished, only to discover in retyping that I've tightened it, or added something that, in retrospect, seems obvious and necessary.

WD: Can you talk about the different sorts of writing projects you undertake? Let's start with the short story. What role does the short story play in your activity as a writer?

OATES: I seem to have published more than three hundred short stories since 1963, so their *role* is virtually indistinguishable from my life! Most obviously, the short story is a short run—a single idea and mood, usually no more than two or three characters, an abbreviated space of time. The short story lends itself most gracefully to experimentation, too. If you think about it, the story can't be defined, and hence is open, still in the making. Radical experimentation, which might be ill-advised in the novel, is well suited for the short story. I like the freedom and promise of the form.

WD: Do you find that, like a painter, you consciously work your stories into series of common themes or colors—such as in *Crossing the Border* and *Night-Side*—or do they sort of gather that way after a period of time?

OATES: Yes, I think the process is rather like that of a painter's: There are common concerns, common themes and obsessions, in a certain period of time. I collect only a few stories in proportion to the number I publish. To me, hardcover publication is the final imprimatur. When I assemble stories, as in *Last Days* and *A Sentimental Education*, my most recent collections, I rewrite them, at least in part, and arrange them in a specific order. My story collections are not at all mere collections; they are meant to be books, consciously organized. Unfortunately, a number of stories I am fond of have never found their way into hardcover print because their themes or voices were unsuited for a volume.

WD: You've written a substantial amount of poetry—enough to merit a volume of collected poems. How does poetry fit into your life as a writer?

OATES: Poetry is my *other* world, my solace of a kind. I love both to read and to write—or to attempt to write—poetry as a means of escape from the strain of prose fiction. It is also an extremely personal mode for me, as fiction is not. I can employ autobiographical landscapes and even experiences in my fiction, but *I* never exist—there is no place for *I*.

In a phase of poetry writing, I feel that I am most at home in poetry. There is something truly enthralling about the process—the very finitude of the form, the opportunity for constant revision—an incantatory solace generally missing in fiction. Poetry requires no time in the reading as prose fiction always does, particularly the novel; the demands of the novel on both reader and writer are considerable, after all. After finishing a long, difficult novel, I always enter a phase of poetry. It can last for perhaps six or eight weeks. Of course, this phase is by no means without its own difficulties, but its pleasures are more immediate and forthcoming. One can even see a poem in its entirety—a source of amazement to the novelist.

WD: What about book reviews and literary essays? What function do they serve in your career?

OATES: I don't know that they serve any *function*; they are vehicles for my more discursive voice, I suppose. Like most critics, I write about what I like and hope to know more thoroughly by way of writing and analysis.

WD: One final question: If and when you write your memoirs, what period of your career would you consider to be your happiest?

OATES: I can't have that—perhaps I don't yet have the perspective to make such a judgment. My husband and I are quite happy here in Princeton, and I've been extremely productive here, but I well remember feeling idyllic in Windsor, if not always in Detroit, where we lived from 1962 to 1968. Also, the concept of a *career* is rather foreign to me since a *career* is so outward, while *life* is so inward, a matter of daily experience. Many a writer has enjoyed an outwardly successful career while being personally unhappy, and the reverse might well be true. The most sustained and experimental—if not audacious—work of my career is the five-volume sequence of novels written here in Princeton. So I suppose this period, from 1978 onward, might be later seen as my "happiest" time.

Classifieds & Personals

JANUARY 1934

WRITER'S SECRETARY—Was Jack London's secretary three years; Rupert Hughes's, off and on two years. Will travel. Dictaphone; dictation; grammar perfect. No propositions. Not good looking. Box YO.

FULL DRESS SUIT—Six months old. Fits man 5 feet, 5 inches, 150 pounds. Waist, 32; Chest, 35. Will clean and press. Made by firm that sells to Brooks. Box M.X.

GIRL, 26—Portland, Oregon—Attractive; Creative. Have published one novel: Lothrop, Lee, and Shepard. Interested in corresponding to single engineer. Not choo-choo. Box E.

WRITER HOBO—Man, 36—2 years Michigan State. Not prison. Correspond writers with view to saying hello if I pass your way. Box 9-M.

STUCK in God-forsaken, small town. No library; no stores; not even a marshal. Girl, 18. Wanted to be fashion designer; lost job. Shipped myself home collect. Correspond interesting writers. Box L.F.

AMAZING LIFE STORY—Traveled Tibet, Siberia. Fought as Chinese general. Am Russian. Cannot write English well. Educated. Sell facts of my life for cash. Box I.C.M.

FEBRUARY 1934

WILL SWAP—Ten dollar plot device. Clean—no egg stains! Nicholas Wells, 132 Adams Street, Lynn, Mass.

WIDOWER—Over fifty, bordering on moronic, thinks he can write. Would correspond with another similarly situated. Box F-2.

RETIRED DETECTIVE (Formerly Assistant Manager, William J. Burns, International Detective Agency, Tenn., Vice President International Association for criminal investigation, fingerprint expert). Spent best part of life making criminal investigations. Will furnish skeleton of detective stories for writers to build into fiction—$1.00. Murder, burglary, confidence game, pickpockets, diamond robbery, insurance grafters, state which. Send cash and 3¢ postage first letter. Park Summers, 333 Curry St., West Plains, Mo.

MARCH 1934

BODYGUARD, GHOST-BUSTER, ADVENTURER, expert gunrunner, 33; available May 1. Write. Box M-7.

MAN, 28—Stories in ten publications. Interested in contacting a woman, 23-33, who has extensively studied Edmund Shaftesbury's philosophies. Box M-12.

AUGUST 1934

OLD MAID—Owns home and typewriter. That's all. Desires intellectual bachelor correspondents. Roman Catholics preferred. G.L. Olmstead, R.F.D. No. 1, Mayfield, N.Y.

FEBRUARY 1937

PROSTITUTE'S LINGO—Valuable to writers, 20c. Box O-3.

OCTOBER 1937

ARE YOU A ROVING WANDERER without permanent address? Postcard will bring good news. Box 91, Station D, New York City.

MARCH 1939

INFANT, male, 20, published. Unfortunately traveled. Badly needs correspondence from intelligent damsel. Has nothing to offer. Box B-10.

DON'T SHOOT! Living is more fun than anything. Understandable psychological solutions to your perplexing problems, 50¢ each. Competent, confidential, Psychology Service, 819 Lincoln Avenue, Pasadena, California.

JANUARY 1941

LISTEN, my little puss, this sounds like mystery on the bridge at moonlight, but if you will look in my bureau under the third rafter from the left, by the place where it was repaired, you will find my novel. Please send it. And I am not going to take care of Hobart forever. Why don't you settle down so I don't have to write you like this? Spiegelbaum.

MARTHA. Am leaving Peking in November. Will return Peking overland from India coming up from Tibet, we allege. Make it August at Ayer Itam.

MAY 1941

STRUGGLING LOVE-PULP AUTHORS—Love-Pulps demand a Particular emotional problem! Most stories rejected because writers Don't Know what This is. We explain it thoroughly; simple, fool-proof ten-second Test, to make Sure it is a Love-Pulp emotional problem, enclosed. Price: $2.00. FMR Service, 1457 Broadway, N.T.C.

JULY 1941

ST. BERNARD DOG wants job. Can count, whistle, and play accordion. Box V-8.

A BILLION PLOTS FROM SEARS' CATALOGUE! How to write any kind original plot from Sears, Roebuck catalogue, $1. This is no hokum—it actually works! Mailed postpaid. Plotamatic, Box 1272, Columbus, Ga.

FEBRUARY 1942

SPEECH—Will someone write one for me; subject on Life in General, in a semi-serious-humorous vein, for a reasonable fee? F-4.

IMAGINATIVE MALE (inventive, 32), interested in story collaboration with "Manhattan residing" female—one slimishly chic, attractive, inspiring, philosophically mature and ready to write. Box F-3.

MARCH 1942

TSK TSK—"SEX AND THE WRITER" tells authors' facts of life. Practical—Increases your output. Send 35¢ for it today. Don't be a sissy! Hallack McCord, 727 Pearl, Denver, Colorado.

OCTOBER 1942

LADY HORTICULTURIST, writer, esthlete, metaphysician wishes to contact unusual individual, but doubts whether one meeting specific qualifications exists on Planet Earth. Box O-7.

NOVEMBER 1942

JOIN THE HUMPHREY BOGART FAN CLUB. Many members. Enjoy club news. Details, stamp. Eloise Coats, 341 N. Gregory, Whittier, Calif.

MAY 1945

WANTED: Young man, 21-24, lonely, disgusted, homeless who wishes a home, large library and time, help in writing. I need someone to help on writing books, handling confidential correspondence. Live in S.W., and want someone around the place to care for pups when I'm gone, play a musical instrument when I'm exhausted. Not a job but an opportunity for young chap with writing ability, a flair for publicity. M.N. bunker, Box 1150, Joplin, Mo.

FEBRUARY 1950

DON'T FUSS! SPANK! Let the "Spencer Spanking Plan" insure your domestic happiness. In plain sealed envelope, $2. Naboma Company, Box 3181, Terminal Annex A, Los Angeles 54, Calif.

MARCH 1950

YOU CREATE BILLIONS REALISTIC characters with "Spinit Character Builder." Booklet, wheel, charts, etc. Limited quantity, $1 per set. "Calendar

Reckoner" locates any date, A.D., 25¢. Blois, 16 Norman, Ottawa, Ontario.

NOVEMBER 1950

STRUGGLING YOUNG WRITER would like to struggle through the winter in Florida. Married, veteran, journalism school graduate. Experience—magazine editing and public relations. Any suggestions? H. Dumbleton, 30 S. Maple St., Warsaw, New York.

MAY 1951

SLUMPED! WHO WILL GIVE ME a kind hand, Pep Talk, or Swift Kick? Box S-3.

AUGUST 1951

ARTICULATE comic magazine factory factotum, marooned for years on graveyard shift and somewhat interested in writing, desires interesting correspondence. Box X-3.

NOVEMBER 1951

I WRITE POETRY, advertising jingles... any subject. Sublime ... Ridiculous. What's it worth to you? Make offer. M. Friedebach, 1604 S. Osage, Sedalia, Mo.

FEBRUARY 1952

NEED MONEY? Can't Write? Try Clay-craft. Products sell good. Instructions 50¢. Mrs. Ruth H. Painter, Jadwin, Mo.

SINGLE MAN, 34, needs life, love, health, happiness. Destitute. More than decade of poverty. Cannot obtain employment locally because of his refusal to practice racial intolerance. How can he raise honest dollars for suitable clothes and one-way bus fare to new life elsewhere? Must make change. No future here. Sealed, sincere letters of advice deeply appreciated. Box F-1.

DRAW PRETTY GIRLS—An interesting and fascinating hobby. Prepare to draw from beautiful models! Send immediately for "How To Draw Pretty Girls." Complete course $2. Cartoon Club, Dept. B-1. 1506 Goodlet Street, San Bernardino, California.

RECLUSE WRITER INVITES correspondence like-minded spinsters. Writer, Blue Ridge Lodge, Idlewild, NC.

JANUARY 1960

WRITERS! SLIGHTLY USED quality Carbon Paper, generous supply $1. 618 Gold, S.W. Albuquerque, N.M.

HAVE YOU fiction-writing talent? I'll tell you—send two pages your handwriting and dollar-bill. Mike Hoelt, Box 602, Upland, California.

UNUSUAL BOOK FOR NEW WRITERS! Tells true "inside" stories how famous authors learned to write and sell. Gives special advice from O. Henry, Kathleen

Norris, Somerset Maugham, and others. Helpful. Inspiring. Only 10¢. Money-back guarantee. Comfort Writer's Service, Dept. B-207, St. Louis, Mo.

U.S. MARINE CORPS—Ex-First Sergeant, honorably discharged October 17, 1941, for physical disability, has 13 years actual, regular service on stations from Boston to China. Will answer 3 questions about Marine Corps for $1. My experiences in Haitian revolt, 1929, and 3 years continuous duty in Shanghai alone will fill a book. Interested? Larry LaVoy, 1725 Church St., N.W., Washington, D.C.

FEBRUARY 1960

EDITORS RECOMMEND our specially designed 9x12 and 10x13 "Protect-O-Script" envelopes for mailing manuscripts flat. Special offer. 24 for $1 postpaid. 100 for $4 postpaid. TASKER SUPPLIES, Box 3131, Alexandria, Virginia.

WRITERS! Do as I do. Live in Mexico while working on your next manuscript. My booklet describes a hidden paradise, names specific persons to contact, tells how to live—with servants—on $150.00 monthly. Yours for $1. Haller, 706 Park Place, Austin, Texas.

APRIL 1960

WRITERS! INCREASE YOUR CREATIVE ABILITY! Find Complete Happiness! Develop the Supraconscious Powers within you! Write for free catalog of helpful books, tapes, recordings. Philanthropic Library, Drawer W697, Ruidoso, New Mexico.

MAY 1960

WILL THE PERSON WHO, several years ago, wrote a piece for Writer's Digest about articles of approximately 800 words he was doing for newspapers on the early history of Virginia (or W. Virginia) please contact me. Box No. E-30.

OCTOBER 1960

HAKO-SHAYR MO-IL M-ODE! TRANSLATION: In Israel, all writers write with The Plotter! See our ad. Creative Features, Potomac P.O. Box 2121, Alexandria, Va.

NOVEMBER 1960

POSITION WANTED by ex-political speech writer. Former employer wasn't elected.

FEBRUARY 1961

ATTENTION WRITERS! Do NOT write to me. Come and see if you are near. Free materials (verbal) for sympathetic writers and photographers. We have two gorillas—some chimps—two Orangutans—monkeys—baboons—birds and alligators. Each has a story. Winter quarters at Tarpon Springs, Florida, until March 15. Bring samples to prove authorship and ask for Mrs. Robert Noell at The Monkey Ranch.

JUNE 1961

36 SURPRISE ENDINGS. The One Thing Every Story Must Have To Sell. 75¢ Each. Two, $1.40. All, $2.10. Delano Publishers, 232 Delano, Yonkers, N.Y.

AUGUST 1961

SKYWRITING POSITION OPEN. Must be able to spell Russian while flying up-side-down. Write Smrynsk Grobsdt, Moscow.

JUNE 1963

NEW WRITERS! Preserve your brainchild on a hand-crafted antique wall plaque. Poems, recipes especially effective. Promising rejection slips make quaint objects from the past; reminders to try again. $3.95 for each. Senlore Studios, 129 Parkway Drive, Eastlake, Ohio.

SEPTEMBER 1963

NEW "PROTECT-O-SCRIPT" mailing labels. Protect your valuable manuscripts and guarantee safe arrival. Several actual sample labels sent absolutely free. Simply write Charles S. Shaffer, 119 Register Ave., Baltimore 12, Md.

OCTOBER 1963

JUST PUBLISHED! "The Alabaster Bambino." Powerful novel of sex-ridden small-town youth. Exciting episodes comparing favorably with "Peyton Place" and "From Here To Eternity"... Hard cover ... Over 280 pages ... $5 Postpaid ... Cash, money order, check ... Frank J. Pepe ... 216, Cedar St., Watertown, New York.

EUROPEAN WRITER (fiction) looking for someone with writing gift, good imagination, near N.Y.C. to rewrite his stuff. (Please—not a ghostwriter, retired teacher.) Will pay according to ability. *Writer's Digest*, Box 120-J-3.

MAY 1964

TARZAN. I will give $5.00 to the writer sending me the best elephant joke which mentions manuscript envelopes. Holly Knoll, Woodstock, Georgia.

OCTOBER 1965

OLD TIMERS. Many years ago, *Writer's Digest* published a book by Fred Ziv called "The Business of Writing." We will pay $5 for a copy. Address Aron M. Mathieu, Writer's Digest, 22 East 12th St., Cincinnati, Ohio 45210.

APRIL 1966

TYPEWRITER RIBBON—Factory Fresh, any machine, 50¢, $5.00 dozen postpaid. KOPPEL, 1191 N.W. 112th Terrace, Miami, Florida 33168.

Index

BY PERRI WEINBERG-SCHENKER

About the Author

Phillip Sexton is one of the founders and editors of *Fresh Boiled Peanuts*, a literary journal. He is also the author of *A Picture Is Worth 1,000 Words: Image-Driven Story Prompts and Exercises for Writers*, and co-author of *The Writer's Book of Matches*. He lives in Cincinnati, Ohio, where he is currently at work on his next book.